Peter Cumberlidge

Waypoint Directory English Channel

**Over 600 passage and coastal waypoints
for the English Channel**

- **Isles of Scilly to North Foreland**
- **Calais to the Chenal du Four**
  including the Channel Islands

Charts devised by Jane Cumberlidge and drawn by Maggie Nelson

Adlard Coles Nautical • London

This edition published 2000 by Adlard Coles Nautical
an imprint of A & C Black (Publishers) Ltd
35 Bedford Row, London WC1R 4JH
www.adlardcoles.co.uk

ISBN 0-7136-54384

A CIP catalogue record for this book is available from the
British Library.

Typeset in Baskerville on 12½ by Falcon Oast Graphic Art
Printed and bound in Great Britain by Bell & Bain, Glasgow

Cover photograph courtesy of Garmin Europe Ltd

Contents

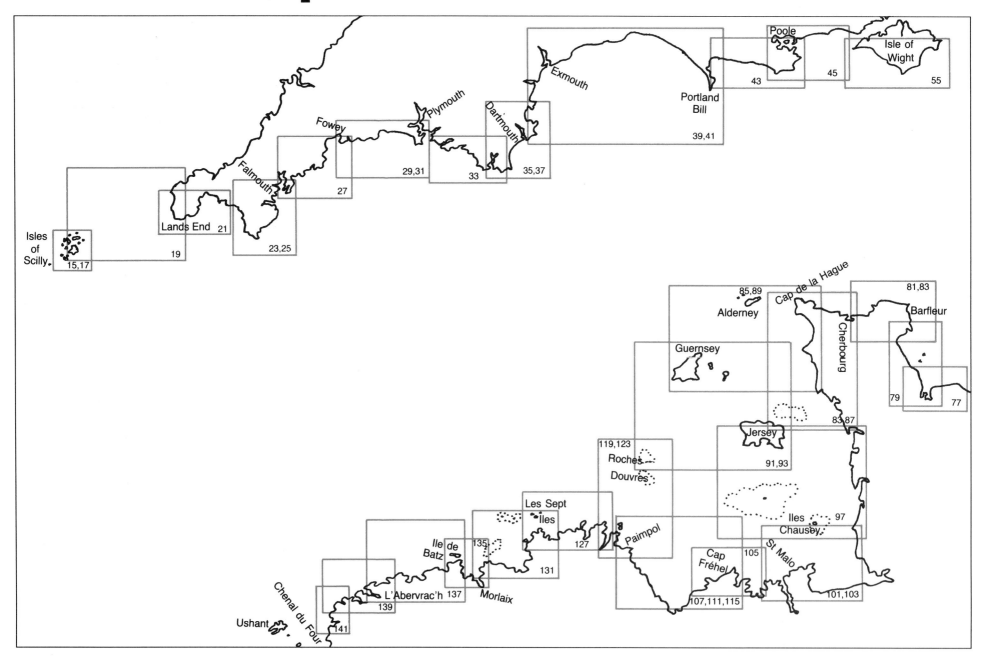

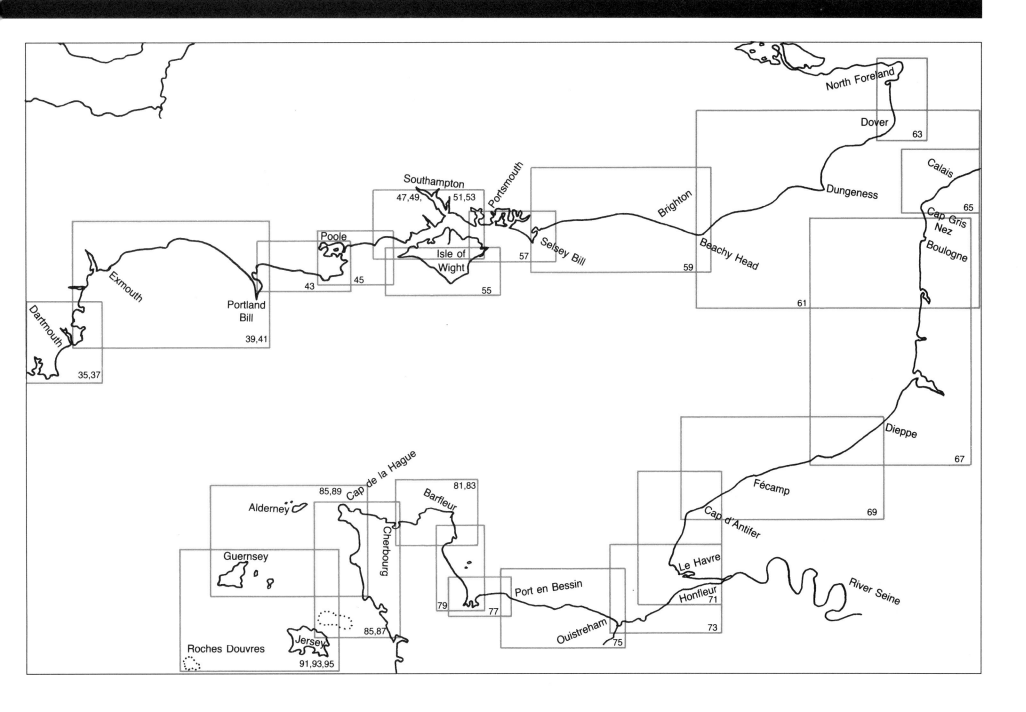

North Foreland

Dover 63

Calais

Dungeness

Cap Gris Nez 65

Boulogne

Southampton
47,49, 51,53

Portsmouth

Brighton

Beachy Head

Selsey Bill

Poole

57 59

Isle of Wight

61

43 45

55

Exmouth

Portland Bill

39,41

Dartmouth

35,37

Dieppe

67

Fécamp

69

Cap de la Hague

85,89

Barfleur 81,83

Alderney

Cherbourg

Cap d'Antifer

Guernsey

Le Havre

Port en Bessin

Honfleur 71

River Seine

79 77

Ouistreham

73

Roches Douvres

Jersey

85,87

91,93,95

75

Introduction

ELECTRONIC NAVIGATION

All navigation, 'manual' or electronic, has the common purpose of directing a craft safely from place to place and keeping track of where you are on the way. The aims of modern navigation are identical to those of traditional navigation. Technology simply enables us to do this more easily, accurately and, on the whole, more safely. Remember the basic objectives of any navigation:

1. Planning a safe route
2. Position fixing and monitoring your route
3. Safe pilotage and avoiding traffic

Principles of seamanship don't change for electronic navigation. Linked to the basic skills and an awareness of error must be a sense of strategy and an understanding of the potential risks posed by a particular sea area at a given time in the conditions likely to be prevailing.

Even using GPS, you still need to give a wide berth to dangerous reefs and banks, passing down-tide or to leeward if possible. You should be wary of certain headlands in wind-over-tide conditions, cautious about approaching rocky coasts at night, in murky visibility or in strong onshore winds.

You have to allow for possible weather shifts, make best use of tides, plan landfalls carefully and work out alternative bolt holes. Flexibility is easier with modern electronics, but navigators must always remain a bit pessimistic, ready for unforeseen complications and prepared for diversions in the event of mechanical problems or a threatening forecast.

It certainly makes sense for navigators to use any modern equipment to best advantage.

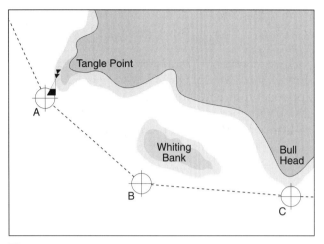

Fig 1

There is nothing wrong with making GPS central to your navigation, so long as:

(a) Equipment is carefully installed to reduce the risk of power failure, aerial problems or damage by seawater or corrosion.
(b) You keep a regular record of displayed latitude and longitude, at least every hour for a displacement boat and more frequently aboard high-speed boats, so that if all systems should fail you can carry on navigating manually.

WAYPOINT THINKING

Although navigators have always used buoys and other seamarks as signposts on passage, the waypoint concept has taken on a wider meaning since its incorporation into GPS sailplan software. Waypoints are used to represent both tangible navigation marks along a route and more arbitrary positions that serve as convenient turning points between successive stages of a passage.

Fig 1 shows examples of three different types of waypoint, using a coastal passage eastward round Tangle Point and Bull Head.

Waypoint A is the south-cardinal buoy off Tangle Point, either its actual latitude and longitude or a position slightly to seaward of the buoy. Waypoint B is a clearing waypoint set a safe distance seaward of Whiting Bank so that the passage legs approaching and leaving B both lie in safe water. Waypoint C is a headland waypoint whose distance offshore will depend on how steep the coast is, and whether there are any tidal overfalls or crab-pots to avoid.

Once you start using waypoints as a matter of routine, it soon becomes apparent that different types of waypoint tend to be used in different circumstances.

Seamark waypoints

Seamark waypoints may be buoys, beacons, light floats, lightships, and so on. Some naviga tors set actual positions for seamark waypoints, to maximise the chance of finding the mark. Others prefer offset waypoints, to be sure of staying in safe water – and, in poor visibility, to reduce the risk of collision with the waypoint!

Clearing waypoints

Danger clearing waypoints are set a safe but arbitrarily judged distance clear of navigational dangers such as sandbanks, reefs, headlands or races off headlands. Because clearing waypoints are often positions at which you change course, they must be set so that your tracks approaching and leaving the waypoint both lie in safe water ie with no dangerous cutting of corners.

The distance off for clearing waypoints may depend on weather and sea-state, wind direction, visibility, whether the headland is a popular area for crab-pots, the type of boat (deep or shallow draught) and her general manoeuvrability and cruising speed.

Setting the right distance off involves judgment. You don't want to shave a danger area too close, and yet taking too wide a sweep adds extra distance and time that may be crucial later in the passage. Even half an hour at sea may have a significant bearing on future events in the lottery of changing weather and sea conditions.

Turning waypoints

Some waypoints are arbitrarily chosen positions at which it is simply convenient to alter course: for example, off a bulge in the coast where the shoreline changes direction, or perhaps on the edge of a traffic separation scheme within which your heading is constrained at right-angles to the direction of the scheme.

Departure waypoints

When starting an open sea passage, navigators have traditionally taken a final departure from some convenient known point, such as an outer channel buoy or a fix position off a headland. You should also set departure waypoints when using GPS, rather than allowing the system to take its own departure from wherever you switch on. The cross-track error display will then make full sense, relating to the open sea track once you are properly on passage.

Landfall waypoints

These are carefully chosen positions out in safe water, perhaps within a few miles of the coast you are heading for. Landfall waypoints may be seamarks, such as fairway buoys or outer channel buoys, but they may also just be convenient positions on the chart that are far enough offshore to be safe destinations in any weather, but

close enough inshore that you can identify landmarks and get your bearings before closing the coast.

When specifying landfall waypoints, much depends on the type of coastline you are approaching: whether steep-to or gradually shoaling; whether it is free of offshore dangers or littered with rocks or sandbanks; whether it is high and fairly easy to identify or low, featureless and enigmatic.

Also consider what the tide will be doing as you approach the coast. Where streams are powerful, such as in the Dover Strait, around the Channel Islands or along the North Brittany coast, it's usually best to arrive a little up-tide of your destination (easier by far to drop down half-a-mile with a three-knot stream than push back against it).

Approach waypoints

You need to have done your homework for the final approach and carefully worked out any inshore waypoints that may be useful, for example, in leading along a harbour entrance channel or into a river mouth in poor visibility. Don't worry about over-preparing an approach. To my mind, it doesn't make sense to use GPS to arrive precisely at an outer fairway buoy and then risk getting lost or confused in the more intricate coastal buoyage simply through lack of preparation. Used with care, GPS waypoints can be helpful in close-quarters pilotage, keeping you oriented while you identify important marks.

I prefer to enter a complete set of waypoints for a passage – a door-to-door route that can, if necessary, take you right up to the marina entrance. Such detailed waypoint planning will be appreciated if the weather turns foul during a landfall, when the coast you have successfully

found and identified vanishes in driving rain, along with the next critical buoy you thought you'd just spotted a mile away.

Of course you need to be careful using waypoints close inshore and along narrow channels, since the normal limits of system accuracy can take you the wrong side of a buoy as easily as the right side. However, close-quarters waypoints can at least set you off in the right direction towards the next mark, until you identify it for certain by eye.

Marking waypoints on the chart

Having decided on a set of waypoints for a passage, I like to pencil them on the charts in black-and-white, using the now conventional waypoint symbol and with the GPS identifier written against each waypoint – for example P1, P2, P3, P4 etc, or the relevant reference numbers from a waypoint directory.

Entering and checking waypoints

Using electronic systems as primary means of position fixing, it's vital to double-check, slowly and carefully, that you have entered your selected waypoints accurately. One wrong digit can lead you into trouble, and a slight error in a waypoint position can be more dangerous than a large error that may often reveal itself as such in good time.

Make sure you key in the decimal point correctly, and check that you are entering latitude when your system is expecting latitude, and longitude when it is expecting longitude. Most longitudes in this book are west of Greenwich, so you need to know whether your program assumes west or east longitude as a default entry – remember to change this if necessary with the ± or E/W key.

Once all waypoints for a passage have been

entered, scroll them across the display to double-check the latitudes and longitudes against your list. Check and double-check are the watchwords with electronic navigation, a way of thinking that should continue throughout a passage. For example, a gradually increasing discrepancy between a charted course to steer and the displayed 'course to next waypoint' is usually the result of a cross-tide. If you know from the tidal atlas what the stream should be doing and if the difference between the displayed and charted courses to steer develops as expected, you have an explainable consistency between different sources of information which strengthens the reliability of the navigational conclusions you can draw. The habit of looking for consistency, or inconsistency, between different sources of navigational information is just as important as it always was, perhaps more important now that we are tending to use electronic systems as the primary method of navigation.

Conclusions on choosing and using waypoints

Waypoint thinking has become a normal part of navigation for those who use electronics as a matter of course, but it's important to remember that GPS sailplan displays depend crucially on the care and accuracy with which waypoints are specified, stored and handled.

Although some traditional navigational methods and skills are falling naturally into disuse, many new kinds of expertise are emerging. Perhaps the most important of these centre on the whole business of passage planning and setting up the ship's navigation system so that it can handle likely changes of route without significant reprogramming or data entry at sea. A vital consideration here lies in specifying safe individual waypoints that can also be incorporated into safe and efficient waypoint networks.

Although the process of setting a waypoint may seem routine, there can be many strategic implications in the selection of even a single waypoint, especially off a tricky coast. How a number of waypoints then fit together to form a route can be critical to the value and flexibility of a passage plan.

ELECTRONIC NAVIGATION IN PRACTICE

The power of GPS comes not just from the amazing facility of having your position displayed continuously to two decimal places of a minute, but also from the sophisticated passage planning software which has introduced the concepts of 'waypoint' and 'cross-track error', and which brings into sharp focus the idea of 'course and speed made good'.

The displays of 'distance to next waypoint' and 'bearing to next waypoint' are important sailplan features, and electronic navigators now visualise, and hence plan, their passages in a different kind of way. Destinations seem more precise, with waypoints normally specified to two decimal places of a minute.

One side effect of such accurate navigation comes from greatly increased expectations of a precisely ordered passage. Even fairly minor incidents or problems causing deviations from plan can now instil a sense of 'distress', whereas they would once have been accepted as a normal part of passage-making and being at sea. Always remember that you are not necessarily in danger just because a system has failed and you suddenly don't know exactly where you are.

Allowing for tide

Tide doesn't vanish because you are using a precise position-fixing system. For passage making in tidal waters, you still have to assess the net tidal effect in advance, as you would if navigating the traditional way. Indeed a full understanding of tidal streams is important for interpreting changing GPS displays, especially 'cross-track error' displays.

Novice navigators sometimes regard 'cross-track error' as a navigational error or an off-course warning needing immediate correction, but this is usually not the case on a longish passage. Cross-track error is not an error if, for example, the tide is setting west for the first half of a Channel crossing, then slack for an hour, then setting east for the second half.

Working out the best course to start steering involves the same calculations as if you were navigating by traditional methods. The tidal vectors are compounded for the estimated duration of your passage, and the course to steer laid off on the chart in the usual way.

Monitoring tide

Accurate position-fixing systems allow you to monitor the effect of tidal streams quite precisely. With GPS interfaced to an electronic compass and log, some systems can display the tidal direction and rate you are experiencing at any given time, by calculating the vector difference between the course steered and speed through the water and your actual course and speed made good.

Even without this facility, an experienced navigator can soon tell from the 'cross-track error' and 'bearing to next waypoint' displays whether he is experiencing more or less tide than predicted and can then adjust his course in good time.

Landfall procedures

The satisfaction of a good landfall never palls, although a landfall on instruments has a different quality to the traditional style of arrival when you were often not too sure which section of coast would lift above the horizon.

Using GPS, especially linked to a chart plotter, you make a landfall more gradually, well in advance of seeing land. The flashing blip edges closer to your approach waypoint, converging with the video outline of the coast. The first radar echoes of the coast may turn up long before you glimpse land over the bow. A radar scan somehow has a genuine solid feel about it, a real but invisible sighting. Yet even knowing your position every step of the way, it's always exhilarating when the first smudge of land appears ahead.

As you draw closer inshore, you should plot the GPS latitude and longitude on a large-scale chart from time to time, rather than rely on the 'distance and bearing to next waypoint' display; remember that an approach waypoint may be slightly in error and this might not show up until you get close in amongst hazards.

A traditional danger about landfalls is that, suddenly, the passage may feel almost over and the navigator starts to relax, imagining himself to have arrived just as the boat is entering the most risky part of the trip. This tendency is equally relevant to instrument landfalls, sometimes more so because a navigator using GPS usually feels certain about his position and confident about picking up whatever marks he has set as waypoints. Guard against overconfidence and keep double-checking the navigation until you really do arrive.

Heavy weather

Good electronics really come into their own in heavy weather, especially with position-fixing systems duplicated for peace of mind. The main requirement for navigation in heavy weather is that your passage planning should be even more conscientious than usual.

The classic landfall risk, of trying to reach a nearby harbour that is inherently unsafe in the prevailing conditions, can actually be increased when you have accurate position-fixing systems – when anything seems possible. This is a question of seamanship rather than navigation, but there are cases every season where skippers using GPS have diverted, in deteriorating weather, for dangerous entrances they would never have considered if navigating by traditional methods.

Even with high technology, prudent seamanship should rule the day. Beware of closing a tide-swept rocky coast in rising onshore winds, or making for a shallow river mouth where the seas are liable to break over a bar. Don't risk being guided with digital accuracy into a traditional seaman's death-trap.

The danger of 'auto-steering'

Perhaps one of the greatest hazards from increasingly integrated systems is the risk from boats being steered on autopilot directly from GPS, when you select a particular waypoint and tell the boat to go there automatically. This auto-track facility must be used with great caution, not only in terms of always keeping a good lookout at sea, but also in the care given to data input so that you are not sent off in an inadvertently dangerous direction. All kinds of dramatic nightmare scenarios can be imagined when technology gives you the facility, as it were, to dial-a-destination.

Regular manual back-up

Even if you have fully duplicated position-fixing systems, it's vital to keep a regular note of the minimum data that would enable you to carry on navigating manually should all your equipment fail. The minimum safe record is to write down every hour, against the time, your course, log reading and latitude and longitude by GPS, having first checked that, if you have duplicate systems, the two displays are giving practically the same readings.

By keeping up this minimum log as a routine, you'll never be more than an hour away from an accurate position, and you can quickly use your course steered and present log reading to work out an estimated position if your electronics go down.

USING THE WAYPOINT DIRECTORY

This *Directory* has been compiled for the convenience of anyone who uses electronic systems for navigating the popular cruising areas of the English Channel, under sail or power. As I have indicated, choosing and specifying waypoints, especially landfall waypoints, needs care and consideration. The waypoints presented in this *Directory* have certainly been set with safety in mind, but they have also been chosen to be practical in all kinds of passage-making circumstances, whether yachts are coasting in a local area between successive waypoints, or whether the navigator is arriving on a particular stretch of coast after a longish offshore passage.

It's not enough to present waypoints in a long list with rather vague labels. A navigator has to see where a waypoint lies in relation to a harbour entrance, in relation to coastal dangers, and in relation to other waypoints. Each double page spread in this book therefore deals with a particular section of coast in some detail. A scale chart on the right-hand page shows the location of all the chosen waypoints in that area, and the positions of these waypoints are given in a table on the corresponding left-hand page.

Of course the latitude and longitude of every waypoint is given to two decimal places of a minute, ready for immediate entry into a GPS sailplan. However, it is also important for a navigator to know exactly where each waypoint can be located and plotted on an Admiralty chart. Therefore, the charted position of every waypoint is also included in the tables, precisely related by bearing and distance to some readily identifiable landmark or seamark. You therefore know exactly which waypoint you are dealing with and can readily judge whether it is safe and suitable for your purpose.

Also on the left-hand page of each spread, I give a brief résumé of the significant dangers for that area, together with a list of the relevant Admiralty charts, so that the navigator has these summarised conveniently to hand.

DATUM OF CHARTED POSITIONS

The latitudes and longitudes of all the waypoints in this *Directory* have been taken from and cross-checked with the most recent large-scale charts of the coastal areas concerned. However, remember that positions derived from GPS are based on the world datum known as WGS 84 (World Geodetic System 1984) whereas at the time of writing most Admiralty

charts of UK waters were still based on datum OSGB 36 (Ordnance Survey of Great Britain 1936), while those covering French and Channel Island waters were generally referred to ED 50 (European Datum 1950).

The British Admiralty are currently reprinting all their UK charts using WGS 84 datum, a process that will take until about the end of 2002. The Channel Island charts will be next in line for reprinting. GPS derived positions can be plotted directly on WGS 84 charts without correction, but during the longish transitional period most cruising yachtsmen will have some English Channel charts that refer to OSGB 36 datum, some to ED 50 and some to WGS 84. The datum to which a particular Admiralty chart refers is printed in the notes immediately under the chart title. Also given, in a note titled 'Satellite-Derived Positions', are the corrections required to convert between GPS datum and charted datum.

Selecting the correct datum on your GPS set

Most GPS receivers allow you to specify position output in different selected chart datums. For the practical purposes of using the waypoints in this edition, set your GPS to work in OSGB 36 datum when you are using waypoints along the English coast, for the Dover Strait and for the area between Calais and Cap Gris-Nez. For the French coast west of Cap Gris-Nez, and for the Channel Islands, set your GPS to work in ED 50 datum.

WAYPOINTS FOR CHART PLOTTERS

Compact chart plotters and PC-based navigation systems are becoming increasingly acceptable

and popular aboard boats of all sizes as the principal means of passage planning, position finding and track monitoring. Linked to GPS, whose differential 'error' has now been removed, carefully set up plotters and computer systems can give amazing results. Many plotter displays are capable of showing your boat moored neatly alongside the exact pontoon in a marina.

Most compact chart plotters use Navionics electronic charts, while computer-based systems such as those pioneered by PC Maritime use Admiralty Raster charts and navigation software written around Windows operating systems. I have used both kinds of plotters and been greatly reassured by their implacable displays of our position and progress in some miserable weather conditions that would otherwise have had the navigator hopping about with a nervous twitch.

These systems make it easy to enter waypoints on the screen directly, by a couple of keystrokes or the click of a mouse, and then join up selected waypoints to form passage routes. But in practice, it's not quite so simple to judge, from the screen alone, whether that waypoint is in the best or safest position for the passage as a whole.

With compact chart plotters in particular, whose cartography (while certainly impressive) is not so clear or familiar as a large display of an Admiralty chart, it can be all too easy to join two waypoints to form a neat looking track that passes unintentionally close to some charted but difficult-to-spot danger. You also need to be sure that, at the end of one passage leg, you are in a safe position to set off on the following leg and are not starting from somewhere that gives a tricky angle on your next target waypoint.

Even when using plotters or computer

systems, I like to choose my passage waypoints with reference to the Admiralty charts of the area concerned. In preparing this Waypoint Directory, I have considered routes and passages to and from all directions, and potentially undertaken in a wide range of weather and tidal conditions. I have selected waypoints that I use myself and would be happy to rely on under most conceivable circumstances. If you regularly use a chart plotter to find your way about, this Directory will provide an ideal source of waypoints for passage planning and landfalls in the English Channel cruising area.

Enter and edit

While it's now very easy to click on a plotter screen to enter a waypoint, you usually find the initial waypoint position is not quite what you'd have marked on a paper chart with a pencil and the benefit of the clear overview that such a chart provides. Moving a cursor across a small screen is not a particularly precise business and you often find that a selected waypoint is not quite the right distance off a headland or perhaps doesn't give the best turning-point between two successive legs in a route. While you don't want to pass precariously close to a reef or sandbank, there's also no point in rounding such dangers too far off. Strangely enough, waypoint routes entered directly onto a screen often pass much further away from given buoys, headlands or dangers than you'd want to in practice.

Once you have entered a waypoint into a plotter system by clicking on the cursor position, you can easily edit the waypoint using this Directory, fine-tuning the numbers of latitude and longitude so that you'll be happy with that waypoint position not just for the passage in hand, but also for future passages that may use

that particular waypoint. A navigator must be sure that stored waypoints are *quality* waypoints that will serve him safely in future passages if he clicks them into a different route. The waypoints in this Directory have been selected with that important criterion in mind.

Waypoint naming

As anyone who uses computer systems quickly discovers, it doesn't take long to build up large directories of material, whether you are talking about documents and folders in a word processing system or waypoints and routes in a navigation system. As you accumulate more and more waypoints in different cruising areas, it's vital to be certain, not only that you are saving quality data, but that you label this data clearly to make it unambiguously identifiable when you come to use it much later. Compact chart plotters only allow limited fields for waypoint names, so you may find it convenient to use the waypoint reference numbers in this Directory as identifiers. Computer-based systems allow more generous 'comment' space for waypoint descriptions, so with these you can easily enter the 'Waypoint names and positions' that are given in the second columns of the Directory tables.

And always remember, as with any vital data punched into a computer, check and double-check to make sure that the latitude and longitude you have entered and stored is exactly correct.

GENERAL CAUTION

All the waypoints in this Directory have been chosen and specified with great care, to be safe, suitable and convenient when used in conjunction with GPS, either for making a landfall on

the relevant section of coast or for cruising between sections. However, it is never necessarily safe to approach any waypoint from all directions. Navigators must always refer to the appropriate large-scale Admiralty charts when planning landfalls or passages in any of the areas covered by this *Directory*.

On the question of published accuracy, it is also important to remember that, while the marked positions of all waypoints and the accuracy of their latitudes and longitudes have been exhaustively checked before publication, the small risk of errors can never be eliminated entirely. This *Waypoint Directory* is presented in good faith as a considerable aid and convenience to navigators, but neither the Author nor the Publishers can hold themselves responsible for any accident or misadventure allegedly attributable, wholly or partly, to the use of any waypoint contained herein, whether or not there was any Author's or Publisher's error in specifying or printing the waypoint positions or their latitudes and longitudes.

All navigators at sea are ultimately responsible for their own safety and must assure themselves of the accuracy and relevance of published information before acting upon it. In particular, any published waypoint from whatever source must always be used in a seamanlike manner, and its accuracy and suitability for a specific navigational purpose verified by reference to the largest scale Admiralty charts of the area.

WP No	Waypoint name and position	Latitude	Longitude
1-1	Crow Sound approach, 1 M due E of Tolls Island	49°55.68'N	06°14.98'W
1-2	Crow Sound inner, close SW of Hats S-card buoy	49°56.16'N	06°17.10'W
1-3	Crow Bar, 4½ ca 296° from Hats buoy	49°56.38'N	06°17.70'W
1-4	Tresco South, 1½ ca due E of Nut Rock	49°55.86'N	06°19.90'W
1-5	Hugh Town approach, 4 ca 284° from b/water head	49°55.17'N	06°19.54'W
1-6	Hugh Town entrance, ½ ca due N of b/water head	49°55.12'N	06°18.93'W
1-7	North Channel outer, 1 M W of Biggal Rock on leading line	49°55.84'N	06°24.98'W
1-8	Maiden Bower clearing, ¾ M W of Maiden Bower summit	49°56.78'N	06°24.69'W
1-9	New Grimsby outer, 4 ca NW of Kettle Rock	49°58.40'N	06°21.49'W
1-10	New Grimsby entrance, 1 ca NE of Shipman Head	49°58.07'N	06°21.36'W
1-11	Old Grimsby outer, ½ M NW of Golden Ball	49°58.77'N	06°20.86'W
1-12	Old Grimsby entrance, 3 ca SSW of Golden Ball	49°58.13'N	06°20.50'W
1-13	Round Island clearing, 6 ca due N of lighthouse	49°59.31'N	06°19.34'W
1-14	White Island clearing, 6 ca NE of Baker Rock	49°59.28'N	06°16.65'W
1-15	St Martin's north-east, 1 M NE of St Martin's daymark	49°58.67'N	06°14.82'W
1-16	St Martin's east, 1½ M E of St Martin's daymark	49°57.95'N	06°13.58'W
1-17	Eastern Isles clearing, 6 ca E of Mouls Rock	49°57.12'N	06°13.58'W

COASTAL DANGERS

Refer to Admiralty charts 34, 883

The Isles of Scilly are littered with rocks and ledges, so great care is needed both when approaching the archipelago and when piloting the channels between the islands. There are too many dangers to list here, but the following are particularly important to watch on a normal cruise to the islands.

Eastern rocks

Approaching Crow Sound from off Land's End or the Lizard, take care not to make a landfall north of the Eastern Isles. Various drying hazards lie up to ¾ mile east and south-east of St Martin's Head, dangerous if you were approaching this stretch in a mist of summer haze.

The Hats

The Hats ledge lies across Crow Sound as you approach the north end of St Mary's island from eastward. Be sure to pass close south and west of Hats S-cardinal buoy before skirting round Bar Point.

Crow Bar

This shallow and partly drying sandbank lies north and a shade west of Bar Point. The shallowest parts dry at chart datum from between 0.5 metres and 0.8 metres. For passing the bar, much depends on the swell and sea state. In quiet weather, some yachts and motorboats will be able to creep over 1½–2 hours after a mean low water, but with any swell strangers should wait until half-flood or later. Some 3 cables south-west of Crow Bar, Crow Rock isolated danger beacon may be passed fairly close either side.

Steeple Rock

This head (0.1 metres over it) needs watching near LW in the North Channel. Steeple Rock lies 7 cables south-west of the highest point of Mincarlo islet and is cleared by the North Channel leading line – St Agnes old lighthouse in transit with the gap between the two summits of Great Smith Rocks bearing 130°T.

Kettle Bottom Rocks

This ledge of drying rocks extends 2 cables north-west of Kettle Point, the north-west tip of Tresco; it needs watching when entering New Grimsby Sound from northward. The leading marks for New Grimsby can be tricky to make out (Star Castle Hotel on St Mary's in transit with the west side of Hangman Island bearing 157°T) so it is simplest to keep fairly close to Shipman Head when coming into New Grimsby from the north-west.

Deep Ledges

Deep Ledges and Tide Rock lie within 4 cables ENE and east of Round Island and jut out beyond a direct line struck between the north tip of Round Island and the outer Lion Rock; ¾ mile just east of north from Round Island. These dangers are important for boats skirting close round the north or for those entering St Helen's Pool through the Gap.

St Martin's Head

This distinctive headland, marked by a prominent red-and-white daymark, has Deep Ledge (0.9 metres over it) not quite ½ mile to the north; the Chapel Rocks and Little Ledge close on its north-east side; Flat Ledge ½ mile east by north of the daymark; and the various Eastern Rocks – up to ¾ mile east of the Head.

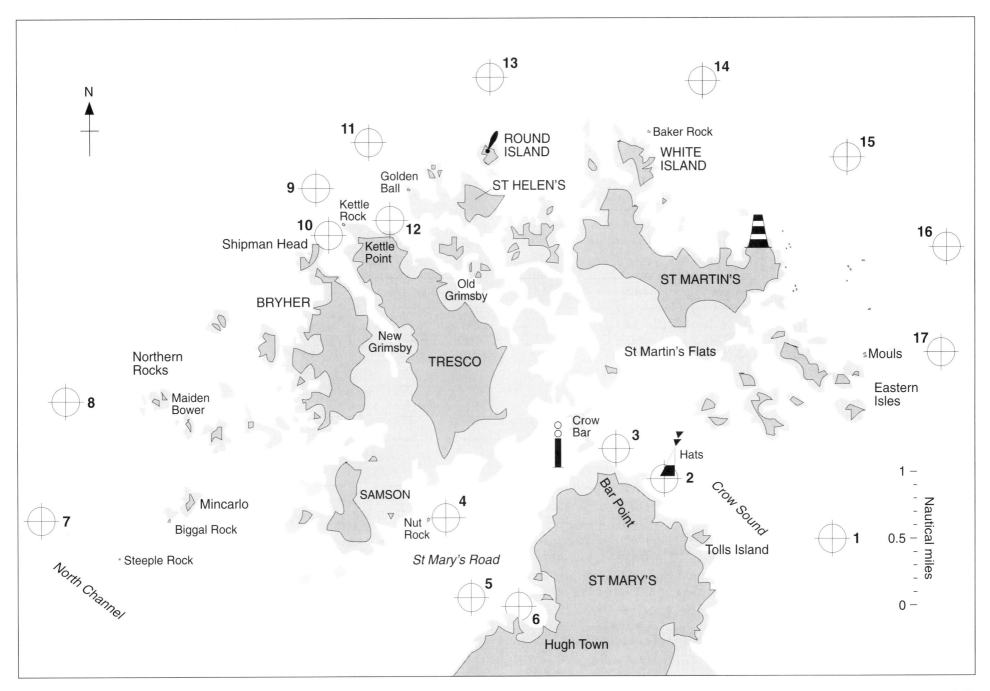

N

13

14

11

ROUND ISLAND

Baker Rock

WHITE ISLAND

15

Golden Ball

ST HELEN'S

9

Kettle Rock

10   **12**

Shipman Head

Kettle Point

16

Old Grimsby

ST MARTIN'S

BRYHER

New Grimsby

TRESCO

St Martin's Flats

Mouls   **17**

Northern Rocks

Eastern Isles

Maiden Bower

8

Crow Bar

3

Hats

2

Crow Sound

Mincarlo

SAMSON

4

Bar Point

7

Biggal Rock

Nut Rock

Tolls Island

1

Steeple Rock

St Mary's Road

ST MARY'S

North Channel

5

6

Hugh Town

1 —

Nautical miles

0.5 —

0 —

Isles of Scilly South

WP No	Waypoint name and position	Latitude	Longitude
2-1	Crow Sound approach, 1 M due E of Tolls Island	49°55.68'N	06°14.98'W
2-2	St Mary's Sound outer, 4 ca due S of Peninnis Head L/H	49°53.84'N	06°18.17'W
2-3	Porth Cressa entrance, 1 ca due E of Biggal Rock	49°54.33'N	06°18.70'W
2-4	Porth Conger South, ¼ M due S of The Hoe	49°53.03'N	06°19.70'W
2-5	Smith Sound South, ½ M due E of Flat Carn Rock	49°52.50'N	06°21.26'W
2-6	Western Rocks South, ¾ M due S of Black Rock	49°51.08'N	06°23.87'W
2-7	Bishop Rock clearing, 1 M SW of Bishop Rock lighthouse	49°51.63'N	06°27.78'W
2-8	Broad Sound outer, 4 ca NW of Bishop Rock lighthouse	49°52.62'N	06°27.12'W
2-9	Crim Rocks clearing, ¾ M due W of the Peaked Rock	49°53.75'N	06°28.45'W
2-10	North Channel outer, 1 M W of Biggal Rock on leading line	49°55.84'N	06°24.98'W
2-11	Broad Sound middle, 1½ ca S of Gunner S-card buoy	49°53.45'N	06°25.02'W
2-12	Broad Sound inner, ½ ca NW of Old Wreck N-card buoy	49°54.27'N	06°22.82'W
2-13	North Channel inner, 4 ca NE of Old Wreck N-card buoy	49°54.51'N	06°22.32'W
2-14	Smith Sound North, ¼ M NW of Great Smith Rock	49°54.27'N	06°22.00'W
2-15	Porth Conger North, 1 ca NNW of The Cow Rock	49°53.94'N	06°20.44'W
2-16	St Mary's Sound inner, 2 ca NW of Bartholomew red buoy	49°54.53'N	06°20.02'W
2-17	Hugh Town approach, 4 ca 284°T from b/water head	49°55.17'N	06°19.54'W
2-18	Hugh Town entrance, ½ ca due N of b/water head	49°55.12'N	06°18.93'W
2-19	Tresco South, 1½ ca due E of Nut Rock	49°55.86'N	06°19.90'W

COASTAL DANGERS

Refer to Admiralty charts 34, 883

Spanish Ledges

In St Mary's Sound, the south approach round St Mary's island, the Spanish Ledges, lie about ½ mile south-west of Peninnis Head, marked on their east side by an E-cardinal bell buoy. Coming into St Mary's Sound from seaward, it is important to pass between Peninnis Head and the Spanish Ledge buoy; then, continuing north-west, leave the Bartholomew red buoy to port as you round the south-west corner of St Mary's.

Western Rocks

This far south-western group of reefs and islets, about 1½ miles east of the Bishop Rock, have numerous dangers around them and unpredictable tidal streams running through them. On a circumnavigation of the archipelago, keep a good ¾ mile south of the group.

The Bishop Rock

This famous, prominent lighthouse on the south-west edge of the Isles of Scilly is easily recognised. However, boats rounding this south-west corner should avoid the area of overfalls which can extend nearly ½ mile south of the Bishop. There are also overfalls close north of the Bishop, and on the north side of Broad Sound over Flemming's Ledge.

Crim Rocks

The most westerly dangers of the Isles of Scilly, the Crim Rocks, are unmarked except by their position about 1½ miles north and a shade west of Bishop Rock lighthouse, and by the only above-water head known as the Peaked Rock (2 metres high). Boats approaching the islands from westward or making a circumnavigation of the group must take great care to avoid the Crim Rocks. The whole area around these reefs is uneasy with breaking swell and overfalls.

Gunners Ledge

The Gunners Rock and Gunners Ledge lie not quite 1½ miles east of the Crim Peaked Rock, marked on their south side by the Gunner S-cardinal buoy. Coming into Broad Sound from the south-west, passing 4 cables or so to the north-west of Bishop Rock lighthouse, be sure to pass between Gunner S-cardinal and Round Rock N-cardinal buoys; be careful, as it is easy to confuse the two from a distance.

Jeffrey Rock

Along the inner end of Broad Sound, passing to the north of Annet island, steer to leave the Old Wreck N-cardinal buoy fairly close to the south-east and so avoid Jeffrey Rock (with only 0.9 metres over it) which lurks 4 cables west of the Old Wreck buoy.

Steeple Rock

This head (0.1 metres over it) needs watching near LW in the North Channel. Steeple Rock lies 7 cables south-west of the highest point of Mincarlo islet and is cleared by the North Channel leading line – St Agnes old lighthouse in transit with the gap between the two summits of Great Smith rocks bearing 130°T.

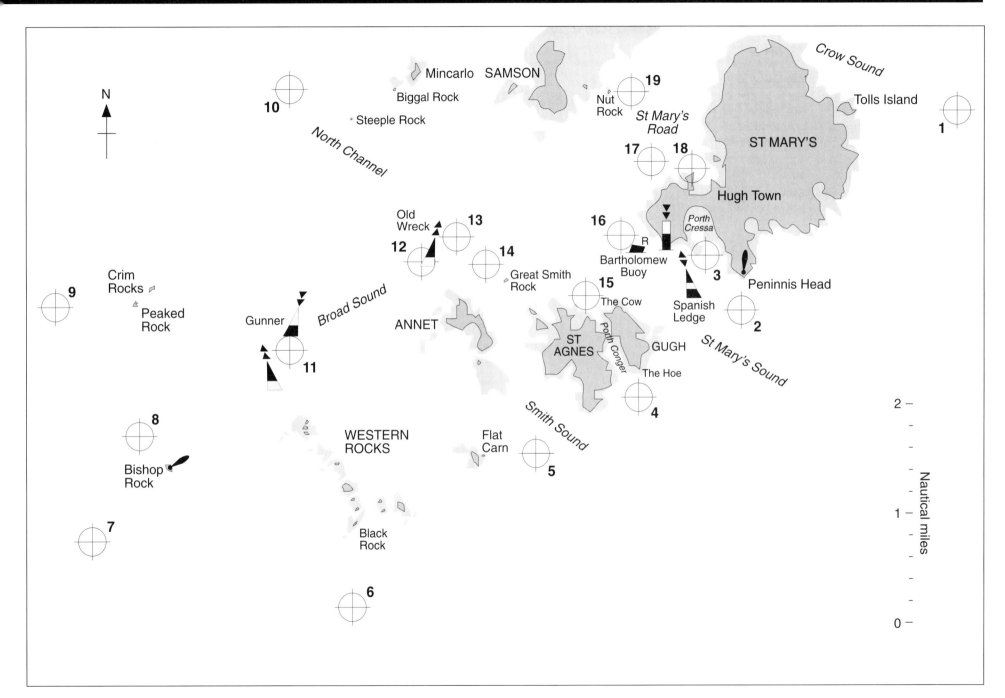

N

Crow Sound

Mincarlo   SAMSON

Biggal Rock

Steeple Rock

10

19

Nut
Rock

Tolls Island

St Mary's
Road

ST MARY'S

1

North Channel

17   18

Hugh Town

Old
Wreck   13

16

Porth
Cressa

12

14

R

Bartholomew
Buoy

3

Crim
Rocks

Great Smith
Rock

15

Peninnis Head

9

Peaked
Rock

Broad Sound

The Cow

Spanish
Ledge

2

ANNET

ST
AGNES

GUGH

St Mary's Sound

Gunner

Porth Conger

The Hoe

11

4

8

WESTERN
ROCKS

Flat
Carn

Smith Sound

5

Bishop
Rock

1

Nautical miles

7

Black
Rock

6

0

Isles of Scilly to Land's End

WP No	Waypoint name and position	Latitude	Longitude
3-1	Crow Sound approach, 1 M due E of Tolls Island	49°55.68'N	06°14.98'W
3-2	St Mary's Sound outer, 4 ca due S of Peninnis Head L/H	49°53.84'N	06°18.17'W
3-3	Porth Conger South, ¼ M due S of The Hoe	49°53.03'N	06°19.70'W
3-4	Round Island clearing, 6 ca due N of lighthouse	49°59.31'N	06°19.34'W
3-5	White Island clearing, 6 ca NE of Baker Rock	49°59.28'N	06°16.65'W
3-6	St Martin's north-east, 1 M NE of St Martin's daymark	49°58.67'N	06°14.82'W
3-7	St Martin's east, 1½ M E of St Martin's daymark	49°57.95'N	06°13.58'W
3-8	Eastern Isles clearing, 6 ca E of Mouls Rock	49°57.12'N	06°13.58'W
3-9	Seven Stones North, 4 M due N of light-float	50°07.58'N	06°04.28'W
3-10	Seven Stones light-float, ½ M due E of float position	50°03.58'N	06°03.50'W
3-11	Seven Stones South, 4 M due S of light-float	49°59.58'N	06°04.28'W
3-12	Wolf Rock North, 2 M due N of lighthouse	49°58.70'N	05°48.50'W
3-13	Wolf Rock South, 2 M due S of lighthouse	49°54.70'N	05°48.50'W
3-14	Pendeen clearing, 2½ M 300°T from lighthouse	50°11.15'N	05°43.62'W
3-15	Cape Cornwall clearing, 2 M due W of old chimney	50°07.59'N	05°45.65'W
3-16	Longships clearing, ¾ M due W of lighthouse	50°04.00'N	05°45.89'W
3-17	Runnel Stone SW, ½ M SW of S-card buoy	50°00.85'N	05°40.88'W

COASTAL DANGERS
Refer to Admiralty charts 2565, 1148

Seven Stones reef
This notorious reef lies 6–7 miles north-east of St Martin's Head, and is marked on its north-east side by the Seven Stones light-float. Boats approaching the Isles of Scilly from the south coast of England would not normally stray near the Seven Stones, but those on passage to and from the south-west coast of Ireland need to watch the Seven Stones. In particular, boats making for the Isles of Scilly direct from Ireland need to watch their longitude carefully as they approach the Scillies.

Eastern Rocks
Approaching Crow Sound from off Land's End or the Lizard, take care not to make a landfall north of the Eastern Isles. Various drying hazards lie up to ¾ mile east and south-east of St Martin's Head, dangerous if you were approaching this stretch in a mist of summer haze.

St Martin's Head
This distinctive headland, marked by a prominent red-and-white daymark, has Deep Ledge (0.9 metres over it) not quite ½ mile to the north; the Chapel Rocks and Little Ledge close on its north-east side; Flat Ledge ½ mile east by north of the daymark; and the various Eastern Rocks – Hard Lewis Rocks, Polreath, Southward Ledge – up to ¾ mile east of the Head. All these dangers must be given a wide berth when skirting this north-east corner of the Scillies archipelago.

Wolf Rock
The Wolf is not so much a danger as a signpost, and the lighthouse is a useful mark if bound directly between the Lizard and the Isles of Scilly. The Wolf Rock lies just over 7 miles south-west of Gwennap Head, the southern tip of the Land's End peninsula, and is fairly steep-to on all sides.

The Longships
The Longships Rocks extend just over 1 mile west from Land's End. The westernmost rock is marked by the famous lighthouse, which can be passed fairly close on its west side. There is a passage inside the Longships in quiet weather, by keeping close to the Land's End shore.

Runnel Stone
This nasty drying rock lies about ¾ mile south of Gwennap Head and is marked on its south side by the Runnel Stone S-cardinal whistle buoy. This buoy is a convenient point of departure for the Isles of Scilly if you are leaving from Penzance or Newlyn.

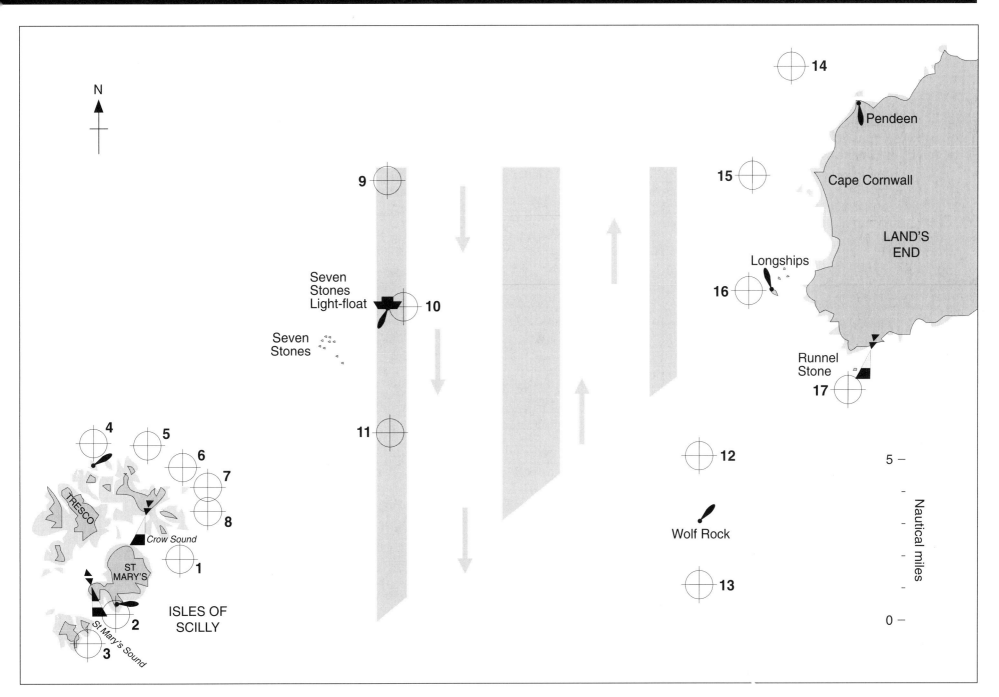

N

9

Seven
Stones
Light-float

Seven
Stones

10

11

14

Pendeen

Cape Cornwall

15

LAND'S
END

Longships

16

Runnel
Stone

17

12

Wolf Rock

13

4

5

6

TRESCO

7

8

Crow Sound

ST
MARY'S

1

2

ISLES OF
SCILLY

St Mary's Sound

3

5 –

–

Nautical miles

–

0 –

Land's End and Mounts Bay

WP No	Waypoint name and position	Latitude	Longitude
4-1	Cape Cornwall clearing, 2 M due W of old chimney	50°07.59'N	05°45.65'W
4-2	Longships clearing, ¾ M due W of lighthouse	50°04.00'N	05°45.89'W
4-3	Runnel Stone SW, ½ M SW of S-card buoy	50°00.85'N	05°40.88'W
4-4	Mount's Bay SW, 1M SE of Carn-Du headland	50°02.87'N	05°32.09'W
4-5	Low Lee East, ¼ M due E of E-card buoy	50°05.53'N	05°30.93'W
4-6	Newlyn approach, ½ M 100°T from S pierhead	50°06.06'N	05°31.75'W
4-7	Newlyn entrance, close N of S pierhead	50°06.18'N	05°32.51'W
4-8	Penzance approach, 6 ca SE of S pierhead	50°06.61'N	05°30.97'W
4-9	Penzance entrance, close E of S pierhead	50°07.03'N	05°31.57'W
4-10	St Michael's Mount approach, 4 ca 260°T from tower	50°06.89'N	05°29.24'W
4-11	Mountamopus, ½ M SW of S-card buoy	50°04.28'N	05°26.79'W

COASTAL DANGERS
Refer to Admiralty chart 777

The Longships
The Longships Rocks extend just over 1 mile west from Land's End. The westernmost rock is marked by the famous lighthouse, which can be passed fairly close on its west side. There is a passage inside the Longships in quiet weather, by keeping close to the Land's End shore.

Runnel Stone
This nasty drying rock lies about ¾ mile south of Gwennap Head and is marked on its south side by the Runnel Stone S-cardinal whistle buoy. This buoy is a convenient point of departure for the Isles of Scilly if you are leaving from Penzance or Newlyn.

Newlyn and Penzance approaches
The Low Lee shoal (with 1.1 metres over it) lies 3½ cables ENE of Penlee Point, marked on its north-east side by an E-cardinal buoy. Most boats will prefer to pass outside this buoy when approaching Newlyn from the south or south-east. The Carn Base shoal (with 1.8 metres over it) lies just over 3 cables north-west of the Low Lee E-cardinal buoy, but has plenty of water over it for most craft except near low springs.

If rounding Battery Rocks between Penzance and Newlyn, pass outside Gear Rock isolated danger beacon, which stands not quite ½ mile south of Penzance south pierhead.

St Michael's Mount
If approaching St Michael's Mount from Penzance harbour, keep the tower bearing due east true from Penzance until you are within four cables of the Mount. This will clear the various rocky ledges fringing the bay between Penzance and the Mount, including the Outer Penzeath Rock (awash at chart datum) which lies ½ mile due west from St Michael's harbour west pierhead.

Mountamopus
The Mountamopus shoal (with 1.8 metres over it) lies on the north side of Mount's Bay, about ¾ mile south of Cudden Point. The shoal is marked on its south-west side by a S-cardinal buoy, which makes a useful mark when approaching Penzance from the Lizard.

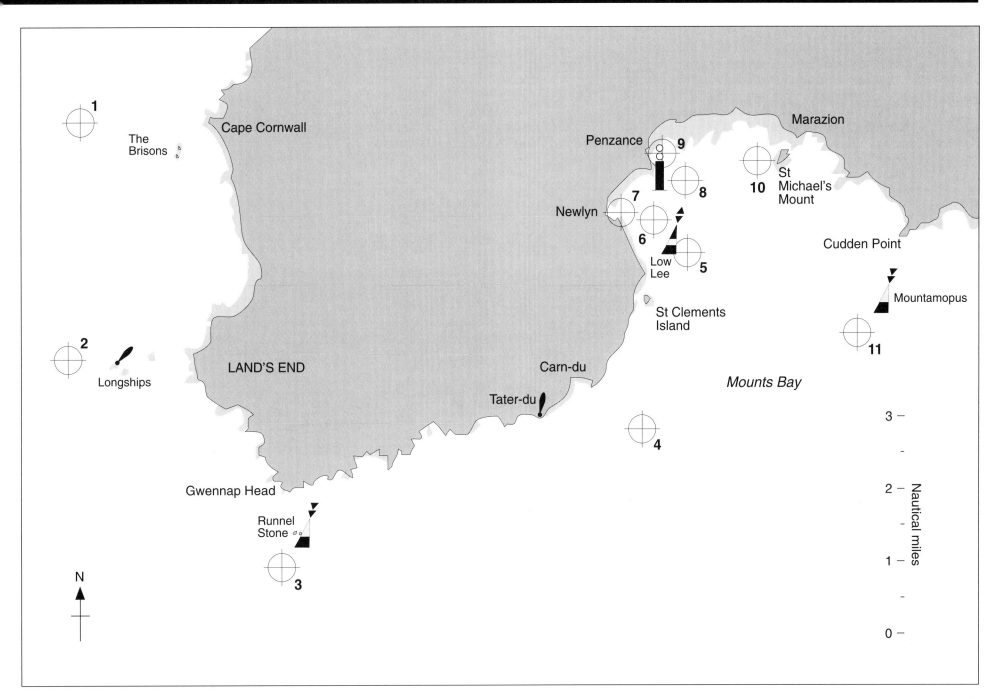

The Brisons

Cape Cornwall

1

Marazion

Penzance **9**

St Michael's Mount

10

8

Newlyn **7**

6

Cudden Point

Low Lee **5**

2

Longships

LAND'S END

St Clements Island

Carn-du

Mountamopus

11

Mounts Bay

Tater-du

4

Gwennap Head

3 –

–

2 –

Nautical miles

Runnel Stone

1 –

N

–

3

0 –

WP No	Waypoint name and position	Latitude	Longitude
5-1	Porthleven approach, 4 ca 240°T from S b/water light	50°04.68'N	05°19.60'W
5-2	Mullion approach, 2 ca NW of N tip of Mullion Island	50°00.90'N	05°16.17'W
5-3	Porth Mellin anchorage, 150 m WSW of harbour entrance	50°00.87'N	05°15.60'W
5-4	Boa West, 4 M due W of Lizard lighthouse	49°57.58'N	05°18.23'W
5-5	Lizard clearing, 3 M due S of lighthouse	49°54.58'N	05°12.08'W
5-6	Lizard inner (calm weather), 1½ M due S of lighthouse	49°56.08'N	05°12.08'W
5-7	Black Head clearing, 1½ M SE of headland	49°59.15'N	05°04.39'W
5-8	Manacles, ½ M due E of E-card buoy	50°02.78'N	05°01.08'W
5-9	Helford River approach, ½ M 020°T from Nare Point	50°05.58'N	05°04.27'W
5-10	Helford River entrance, 300 m due S of Toll Point	50°05.81'N	05°06.02'W
5-11	Falmouth entrance, 4 ca SW of St Anthony Head L/H	50°08.15'N	05°01.34'W

COASTAL DANGERS
Refer to Admiralty charts 154, 777

The Boa
The Boa rocky shoals lie 3 miles or so west of Lizard lighthouse and have plenty of water over them, but there are overfalls in this area during the strongest hours of the tide, especially when the stream is weather-going. Unless conditions are very quiet, it is worth giving the shoals a wide berth using the Boa West clearing waypoint in the table.

Lizard Point
The Lizard has drying rocks extending ½ mile seaward, and a potentially dangerous race which is at its worst when the Channel ebb is running hard against a strong westerly or south-westerly. The race is cleared by staying 3 miles off the Point, although in quiet weather you can cut in closer using the Lizard inner waypoint in the table.

The Manacles
Approaching Falmouth or the Helford River from the south, keep well east of the Manacles Rocks which lurk up to ¾ mile east and south-east from Manacle Point. These dangers are guarded by an E-cardinal bell buoy.

Helford River approaches
Approaching the Helford River from the direction of the Manacles, Nare Point should be given at least ¼ mile clearance since rocky ledges extend east and north-east from the end of the promontory for about 1 cable. On the north side of the Helford estuary, the August Rock (dries 1.4 metre) lurks about 4 cables south of Rosemullion Head. During the summer this Rock is marked on its south-east side by a small green buoy which is not always easy to spot.

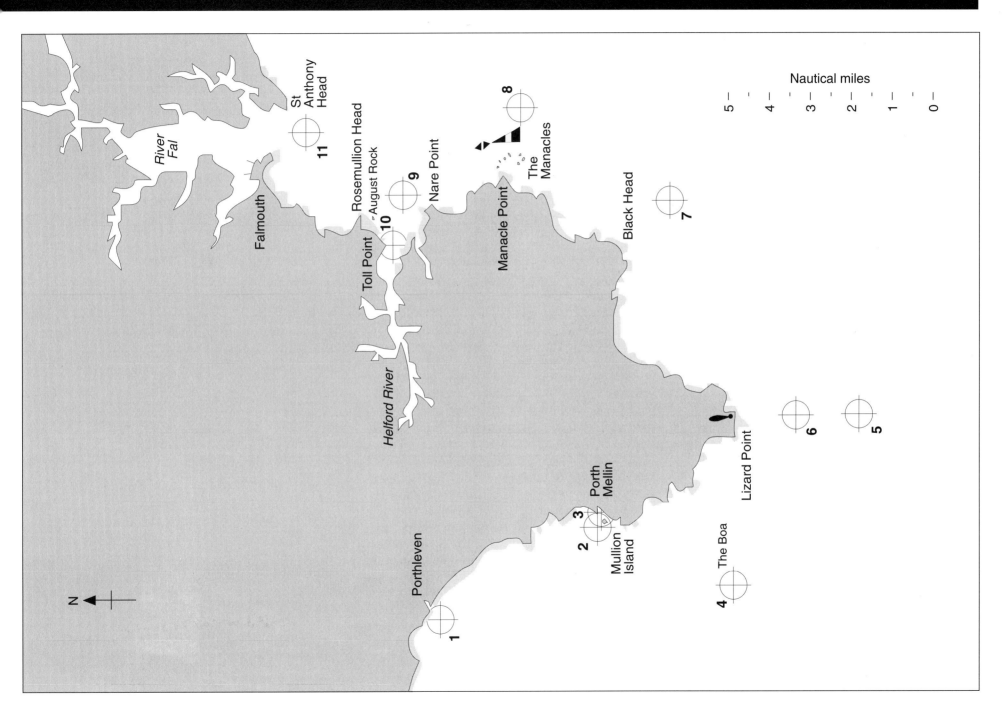

Nautical miles

5 —
4 —
3 —
2 —
1 —
0 —

N

River Fal

St
Anthony
Head

Falmouth

11

Rosemullion Head
August Rock

Toll Point

10

9

Nare Point

Helford River

The Manacles

8

Manacle Point

Black Head

7

Porthleven

Porth
Mellin

3

2

Mullion
Island

The Boa

4

Lizard Point

6

5

1

WP No	Waypoint name and position	Latitude	Longitude
6-1	Falmouth entrance, 4 ca SW of St Anthony Head L/H	50°08.15'N	05°01.34'W
6-2	Black Rock east, 100 m due E of E-card buoy	50°08.65'N	05°01.59'W
6-3	Pendennis Point, 1½ ca due E of E tip of headland	50°08.61'N	05°02.20'W
6-4	The Governor, 100 m due E of Governor E-card buoy	50°09.12'N	05°02.23'W
6-5	Falmouth Eastern b/water, 150 m due N of pierhead	50°09.39'N	05°02.89'W
6-6	Falmouth Inner Harbour, 300 m NW of Queen's Jetty head	50°09.48'N	05°03.65'W
6-7	St Mawes entrance, 100 m due S of St Mawes S-card buoy	50°09.01'N	05°01.35'W
6-8	St Mawes harbour, 1½ ca 170°T from St Mawes pierhead	50°09.31'N	05°00.74'W
6-9	Narrows gap, midway between East and West Narrows buoys	50°09.38'N	05°01.92'W
6-10	Carrick Road, 100 m due W of Vilt green conical buoy	50°09.95'N	05°02.30'W
6-11	St Just Pool, 100 m 100°T from St Just red can buoy	50°10.39'N	05°01.57'W
6-12	St Just entrance, 300 m 200°T from Messack Point	50°10.72'N	05°01.49'W
6-13	Mylor approach, midway between summer fairway buoys	50°10.75'N	05°02.65'W
6-14	Carick Carlys, 100 m 260°T from Carick green buoy	50°11.52'N	05°02.75'W
6-15	Restronguet entrance, 150 m SE of Restronguet Pt SE tip	50°11.51'N	05°03.38'W
6-16	Turnaware approach, 250 m 110°T from Pill Point	50°12.11'N	05°02.38'W

ESTUARY DANGERS

Refer to Admiralty chart 32

The Falmouth estuary is well marked and the pilotage is largely straightforward, but there are a few shoals to bear in mind when you are pottering about, especially near low water.

Lugo Rock

This rocky shoal (with 0.6 metres over it) lies 1½ cables south of Castle Point, just opposite St Mawes Castle. Lugo is marked on its south side by St Mawes S-cardinal buoy. Do not be tempted to cut inside this buoy except above half-tide.

St Mawes Bank

This broad shoal on the east side of Carrick Road can catch you out near low water if you are tacking upstream and not paying full attention to the buoys. In particular, there is a 1.2 metre patch just outside the southernmost of the yellow buoys that are laid in this area during the summer to mark off a water-skiing area.

Mylor approaches

Above Carrick Road, the main river channel trends over to the east shore past Carclase Point and St Just. The west side of the river is very shallow opposite Mylor Creek and between Mylor and Restronguet Creeks. Most boats may cross this area above half-tide, but within a couple of hours of low water deeper draught yachts and motor boats can easily find themselves aground if they stray out of the buoyed channel.

St Just to Turnaware Point

Above St Just, the buoyed channel is about 250 metres wide, with shallow flats on both sides of the river having soundings close to chart datum in parts. Most boats can stray outside the buoys above half-tide, when it is safe to approach Restronguet Creek and moor in the deeper area near the mouth. Further upstream, a drying spit extends some 250 metres north-west from Turnaware Point, marked at its north-west tip by an unlit green buoy.

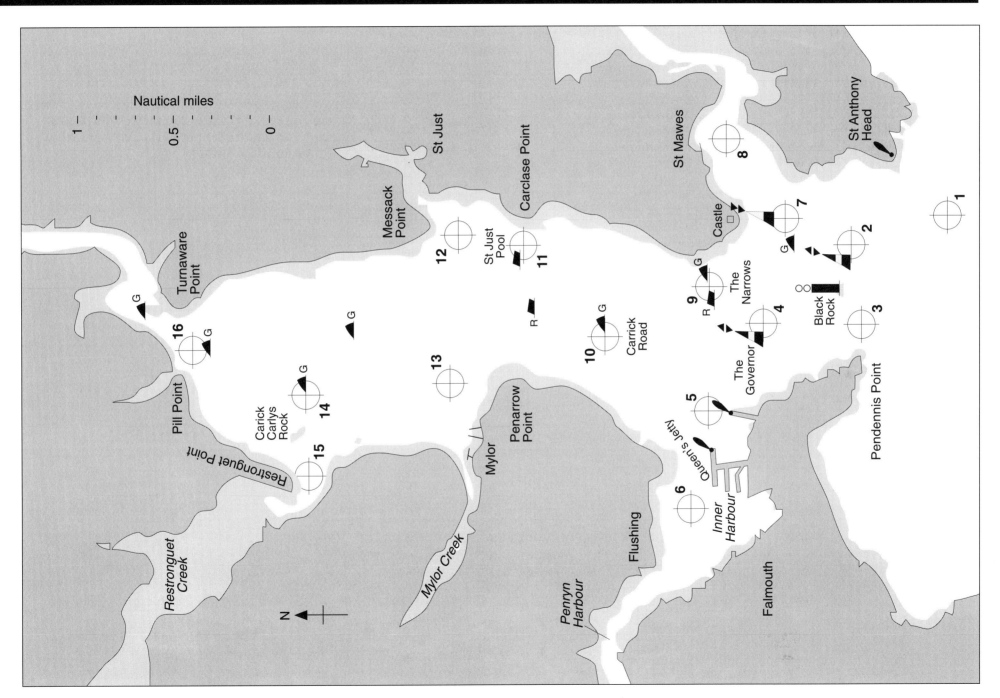

Nautical miles

1   0.5   0

N

St Anthony Head

St Just

Carclase Point

Messack Point

Turnaware Point

Pill Point

Restronguet Point

Restronguet Creek

Mylor Creek

Mylor

Penarrow Point

Penryn Harbour

Flushing

Falmouth

Inner Harbour

Queen's Jetty

Pendennis Point

Black Rock

The Governor

The Narrows

Castle

St Mawes

Carrick Road

St Just Pool

Carick Carlys Rock

1

2

3

4

5

6

7

8

9

10

11

12

13

14

15

16

G

G

G

G

G

G

G

R

R

R

25

WP No	Waypoint name and position	Latitude	Longitude
7-1	Falmouth entrance, 4 ca SW of St Anthony Head L/H	50°08.15'N	05°01.34'W
7-2	St Anthony approach, ¾ M due S of Zone Point	50°07.57'N	05°00.50'W
7-3	Porthscatho anchorage, 2 ca due S of Pednvadan	50°10.88'N	04°58.05'W
7-4	Gull Rock clearing, ¾ M SE of Gull Rock	50°11.18'N	04°53.41'W
7-5	Dodman clearing, 1½ M SE of Dodman Point cross	50°12.12'N	04°46.48'W
7-6	Gwineas clearing, ½ M SE of Gwineas buoy	50°14.12'N	04°44.76'W
7-7	Chapel Point, ¾ M due E of headland	50°15.37'N	04°44.75'W
7-8	Mevagissey entrance, 1 ca NE of south pierhead	50°16.20'N	04°46.75'W
7-9	Charlestown dock, 1 ca SE of pierheads gap	50°19.71'N	04°45.12'W
7-10	Polkerris anchorage, 1½ ca 260°T from pierhead	50°20.21'N	04°41.05'W
7-11	Gribbin Head, 8 ca 145°T from daymark	50°18.33'N	04°39.57'W
7-12	Fowey entrance, 250 m 100°T from Fowey lighthouse	50°19.58'N	04°38.52'W

COASTAL DANGERS

Refer to Admiralty charts 154, 1267

The Whelps

If coasting between Falmouth and Fowey, you need to stay outside The Whelps rocks (drying 4.6 metres) which extend south of Gull Rock (38 metres high) for 3½ cables. Gull Rock is a distinctive islet just over ½ mile east of Nare Head, between Gerrans Bay and Veryan Bay.

Dodman Point

Dodman Point has a race extending ½ mile southward, while the Gwineas Rocks, marked by an E-cardinal buoy, lie 2 miles to the north-east. When approaching Fowey from SSW, bear in mind that the Dodman is unlit, as is most of the coast between Falmouth and Fowey.

Cannis Rock

Cannis Rock (dries 4.6 metres) lies not quite ¼ mile south-east of Gribbin Head, on the west side of the approaches to Fowey. Gribbin Head has a large distinctive daymark with red-and-white horizontal stripes and the Cannis Rock is marked on its south-east side by a S-cardinal buoy.

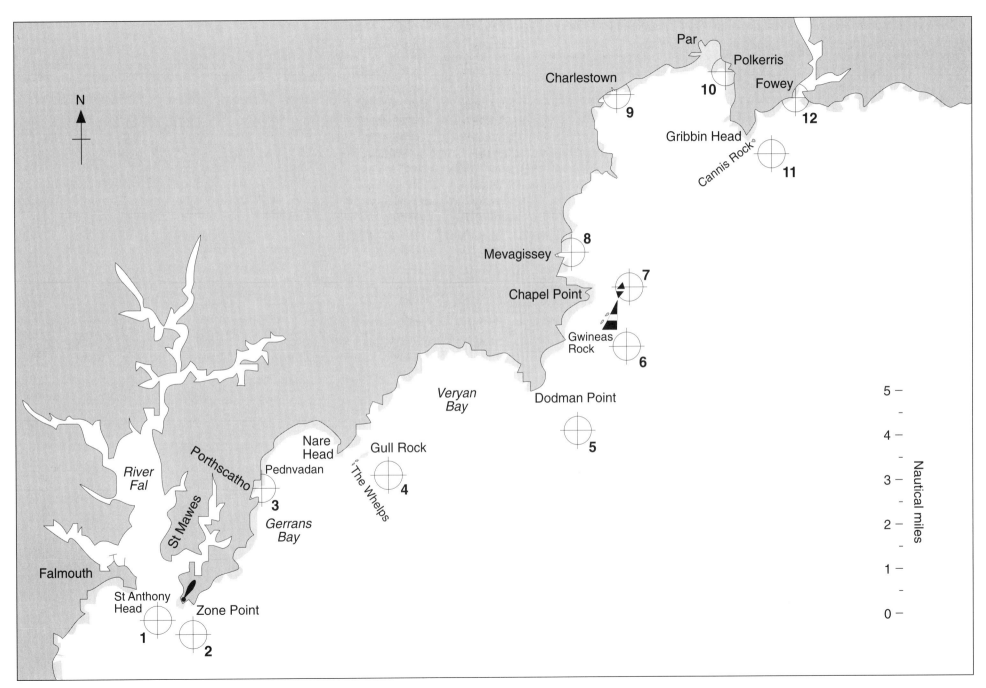

N

Par
Polkerris
Charlestown
10
Fowey
9
12
Gribbin Head
Cannis Rock
11
Mevagissey
8
7
Chapel Point
Gwineas
Rock
6
Veryan
Bay
Dodman Point
5
Nare
Head
Gull Rock
Pednvadan
The Whelps
4
River
Fal
Porthscatho
3
St Mawes
Gerrans
Bay
Falmouth
St Anthony
Head
Zone Point
1
2

5 —
-
4 —
-
Nautical miles
3 —
-
2 —
-
1 —
-
0 —

WP No	Waypoint name and position	Latitude	Longitude
8-1	Gribbin Head, 8 ca 145°T from daymark	50°18.33'N	04°39.57'W
8-2	Fowey entrance, 250 m 100°T from Fowey lighthouse	50°19.58'N	04°38.52'W
8-3	Polperro approach, ¼ M S of Polperro west headland	50°19.54'N	04°30.87'W
8-4	Looe Island south, 1 M S of Looe Island spot height	50°19.19'N	04°26.98'W
8-5	Looe approach, 1½ M SE of Looe Banjo pierhead	50°19.99'N	04°25.33'W
8-6	Looe entrance, 100 m 120°T from Looe Banjo pierhead	50°21.00'N	04°26.83'W
8-7	Eddystone north clearing, 1½ M N of lighthouse	50°12.32'N	04°15.85'W
8-8	Eddystone south clearing, 1½ M S of lighthouse	50°09.32'N	04°15.85'W
8-9	Rame Head clearing, 1 M S of ruined chapel	50°17.81'N	04°13.32'W
8-10	Penlee Point clearing, 1 M S of SE tip of headland	50°18.04'N	04°11.28'W

COASTAL DANGERS

Refer to Admiralty charts 148, 1267

Cannis Rock

Cannis Rock (dries 4.6 metres) lies not quite ¼ mile south-east of Gribbin Head, on the west side of the approaches to Fowey. Gribbin Head has a large distinctive daymark with red-and-white horizontal stripes and the Cannis Rock is marked on its south-east side by a S-cardinal buoy.

Udder Rock

Between Fowey harbour entrance and Polperro, Udder Rock (dries 0.6 metre) lies ½ mile off-shore opposite a white obelisk between Pencarrow Head and Nealand point. Udder Rock is marked on its south side by an unlit S-cardinal buoy, and the white obelisk in transit with a white painted mark on the shore provides a striking mark for the Rock.

St George's or Looe Island

Looe Island, which lies ¾ mile south of Looe harbour entrance, is fringed by a drying rocky shore and has a drying tail of reefs known as the Rennies (drying 4.6 metres) extending a good 3 cables to the south-east. Any boats bound between Looe and further west should round Looe Island by ¾ mile to keep well clear of the Rennies.

Eddystone Rocks

The Eddystone Rocks, marked by a tall light-house, lie 9 miles SSW of Plymouth Sound and should be given a wide berth in heavy weather or poor visibility.

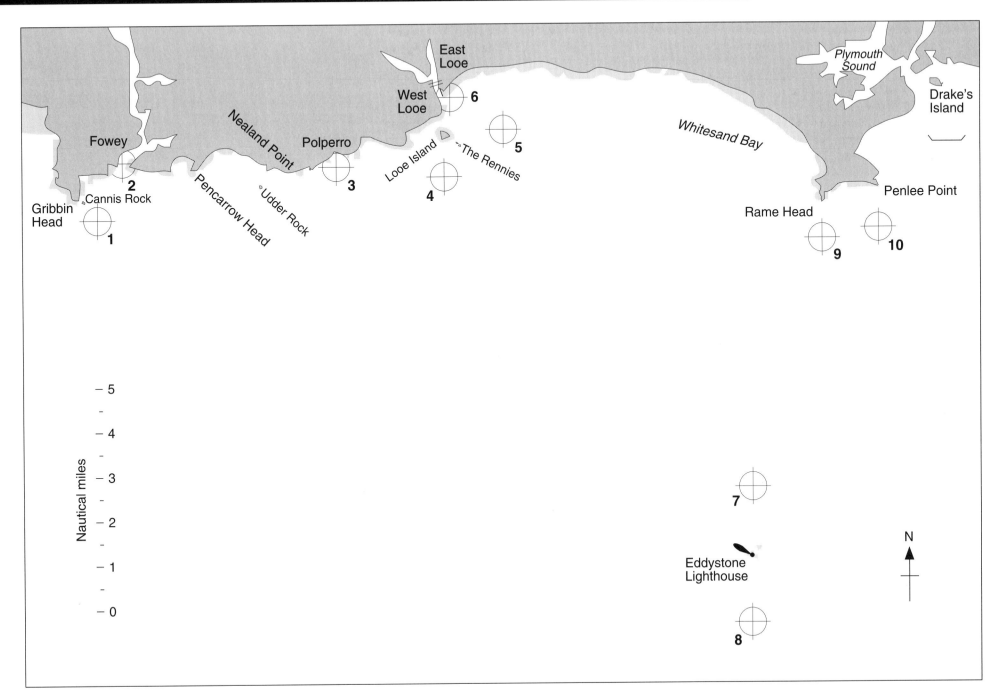

East
Looe

West
Looe

6

Fowey

2

Cannis Rock

Gribbin
Head

1

Nealand Point

Polperro

Pencarrow Head

Udder Rock

3

Looe Island

The Rennies

4

5

Whitesand Bay

Plymouth
Sound

Drake's
Island

Penlee Point

Rame Head

9

10

Nautical miles

− 5

− 4

− 3

− 2

− 1

− 0

7

Eddystone
Lighthouse

8

N

Plymouth Sound

WP No	Waypoint name and position	Latitude	Longitude
9-1	Rame Head clearing, 1 M S of ruined chapel	50°17.81'N	04°13.32'W
9-2	Penlee Point clearing, 1 M S of SE tip of headland	50°18.04'N	04°11.28'W
9-3	Plymouth SE approach, 1 M W of Gt Mewstone summit	50°18.42'N	04°07.92'W
9-4	Great Mewstone SW, 6 ca SW of Gt Mewstone summit	50°17.98'N	04°07.01'W
9-5	Cawsand anchorage, 1½ ca due E of Pemberknowse Pt	50°19.88'N	04°11.72'W
9-6	B/water west, 2 ca due W of W b/water lighthouse	50°20.04'N	04°09.77'W
9-7	B/water east, 1½ ca due E of E b/water lighthouse	50°19.98'N	04°07.94'W
9-8	Melampus, 100 m due E of Melampus red can buoy	50°21.12'N	04°08.57'W
9-9	Smeaton Pass South, 100 m SW of South Mallard S-card buoy	50°21.45'N	04°08.29'W
9-10	Smeaton Pass North, 1 ca due W of Mallard light-tower	50°21.58'N	04°08.41'W
9-11	Sutton approach, 50 m SE of Fisher's Nose lighthouse	50°21.75'N	04°07.91'W
9-12	Millbay approach, 1 ca due S of Millbay pierhead	50°21.62'N	04°09.11'W
9-13	Drake Channel, 75 m NW of NW Drake's Island red buoy	50°21.44'N	04°09.49'W
9-14	West Vanguard, 75 m SW of West Vanguard green buoy	50°21.42'N	04°09.96'W
9-15	Mayflower Marina approach, 250 m 340°T from Devil's Pt	50°21.68'N	04°10.05'W

ESTUARY DANGERS
Refer to Admiralty charts 30, 1967

Plymouth Sound is one of the most easily and safely accessible natural harbours along the south coast, which is why it became such an important naval base in the days of sail. Cawsand Bay, opposite the breakwater on the west side of the Sound, has been a strategic passage anchorage since the times when large unwieldy ships of war could only just work against the wind, and it was not always possible to get in or out of harbour unless conditions were favourable. Cawsand, with its gently shelving bottom and easy access, was a natural holding anchorage for the port of Plymouth.

Because the estuary is so straightforward, boats should stay out of the buoyed channels when possible, leaving them clear for ferries, naval ships and coasters. There are few estuary dangers to mention in Plymouth Sound, but the following are worth watching.

Penlee Point
This headland should not be shaved too close, since it has a small off-lying patch, drying 3.4 metres, within 1 cable due south.

Shagstone
On the east side of the estuary, a drying tail ending at the Shagstone extends west from the Renney Rocks for about 2 cables. This ledge needs avoiding if you are approaching Plymouth Sound from the east round the Great Mewstone and are planning to use the Eastern Channel past the breakwater. Keep a good offing past the Mewstone and then make towards the Tinker green buoy until the east end of the breakwater bears north true. Then it should be safe to alter a shade to starboard for the Eastern Channel.

The Bridge
The Bridge is that narrow neck of shoals and drying rocks which separates Drake's Island from the Mount Edgcumbe shore on the west side of the estuary. It makes a useful short-cut for boats bound up the Tamar, if only as far as the Mayflower Marina. The narrow channel across the Bridge is marked by red and green post beacons and carries a least depth of 2 metres, although the fairway is very fine near low water. The Bridge should only be taken in reasonable visibility when you can pick up the marks safely, but with a couple of hours rise of tide it is perfectly straightforward.

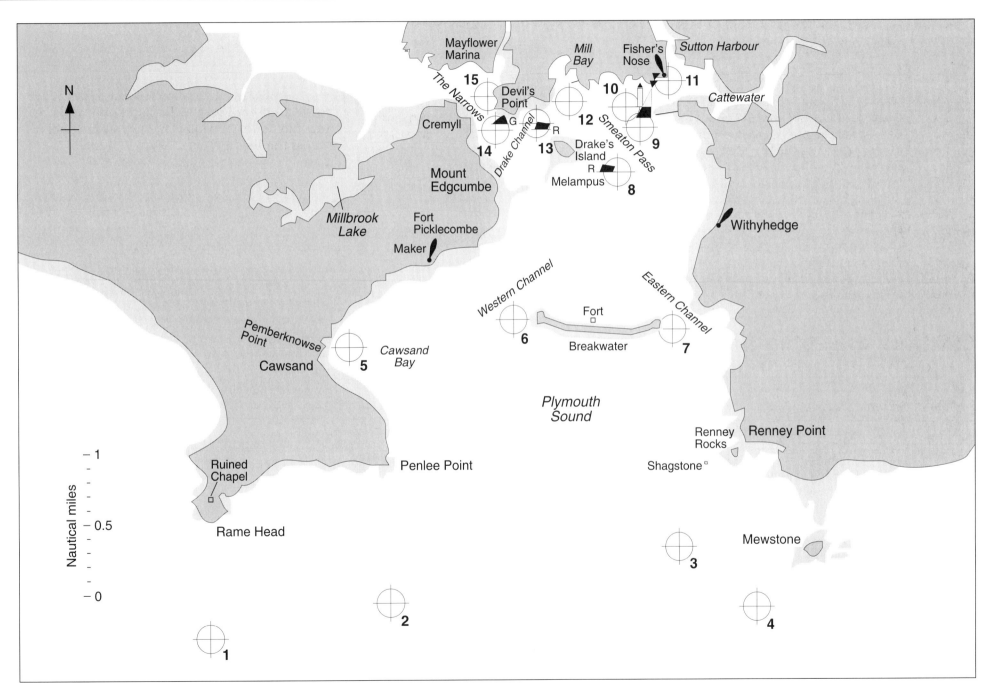

Yealm River to Salcombe

WP No	Waypoint name and position	Latitude	Longitude
10-1	Plymouth SE approach, 1 M W of Gt Mewstone summit	50°18.42'N	04°07.92'W
10-2	Great Mewstone SW, 6 ca SW of Gt Mewstone summit	50°17.98'N	04°07.01'W
10-3	Yealm River approach, 6 ca SE of Gt Mewstone SE shore	50°17.94'N	04°05.58'W
10-4	Yealm entrance, 6 ca 200°T from Wembury church spire	50°18.47'N	04°05.20'W
10-5	Yealm bar, due S of Season Pt SW tip, on leading line	50°18.56'N	04°04.08'W
10-6	Ebb Rocks clearing, ½ M 240°T from Gara Point	50°17.91'N	04°05.07'W
10-7	Hilsea Point clearing, 7 ca due S of Hilsea Point	50°16.93'N	04°02.98'W
10-8	R Erme approach, ½ M SW of Battisborough Is SW tip	50°17.81'N	03°58.23'W
10-9	R Erme entrance, 140 m SE of Battisborough Is SW tip	50°18.14'N	03°57.58'W
10-10	Burgh Island, 3 ca S of SW tip of island	50°16.37'N	03°54.00'W
10-11	Hope Cove outer, 2 ca NW of Bolt Tail NW tip	50°14.66'N	03°52.40'W
10-12	Hope Cove entrance, 2 ca NE of Bolt Tail NW tip	50°14.66'N	03°51.91'W
10-13	Bolt Tail west, ½ M W of Bolt Tail SW tip	50°14.42'N	03°52.92'W
10-14	Bolt Tail south, 1¼ M S of Bolt Tail SW tip	50°13.17'N	03°52.15'W
10-15	Ham Stone clearing, 6 ca 190°T from Ham Stone	50°12.44'N	03°49.90'W
10-16	Bolt Head south, 6 ca due S of Bolt Head SE tip	50°12.01'N	03°47.02'W
10-17	Salcombe approach, 4 ca SE of Bolt Hd on leading line	50°12.32'N	03°46.60'W
10-18	Salcombe entrance, ½ ca S of Poundstone on l/l turn	50°13.55'N	03°46.60'W
10-19	Prawle Point clearing, ½ M due S of headland	50°11.58'N	03°43.15'W

COASTAL DANGERS
Refer to Admiralty charts 28, 1613

Great Mewstone dangers
The prominent Great Mewstone, on the west side of the approaches to the Yealm River, has various dangers around it which need avoiding. On the south-west side of the Great Mewstone, the Little Mewstone ledges extend underwater for a cable or so, so you should not cut this islet too close on this side.

Two drying patches known as the Outer and Inner Slimers lurk a couple of cables from the east side of the Great Mewstone, drying 1.5 metres and 0.3 metre respectively. These heads are only a problem if you arrive a bit early for the Yealm – it is best to approach the estuary at least a couple of hours after low water.

On the east side of the estuary, within 3 cables of Gara Point at the south-west tip of Yealm Head, the Western Ebb and Eastern Ebb Rocks are both awash at chart datum. To the north of the Great Mewstone is the narrow neck across Wembury Ledge, which should only be used with local knowledge within a couple of hours of high water.

Hilsea Point Rock
Not usually a practical problem, Hilsea Point Rock (with 2.1 metres over it) lies ¼ mile off-shore, just under 4 cables south-east of Hilsea Point opposite an old coastguard lookout.

Wells Rock
This head will only need watching by those coasting close inshore in Bigbury Bay. Wells Rock (with only 1.2 metres over it) lies about 1 mile south-east of the estuary of the River Erme, and ½ mile south by east from Beacon Point. In practice, it is only a potential danger for any boat coast hopping between Burgh Island and the Erme.

Greystone Ledge, Ham Stone and Gregory Rocks
Between Bolt Tail and Bolt Head, you should keep at least ½ mile off the cliffs, to clear these various ledges and above-water rocks.

Salcombe bar
Salcombe entrance has a sand bar extending roughly NE-SW across the estuary from Limebury Point on the east side towards the steep cliffs on the west side. The bar is widest off Limebury and narrowest on the leading line. The shallowest soundings are 0.7 metres at chart datum, with a hump of about 1.2 metres as you cross the bar on the leading line.

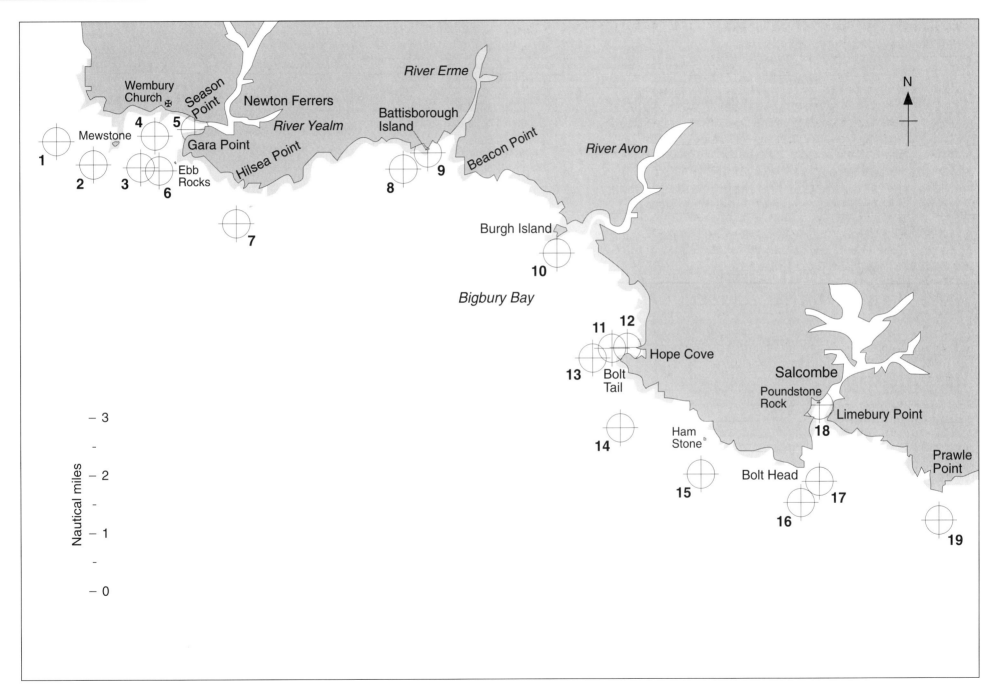

Mewstone

Wembury Church

Season Point

Newton Ferrers

River Yealm

River Erme

Battisborough Island

Beacon Point

River Avon

Gara Point

Hilsea Point

Ebb Rocks

Burgh Island

Bigbury Bay

Hope Cove

Bolt Tail

Salcombe

Poundstone Rock

Limebury Point

Ham Stone

Bolt Head

Prawle Point

N

Nautical miles

— 3

-

— 2

-

— 1

-

— 0

WP No	Waypoint name and position	Latitude	Longitude
11-1	Salcombe approach, 4 ca SE of Bolt Hd on leading line	50°12.32'N	03°46.60'W
11-2	Salcombe entrance, ½ ca S of Poundstone on l/l turn	50°13.55'N	03°46.60'W
11-3	Prawle Point clearing, ½ M due S of headland	50°11.58'N	03°43.15'W
11-4	Start Point outer, 2 M SE of lighthouse	50°11.89'N	03°36.27'W
11-5	Start Point inner, 6 ca SE of lighthouse	50°12.89'N	03°37.82'W
11-6	Hallsands anchorage, close off the village	50°14.10'N	03°39.37'W
11-7	Skerries buoy, actual position	50°16.28'N	03°33.70'W
11-8	Blackpool Sands anchorage, 1 ca off the beach	50°18.98'N	03°36.41'W
11-9	Dartmouth approach, 1 ca W of Castle Ledge green buoy	50°19.97'N	03°33.20'W
11-10	Dart entrance, between Dartmouth Castle and Kettle Point	50°20.52'N	03°33.76'W
11-11	Mew Stone clearing, 4 ca SE of SE tip of Mew Stone	50°19.73'N	03°31.42'W
11-12	Eastern Blackstone clearing, 2 ca SE of eastern rock	50°20.02'N	03°30.90'W

COASTAL DANGERS
Refer to Admiralty chart 1634

Salcombe bar
Salcombe entrance has a sand bar extending roughly NE-SW across the estuary from Limebury Point on the east side towards the steep cliffs on the west side. The bar is widest off Limebury and narrowest on the leading line. The shallowest soundings are 0.7 metres at chart datum, with a hump of about 1.2 metres as you cross the bar on the leading line.

In offshore winds and most moderate weather, the bar is no problem to boats except towards low springs. But in fresh or heavy weather from between south-west and south-east, seas can break steeply and unexpectedly over the bar, especially during a spring ebb. In heavy onshore weather, boats should avoid Salcombe if possible, or at least try to enter well above half-flood.

Start Point Race
A race extends up to 1½ miles SE of Start Point, although its position and severity depend on wind and tide. In moderate weather you can round Start close in, keeping ¼ mile south of the Black Stone to avoid Cherrick Rocks. In fresh wind-over-tide conditions, stay a good 2 miles offshore.

The Skerries Bank
Lying towards the south end of Start Bay, the Skerries Bank is only a danger in strong wind-over-tide conditions, or in strong south-easterlies, when steep breaking seas can build up, especially over the southern tail of the bank. In offshore or quiet weather, boats with normal draught can sail safely over the bank.

Combe Rocks
½ mile west of Dartmouth entrance, this straggling area of drying and above-water rocks juts seaward off Combe Point for well over 1 cable. Boats coasting inshore towards Dartmouth from near Blackpool Sands should give this promontory a wide berth, keeping at least 1 cable off the pinnacle of Old Combe Rock (3 metres high).

The Mew Stone
This prominent islet (35 metres high) off the east side of Dartmouth entrance has a tail of shoals and drying rocks extending more than ¼ mile from its west face. Boats coasting towards Dartmouth from the direction of Tor Bay should give this west side of the Mew Stone a wide berth before turning in towards the Castle Ledge green buoy.

Eastern Blackstone
This two-pronged above-water rock, ½ mile east by north from the Mew Stone, is sometimes difficult to spot from a distance when seen against the coast or the Mew Stone. The Eastern Blackstone is fairly steep to and can be passed either side, although you can easily be carried closer than intended by a strong spring tide.

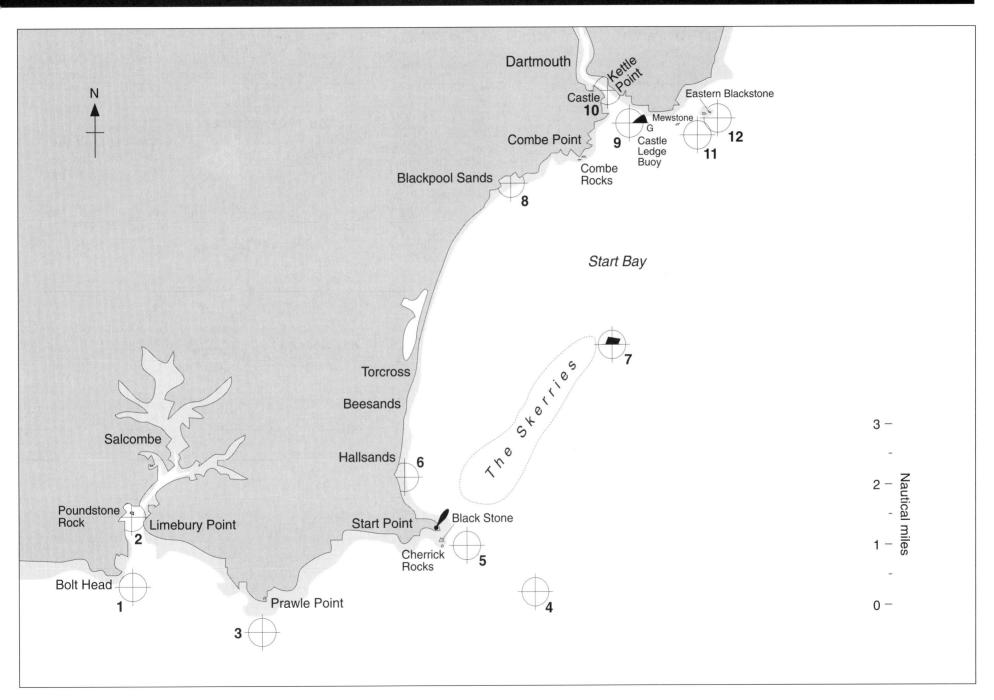

N

Dartmouth

Kettle Point

Castle

Eastern Blackstone

10

Mewstone

9 G

Castle Ledge Buoy

12

Combe Point

11

Combe Rocks

Blackpool Sands

8

Start Bay

Torcross

The Skerries

7

Beesands

Salcombe

Hallsands

6

Poundstone Rock

Limebury Point

2

Start Point

Black Stone

Cherrick Rocks

5

Bolt Head

1

Prawle Point

3

4

3 —

-

2 —

Nautical miles

-

1 —

-

0 —

WP No	Waypoint name and position	Latitude	Longitude
12-1	Dart entrance, between Dartmouth Castle and Kettle Point	50°20.52'N	03°33.76'W
12-2	Dartmouth approach, 1 ca W of Castle Ledge green buoy	50°19.97'N	03°33.20'W
12-3	Mew Stone clearing, 4 ca SE of SE tip of Mew Stone	50°19.73'N	03°31.42'W
12-4	Eastern Blackstone clearing, 2 ca SE of eastern rock	50°20.02'N	03°30.90'W
12-5	Nimble Rock clearing, 8 ca 050°T from E Blackstone	50°20.68'N	03°30.18'W
12-6	Sharkham Point clearing, ½ M SE of Sharkham Point	50°22.51'N	03°29.15'W
12-7	Berry Head east, ½ M due E of lighthouse	50°23.94'N	03°28.16'W
12-8	Berry Head north, 3 ca due N of lighthouse	50°24.24'N	03°28.93'W
12-9	Brixham approach, 1½ ca NW of b/water head	50°24.41'N	03°30.87'W
12-10	Brixham inner, 100 m due N of north fish quay	50°23.97'N	03°30.64'W
12-11	Torquay approach, 50 m due S of green entrance buoy	50°27.37'N	03°31.72'W
12-12	West Shag clearing, 3 ca due S of West Shag rock	50°26.89'N	03°30.71'W
12-13	Thatcher Rock clearing, 3 ca due S of south face	50°26.95'N	03°29.29'W
12-14	Ore Stone south, 4 ca due S of south face	50°26.96'N	03°28.23'W
12-15	Ore Stone east, ½ M due E of east face	50°27.40'N	03°27.42'W
12-16	Hope's Nose, ¾ M 080°T from NE tip of headland	50°27.93'N	03°27.63'W

COASTAL DANGERS

Refer to Admiralty charts 26, 1613, 1634

The Mew Stone

This prominent islet (35 metres high) off the east side of Dartmouth entrance has a tail of shoals and drying rocks extending more than ¼ mile from its west face. Boats coasting towards Dartmouth from the direction of Tor Bay should give this west side of the Mew Stone a wide berth before turning in towards the Castle Ledge green buoy.

Eastern Blackstone

This two-pronged above-water rock, ½ mile east by north from the Mew Stone, is sometimes difficult to spot from a distance when seen against the coast or the Mew Stone. The Eastern Blackstone is fairly steep-to and can be passed either side, although you can easily be carried closer than intended by a strong spring tide.

Nimble Rock

This isolated head, with less than 1 metre over it, lies about ½ mile south-east of Scabbacombe Head. To clear Nimble Rock, keep Start Point lighthouse open either side of the Eastern Blackstone. A striking mark is the cliff summit behind Scabbacombe Bay in transit with Scabbacombe Head bearing 330°T.

Mag Rock

Mag Rock, which dries 3.8 metres, extends up to 1½ cables east of Sharkham Point. This ledge is only a problem if you are coasting close inshore past the bays and coves between Dartmouth and Berry Head.

Morris Rogue

Approaching Torquay harbour along the north side of Tor Bay from the direction of the Ore Stone, you need to stay at least ½ mile offshore to the west of Thatcher Rock, in order to clear Morris Rogue (with 0.8 metre over it).

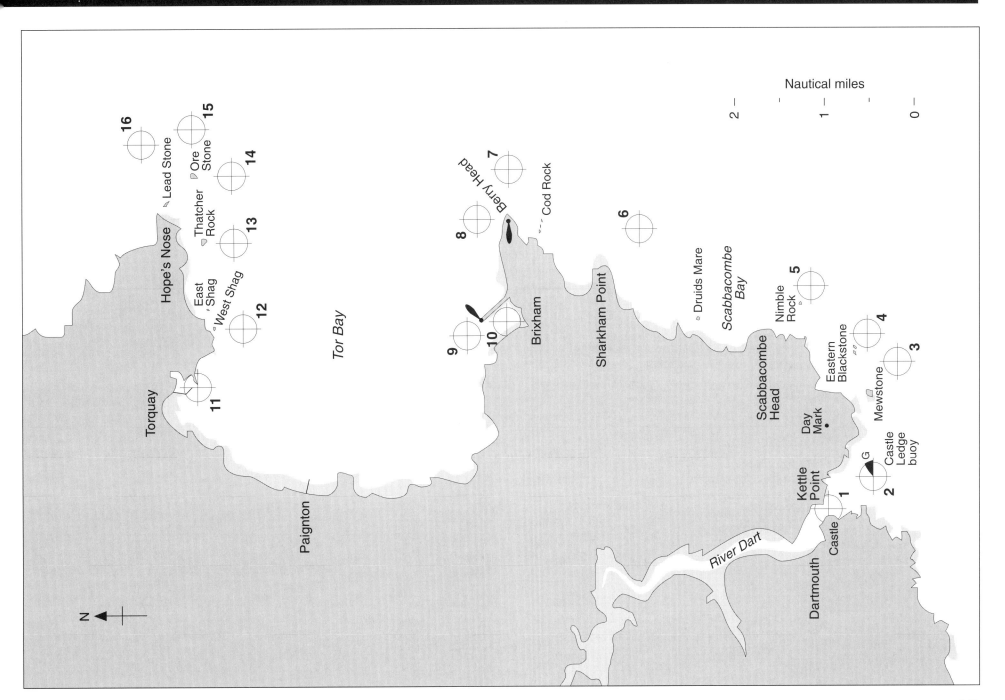

Nautical miles

2 — 1 — 0 —

Torquay

Hope's Nose

Lead Stone

16

Thatcher Rock

Ore Stone

15

14

East Shag

West Shag

13

12

11

Tor Bay

Paignton

Berry Head

Cod Rock

7

8

Brixham

9

10

Sharkham Point

6

Druids Mare

Scabbacombe Bay

Nimble Rock

Scabbacombe Head

5

Day Mark

Eastern Blackstone

4

Mewstone

3

Kettle Point

G

Castle Ledge buoy

1

2

Castle

Dartmouth

River Dart

N

37

Lyme Bay

WP No	Waypoint name and position	Latitude	Longitude
13-1	Mew Stone clearing, 4 ca SE of SE tip of Mew Stone	50°19.73'N	03°31.42'W
13-2	Berry Head east, ½ M due E of lighthouse	50°23.94'N	03°28.16'W
13-3	Berry Head north, 3 ca due N of lighthouse	50°24.24'N	03°28.93'W
13-4	Ore Stone south, 4 ca due S of south face	50°26.96'N	03°28.23'W
13-5	Ore Stone east, ½ M due E of east face	50°27.40'N	03°27.42'W
13-6	Hope's Nose, ¾ M 080°T from NE tip of headland	50°27.93'N	03°27.63'W
13-7	Babbacombe Bay, ½ M 321°T from Long Quarry Point	50°28.90'N	03°30.30'W
13-8	Teignmouth approach, 2 ca SE of the Ness east tip	50°32.08'N	03°29.42'W
13-9	Exe approach, 1 ca due E of Exe E-card buoy	50°35.97'N	03°22.14'W
13-10	Littleham Cove, ½ M NE of Straight Point SE tip	50°36.75'N	03°20.90'W
13-11	River Axe entrance, 3 ca due S of mouth	50°41.82'N	03°03.22'W
13-12	Lyme Regis approach, ½ M 116°T from pierhead on l/line	50°42.95'N	02°55.40'W
13-13	Bridport approach, ½ M 190°T from W pierhead on l/line	50°42.10'N	02°45.90'W
13-14	Portland inner west approach, 1 M NW of lighthouse	50°31.52'N	02°28.41'W
13-15	Portland clearing, 2½ M due S of lighthouse	50°28.32'N	02°27.30'W
13-16	Portland outer clearing, 3½ M due S of lighthouse	50°27.32'N	02°27.30'W
13-17	West Shambles, 1 ca W of W-card buoy	50°29.75'N	02°24.50'W

COASTAL DANGERS

Refer to Admiralty chart 3315

Teignmouth approaches

Teignmouth is an interesting and unspoilt harbour, but the bar at the river mouth requires some care. It is no problem in any winds from a westerly quarter, when strangers should enter above half-tide. In any winds from the east, strangers should stay clear and make for Torquay or Brixham instead.

River Exe approaches

The Exe is one of the most unspoilt estuaries in the West Country, although its bar and shifting sands at the entrance help to keep it so. Strangers should only approach in offshore winds, making for the fairway buoy, not long after low water ideally, when most of the drying banks are visible and should provide some lee in the fairway. Although the channel is lit, you should not attempt the Exe entrance at night unless you have been in a couple of times in daylight.

Portland Race

The worst of Portland Race extends 1½–2 miles south of the Bill. Keep a good 3–3½ miles off the Bill if passing outside, or within ¼ mile if passing inside. If making for the inner passage from Dartmouth or Torbay, use the Portland inner west approach waypoint in order to close the Bill safely north of the Race. Then shave close to the Bill all the way round to the east side, watching out for crab-pot floats all the time.

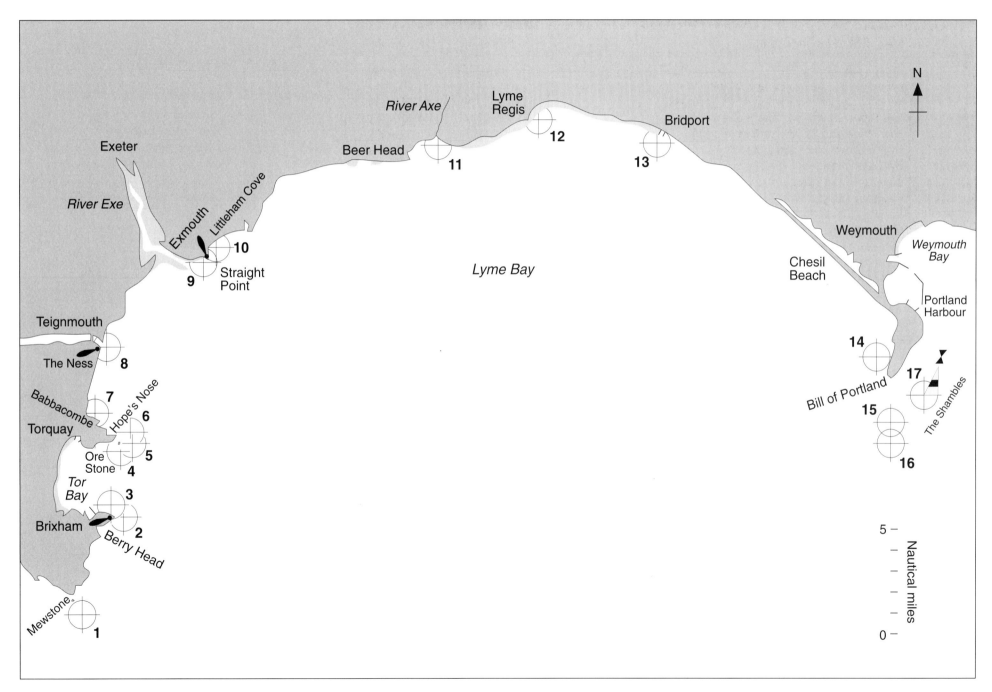

N

Exeter

River Axe

Lyme
Regis

Beer Head

Bridport

12

11

13

River Exe

Weymouth

*Weymouth
Bay*

Exmouth

Littleham Cove

Chesil
Beach

10

Portland
Harbour

Straight
Point

9

Lyme Bay

Teignmouth

The Ness   **8**

14

Babbacombe

7

Hope's Nose

17

Torquay

6

The Shambles

Ore
Stone   **5**

Bill of Portland

4

15

*Tor
Bay*

3

16

Brixham

2

Berry Head

Mewstone

1

5 —

Nautical miles

0 —

WP No	Waypoint name and position	Latitude	Longitude
14-1	Portland inner west approach, 1 M NW of lighthouse	50°31.52'N	02°28.41'W
14-2	Portland inner east approach, ½ M E of Old Low lighthouse	50°31.14'N	02°26.22'W
14-3	Portland clearing, 2½ M due S of lighthouse	50°28.32'N	02°27.30'W
14-4	Portland outer clearing, 3½ M due S of lighthouse	50°27.32'N	02°27.30'W
14-5	West Shambles, 1 ca due W of W-card buoy	50°29.75'N	02°24.50'W
14-6	East Shambles, 1 ca due E of E-card buoy	50°30.76'N	02°19.80'W
14-7	Grove Point clearing, ½ M due E of outer rock	50°32.94'N	02°23.99'W
14-8	Portland Hr, ½ M 080°T from outer b/water north head	50°35.16'N	02°24.00'W
14-9	Weymouth approach, ¼ M due E of South pierhead	50°36.55'N	02°26.01'W

Tides round Portland Bill

The tides are strong round the Bill, whether you are taking the inner or the offshore passage. With the inner passage, it is usually best to go through near slack water just as the stream is starting to run in your favour. If you are staying well offshore, carrying a fair tide round the Bill will take you past and away as quickly as possible.

COASTAL DANGERS

Refer to Admiralty charts 2255, 2610

Portland Race

The worst of Portland Race extends 1½–2 miles south of the Bill. Keep a good 3–3½ miles off the Bill if passing outside, or within ¼ mile if passing inside. If making for the inner passage from Dartmouth or Torbay, use the Portland inner west approach waypoint in order to close the Bill safely north of the Race. Then shave close to the Bill all the way round to the east side, watching out for crab-pot floats all the time.

The Shambles

The Shambles Bank lies from 2½–4 miles E by S of Portland Bill, extending roughly ENE/WSW and marked at either end by the East Shambles E-cardinal buoy and the West Shambles W-cardinal buoy. The lowest soundings are 3.4 metres and local yachts and fishing boats pass over the bank in quiet weather, but it does not take much wind and tide to turn the area into a hostile maelstrom of dangerous white water.

On the east-going stream, the worst of Portland Race lies SSE of the Bill, almost within 1 mile of the West Shambles buoy. Boats coming from the west outside the Race and bound for Weymouth therefore have to be careful if turning in to pass between Portland and the Shambles. Passing east-about the Shambles is usually easier and safer, but adds another 3 miles into Weymouth if coming from the west. In reasonable weather, by far the most efficient route into Weymouth from the west is to take the inner passage round the Bill (see note under Portland Race above). The important tactic in this case is to make your landfall on the Bill well north of the lighthouse and the Race.

Crab-pot buoys

There are numerous crab-pot buoys in the vicinity of Portland Bill, especially close inshore through the inner passage. Take special care to watch out for these buoys, many of which are small and can be pulled half underwater by the tide. With the Race close on one side and the rocky shore of the Bill on the other, a rope snarled round a propeller or rudder could have serious consequences.

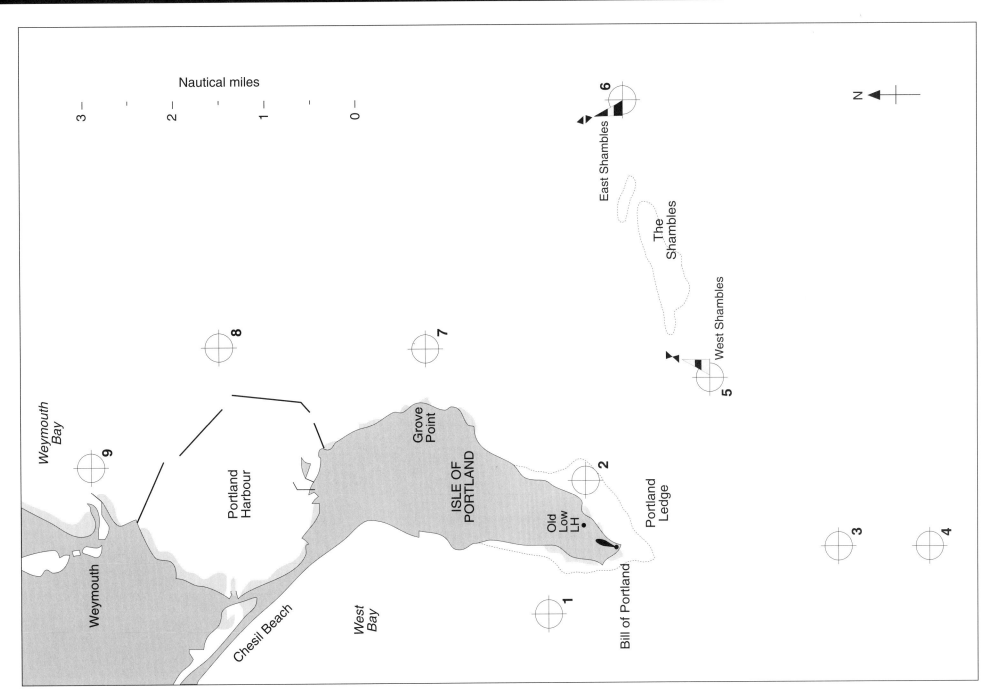

Nautical miles

3 — 2 — 1 — 0 —

N

East Shambles
6

The Shambles

West Shambles
5

8

7

Weymouth Bay

9

Grove Point

ISLE OF PORTLAND

Portland Harbour

Weymouth

Portland Ledge

Old Low LH

2

Bill of Portland

Chesil Beach

West Bay

1

3

4

WP No	Waypoint name and position	Latitude	Longitude
15-1	Weymouth approach, ¼ M due E of South pierhead	50°36.55'N	02°26.01'W
15-2	Portland Hr, ½ M 080°T from outer b/water north head	50°35.16'N	02°24.00'W
15-3	Grove Point clearing, ½ M due E of outer rock	50°32.94'N	02°23.99'W
15-4	East Shambles, 1 ca due E of E-card buoy	50°30.76'N	02°19.80'W
15-5	Lulworth Cove approach, 2 ca S of east headland tip	50°36.78'N	02°14.69'W
15-6	Worbarrow Bay west, ¾ M SE of Bindon Hill occas light	50°36.78'N	02°12.74'W
15-7	Worbarrow Bay east, 3 ca SW of the Tout outer tip	50°36.65'N	02°11.50'W
15-8	Chapman's Pool approach, 6 ca 300°T from St Alban's light	50°35.00'N	02°04.11'W
15-9	St Alban's inner, 1 ca due S of St Alban's Head	50°34.46'N	02°03.22'W
15-10	St Alban's Ledge clearing, 5 M SW of St Alban's light	50°31.19'N	02°08.88'W
15-11	St Alban's Head clearing, 4 M due S of St Alban's Head	50°30.56'N	02°03.22'W
15-12	Anvil Point clearing, 1 M SE of Durlston Head	50°34.94'N	01°55.85'W
15-13	Peveril Point outer, 1.1 M E of Peveril Point	50°36.41'N	01°54.84'W
15-14	Peveril Point inner, 1 ca E of Peveril Ledge red buoy	50°36.38'N	01°55.86'W

COASTAL DANGERS

Refer to Admiralty chart 2610

The Shambles

The Shambles Bank lies from 2½–4 miles E by S of Portland Bill, extending roughly ENE/WSW and marked at either end by the East Shambles E-cardinal buoy and the West Shambles W-cardinal buoy. The lowest soundings are 3.4 metres and local yachts and fishing boats pass over the bank in quiet weather, but it does not take much wind and tide to turn the area into a hostile mass of dangerous white water.

Lulworth Gunnery Ranges

The military practice ranges off Lulworth are used during the week throughout the year except in August, but are only active on a few selected weekends. The planned firing times are published well in advance and the schedule is distributed to Harbourmasters and Yacht Clubs in the area. During firing, the range area is patrolled by the well-known blue-hulled Range Safety Boats, which work on VHF Ch 8.

St Alban's Ledge and Race

St Alban's Ledge extends south-west from St Alban's Head for a good 4 miles. The Ledge has plenty of depth over it, with soundings between about 10–18 metres compared with 25–30 metres in the deeper water on either side. The danger for boats is the overfalls caused by the Ledge, which can be savage at springs with a weather-going stream. The tide can reach 4 knots along this stretch of coast, sometimes more locally over St Alban's Ledge where the flow is squeezed vertically. You need to stay a good 4 miles south of St Alban's Head to avoid the worst of the race (see waypoints 15–10 and 15–11 in the table).

In moderate weather you can take the inner passage close inshore under St Alban's, although there will often be some uneasy water even here (see waypoint 15–9 in the table). You have to shave very close to St Alban's to avoid overfalls altogether, although it is certainly a steep-to headland with no dangers to within about 50 metres of the shore.

Anvil Point Race

There is a much smaller race on the southwest-going stream between Anvil Point and Durlston Head, extending up to ¾ mile offshore and sometimes quite boisterous with wind-over tide. Waypoint 15–12 keeps you 1 mile south-east of Durlston Head, although you can cut much closer inshore in quiet conditions.

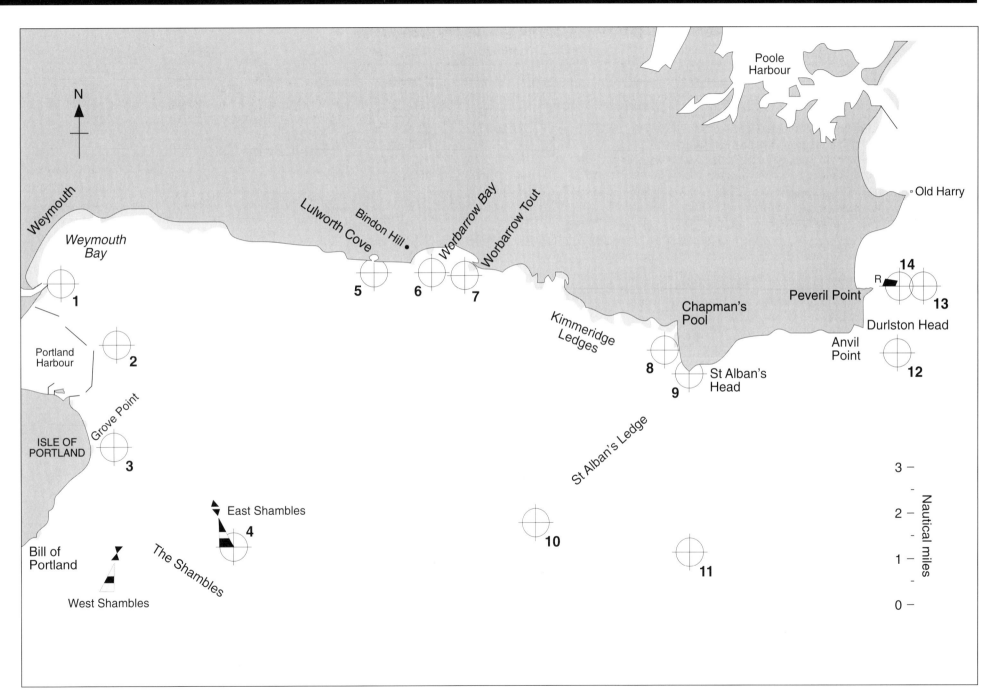

N

Poole Harbour

Weymouth

Weymouth Bay

Lulworth Cove

Bindon Hill •

Worbarrow Bay

Worbarrow Tout

Old Harry

1

2

Portland Harbour

5

6

7

Kimmeridge Ledges

Chapman's Pool

Peveril Point

R

14

13

Durlston Head

Anvil Point

12

Grove Point

ISLE OF PORTLAND

3

8

St Alban's Head

9

St Alban's Ledge

East Shambles

4

Bill of Portland

The Shambles

10

11

West Shambles

3 —

2 —

1 —

0 —

Nautical miles

WP No	Waypoint name and position	Latitude	Longitude
16-1	Anvil Point clearing, 1 M SE of Durlston Head	50°34.94'N	01°55.85'W
16-2	Peveril Point outer, 1.1 M E of Peveril Point	50°36.41'N	01°54.84'W
16-3	Peveril Point inner, 1 ca E of Peveril Ledge red buoy	50°36.38'N	01°55.86'W
16-4	Swash Channel entrance, 100m due S of Poole Bar buoy	50°39.27'N	01°55.17'W
16-5	East Looe approach, 6½ ca 070°T from Haven Hotel	50°41.21'N	01°55.85'W
16-6	Christchurch approach, 4 ca due E of Haven House Inn	50°43.42'N	01°43.78'W
16-7	Christchurch Ledge, Lambeth summer buoy, actual position	50°41.50'N	01°41.62'W

COASTAL DANGERS

Refer to Admiralty charts 2615, 2172, 2611

Tidal races between Anvil Point and Handfast Point

There is quite a localised race on the southwest-going stream between Anvil Point and Durlston Head, extending up to ¾ mile offshore and sometimes quite boisterous with wind-over tide. Waypoint 15–12 keeps you 1 mile south-east of Durlston Head, although you can cut much closer inshore in quiet conditions.

A mile or so further north, the race off Peveril Point, although fairly localised, can be quite savage on the ebb. The tide curving out of Swanage Bay swirls round Peveril Point and across Peveril Ledge, meeting at an angle the main SSW-going stream coming down from Poole Bay. Smaller yachts and motor boats can take a dusting through Peveril race, so give this corner a wide berth during the ebb.

Further north again, there are areas of over-falls on the ebb off Ballard Point and Handfast Point (Old Harry), although at neaps and in quiet weather these areas represent only a slight agitation within a fairly small area.

Hook Sand

The main Swash Channel into Poole Harbour has a long training wall on the west side and the shoals of the Hook Sand on the east. The Swash Channel is well buoyed, but the Hook Sand needs treating with respect, especially by boats working west across Poole Bay towards Poole entrance, perhaps tacking close inshore towards Boscombe and Bournemouth before working out again towards the Poole fairway buoy and the Swash Channel entrance. Craft approaching or skirting the east side of the Hook Sand must always be careful not to stray inside the seaward red buoy and put themselves aground on the *outside edge* of the bank.

Christchurch Ledge

The rocky shoals of Christchurch Ledge extend south-east from Hengistbury Head for almost 3 miles, although the shallowest finger of the ledge (with only 3.8 metres over it) reaches out for 1½ miles. The seas over the ledge can be dangerous in heavy onshore weather, when boats making for the North Channel should stay in the deep water between Christchurch Ledge and the Dolphin Bank. During the summer, a yellow buoy moored not quite 2½ miles south-east of Hengistbury Head gives a useful guide to the outer end of Christchurch Ledge.

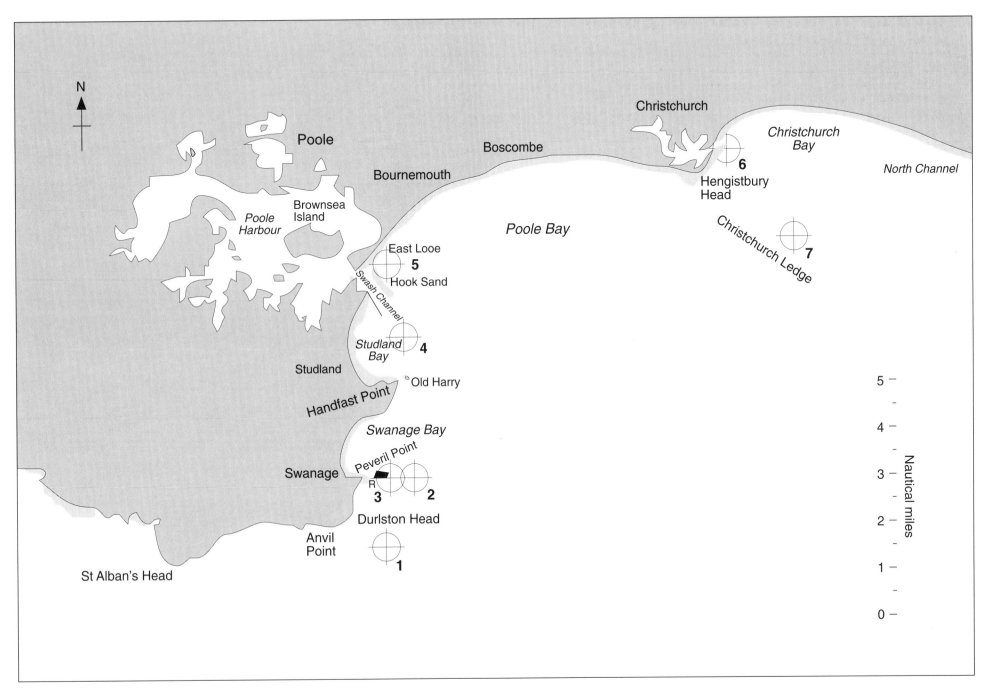

N

Poole

Christchurch

Boscombe

Christchurch Bay

Bournemouth

North Channel

Brownsea Island

Poole Harbour

6

Hengistbury Head

Poole Bay

East Looe

5

Hook Sand

7

Christchurch Ledge

Swash Channel

4

Studland Bay

Studland

Old Harry

5

Handfast Point

Swanage Bay

4

Peveril Point

Swanage

R

3

3

2

2

Durlston Head

2

Anvil Point

St Alban's Head

1

1

0

Nautical miles

WP No	Waypoint name and position	Latitude	Longitude
17-1	Christchurch approach, 4 ca due E of Haven House Inn	50°43.42'N	01°43.78'W
17-2	Christchurch Ledge, Lambeth summer buoy actual position	50°41.50'N	01°41.62'W
17-3	North Channel outer, Woolwich summer buoy actual position	50°43.00'N	01°38.00'W
17-4	North Channel approach, 1 ca W of N Head green buoy	50°42.66'N	01°35.59'W
17-5	North Channel inner, 5½ ca due W of Hurst Low Light	50°42.37'N	01°33.91'W
17-6	Needles fairway buoy, actual position	50°38.20'N	01°38.90'W
17-7	Needles approach, ½ ca W of Bridge W-card buoy	50°39.59'N	01°36.88'W
17-8	Mid Shingles, 1½ ca SE of red buoy	50°41.09'N	01°34.42'W
17-9	Warden clearing, 100 m NW of Warden green bell buoy	50°41.49'N	01°33.52'W
17-10	Hurst Point, 3½ ca SE of Hurst High Light	50°42.20'N	01°32.57'W

COASTAL DANGERS

Refer to Admiralty chart 2219

The Needles Channel

The Needles Channel is rough with wind over tide, especially in a south-westerly over the ebb, when the North Channel is quieter. In heavy weather, seas can break dangerously between the Needles and Hurst Point. Remember that the tide sets across the Shingles bank, so that the ebb through the Needles will be trying to set you west towards the Shingles.

The Bridge Ledge, which extends westward from the Needles lighthouse for almost 1 mile, has overfalls over it with wind over tide, and is dangerous in heavy onshore weather. In such conditions, you should stay in the Needles Channel entrance between the Bridge W-cardinal buoy and the SW Shingles red buoy.

The North Channel

The North Channel into and out of the Solent can be a quieter and safer passage than the Needles Channel in heavy onshore weather. However, approaching the North Channel under these conditions requires care, partly to stay in the deep water between Christchurch Ledge and the Dolphin, and then to pick up the North Head green buoy without straying too close either to the Shingles bank on the south side or the lee shore on the north side.

Alum, Totland and Colwell Bays

Boats tacking through the Needles Channel should obviously take care of the Shingles Bank on the north-west side, but also be wary of tacking too close into the bays on the south-east side between the Needles and Fort Albert. Alum, Totland and Colwell Bays all have rocky shoal areas, especially Colwell Bay, the most northerly of the three. The dangerous Warden ledge, between Totland and Colwell Bays, extends a good four cables north-west towards the Needles Channel from Warden Point.

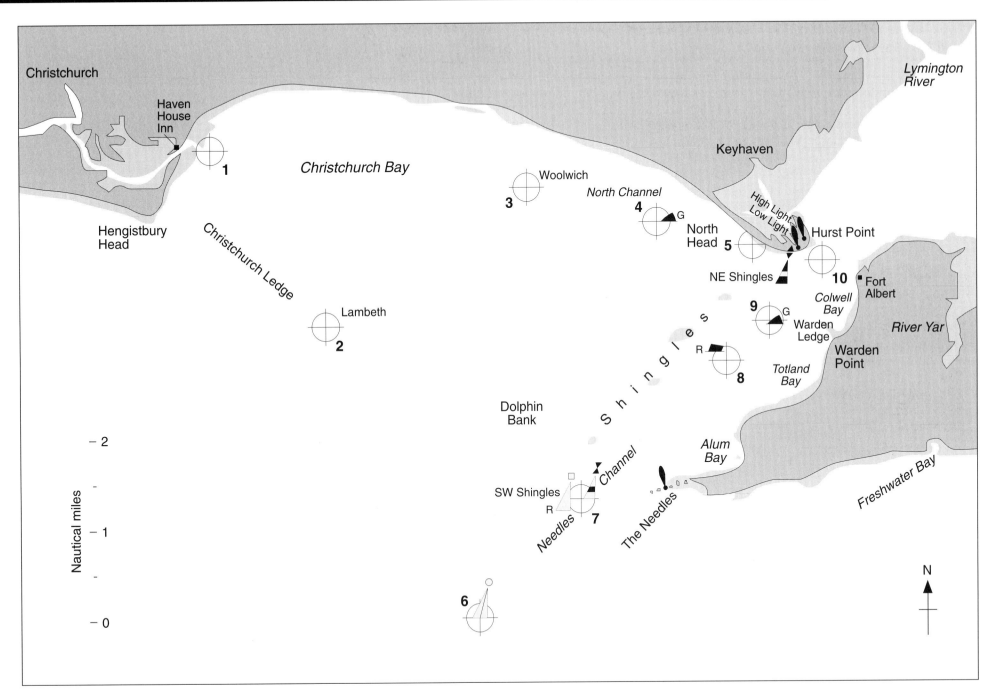

Christchurch

Lymington
River

Haven
House
Inn

1

Christchurch Bay

Keyhaven

Woolwich

North Channel

High Light
Low Light

Hurst Point

3

4 G

North
Head

5

NE Shingles

10 ▪ Fort
Albert

*Colwell
Bay*

Hengistbury
Head

Christchurch Ledge

Lambeth

9 G

Warden
Ledge

River Yar

2

R

8

*Totland
Bay*

Warden
Point

S h i n g l e s

Dolphin
Bank

*Alum
Bay*

SW Shingles

Channel

R

7

Needles

The Needles

Freshwater Bay

— 2

Nautical miles

6

— 1

— 0

N

WP No	Waypoint name and position	Latitude	Longitude
18-1	Hurst Point, 3½ ca SE of Hurst High Light	50°42.20'N	01°32.57'W
18-2	Sconce clearing, 100 m 340°T from N-card buoy	50°42.56'N	01°31.38'W
18-3	Black Rock clearing, 100 m N of green buoy	50°42.61'N	01°30.55'W
18-4	Yarmouth approach, 3 ca 330°T from pierhead NW tip	50°42.74'N	01°30.11'W
18-5	Hurst Road, 2 ca NE of Hurst High Light	50°42.59'N	01°32.71'W
18-6	Keyhaven approach, 2 ca 103°T from entrance buoys	50°42.78'N	01°32.85'W
18-7	Lymington approach, 1 ca E of Jack in the Basket beacon	50°44.26'N	01°30.33'W
18-8	Lymington entrance, midway between Nos 5 and 6 beacons	50°44.59'N	01°30.81'W
18-9	Hamstead Ledge clearing, 1 ca 340°T from green buoy	50°43.91'N	01°26.08'W
18-10	Newtown River approach, 2 ca NW of outer red buoy	50°43.90'N	01°25.04'W
18-11	Salt Mead clearing, 2 ca 340°T from green buoy	50°44.68'N	01°23.06'W
18-12	Gurnard Ledge clearing, 2 ca 340°T from green buoy	50°45.68'N	01°20.61'W
18-13	Egypt Point, 1½ ca 340°T from N-card buoy	50°46.33'N	01°18.83'W
18-14	West Lepe, 100 m 160°T from red buoy	50°45.15'N	01°23.96'W
18-15	East Lepe, 100 m 160°T from red buoy	50°46.04'N	01°20.79'W
18-16	Beaulieu River approach, ½ M 341°T from inner leading mark	50°46.61'N	01°21.53'W
18-17	Beaulieu River entrance, 2 ca 341°T from inner leading mark	50°46.90'N	01°21.70'W
18-18	West Bramble, actual position of W-card buoy	50°47.17'N	01°18.57'W

SHOALS AND DANGERS
Refer to Admiralty charts 2021, 2040

Yarmouth approaches
When approaching Yarmouth from the Needles Channel, stay outside the Black Rock green conical buoy before dropping south of east towards the harbour entrance. The tides are strong off Yarmouth entrance, with overfalls between the Black Rock buoy and the pierhead at springs on a weather-going stream. Because of the strong tides, turn in towards the harbour in good time, allowing for the cross-set as you crab towards the ferry terminal past the pier.

Lymington Flats
The approaches to Lymington are shallow, with wide drying flats on either side of the entrance between Hurst and Pitts Deep. Tacking up towards Lymington from Hurst against a north-easterly, you have to be careful not to stray too far inshore off Pennington Spit and Pennington Marshes. A direct line from Hurst Point towards the Jack in the Basket beacon lies just outside the shoal areas where soundings are down to less than 1 metre.

Lepe Middle and Beaulieu Spit
The approaches to the Beaulieu River are also shallow, and boats making towards Beaulieu entrance from Lymington have to keep out into the Solent a little near low water. The outer mark for Beaulieu entrance is the East Lepe red buoy, which provides a fairway position for the final approaches to the Beaulieu River.

Newtown approaches
The approaches to the Newtown River are shallow. Arriving from the west, you need to pick up the outer red buoy from a position somewhere near Hamstead Ledge green buoy, which lies about ¾ mile just north of west from the Newtown River entrance.

Between the Newtown River and Gurnard Head, the coast within about ½ mile of the Isle of Wight is relatively shallow, with the Salt Mead Ledges marked by Salt Mead green buoy and Thorness Bay awaiting the unwary who tack in too close.

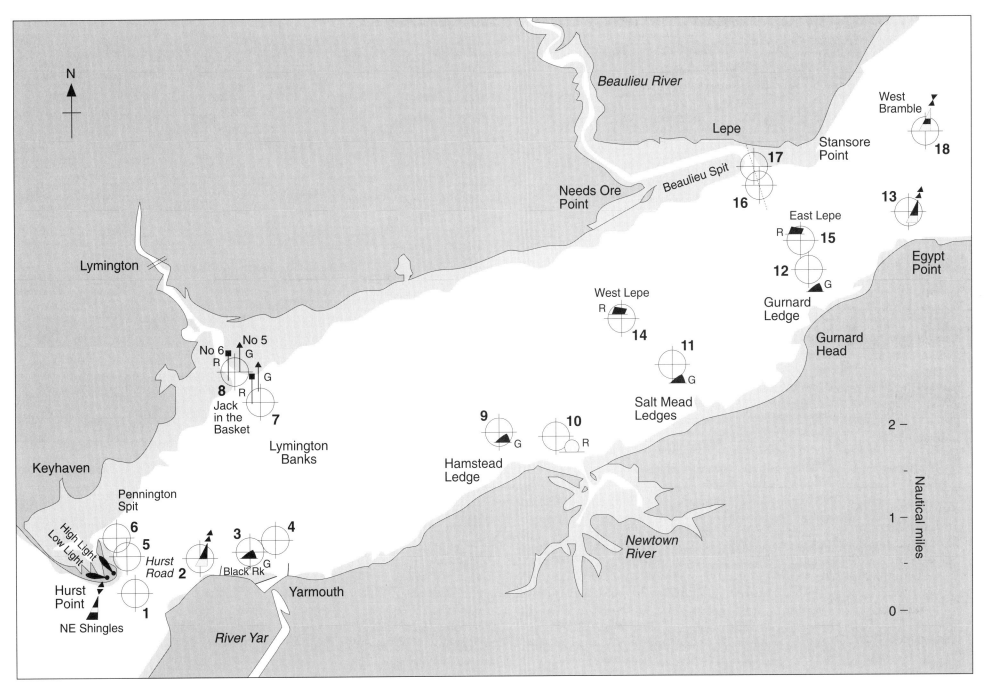

N

Beaulieu River

West Bramble

Lepe

Stansore Point

18

17

Needs Ore Point

Beaulieu Spit

16

13

East Lepe

R **15**

12

G

Gurnard Ledge

Egypt Point

Lymington

West Lepe

R **14**

11

G

Gurnard Head

No 5

No 6
R

G

G

8
R

7

Salt Mead Ledges

Jack in the Basket

Lymington Banks

9
G

10
R

Keyhaven

Hamstead Ledge

Newtown River

Pennington Spit

6

High Light
Low Light

5

Hurst Road

3

4

2

Black Rk

G

Yarmouth

Hurst Point

1

NE Shingles

River Yar

2 —

Nautical miles

1 —

0 —

══Southampton Water══

WP No	Waypoint name and position	Latitude	Longitude
19-1	Calshot Spit, 50 m SE of light-float	50°48.29'N	01°17.51'W
19-2	Calshot Reach, 50 m SW of Reach green buoy	50°49.00'N	01°17.60'W
19-3	Hamble Point, 50 m S of Hamble Point S-card buoy	50°50.09'N	01°18.58'W
19-4	Hound inner, 50 m NE of Hound green buoy	50°51.69'N	01°21.41'W
19-5	NW Netley inner, 50 m NE of NW Netley green buoy	50°52.29'N	01°22.60'W
19-6	Hythe Marina approach, 1 ca NE of Hythe E-card beacon	50°52.67'N	01°23.68'W
19-7	Itchen approach, 1½ ca SE of QEII terminal SW tip	50°52.84'N	01°23.46'W
19-8	Test approach, 150 m SW of QEII terminal SW tip	50°52.89'N	01°23.72'W
19-9	Ocean Village entrance, ½ ca 150°T from N pierhead SE tip	50°53.65'N	01°23.16'W
19-10	Town Quay approach, 1 ca 150°T from pierhead FG lights	50°53.43'N	01°24.17'W

ESTUARY DANGERS
Refer to Admiralty charts 1905, 2041

Bramble Bank
The Bramble Bank is a broad area of shoals, part of which dry, between the south end of Southampton Water and the north corner of the Solent. The Bramble is well marked and straightforward to circumvent, either by the Thorn Channel from the south-west or the North Channel from the south-east. The main significance of the Bramble for boats is that it concentrates shipping bound in or out of Southampton Water into a narrow fairway – the Thorn Channel – which forces ships to make tight turns off Calshot Spit and off the West Bramble buoy.

Yachts and motorboats should therefore navigate the Thorn Channel with great circumspection, following any directions given by the harbour control launches and staying, as far as possible, just outside the marked channel on the 'wrong' side of the buoys.

Fast ferries
Between the West Bramble buoy and Southampton, you are liable to meet fast hydrofoils and catamaran ferries, which are normally very careful to pick their way through the traffic but which can be thrown by sudden changes of course. When a fast hydrofoil or catamaran is approaching, try to maintain a more or less constant course and speed until they have passed.

Ashlett Creek flats
On the west side of Southampton Water, between Calshot Castle and the Esso oil terminal off Fawley, the estuary is very shallow within ½ mile of the shore. Care must be taken in this area if you are tacking up or downstream and tending to hold onto your course at the end of each tack.

Hamble Spit
The approaches to the Hamble River are shallow on both sides, with the Hamble Spit on the west side of the fairway and the banks off Warsash on the east side. Yachts coming up

Southampton Water from Calshot will normally pick up the Hamble Point S-cardinal buoy and then follow the channel past the red and green posts; however, boats arriving from further up Southampton Water must resist the temptation to cut the corner inside the Hamble Point buoy.

Deans Lake
The upper west side of Southampton Water is also shallow, between the Esso oil terminal and the approaches to Hythe Marina Village. Yachts tacking across the estuary must be wary about holding on beyond the channel buoys and beacons on the west side.

Weston Shelf
In the upper reaches of Southampton Water, as you approach the junction between the River Test and the River Itchen, beware of the shallows on the north-east side of the river above Netley. Cutting the corner towards Ocean Village inside the Moorhead and Weston Shelf green buoys can result in a considerable delay.

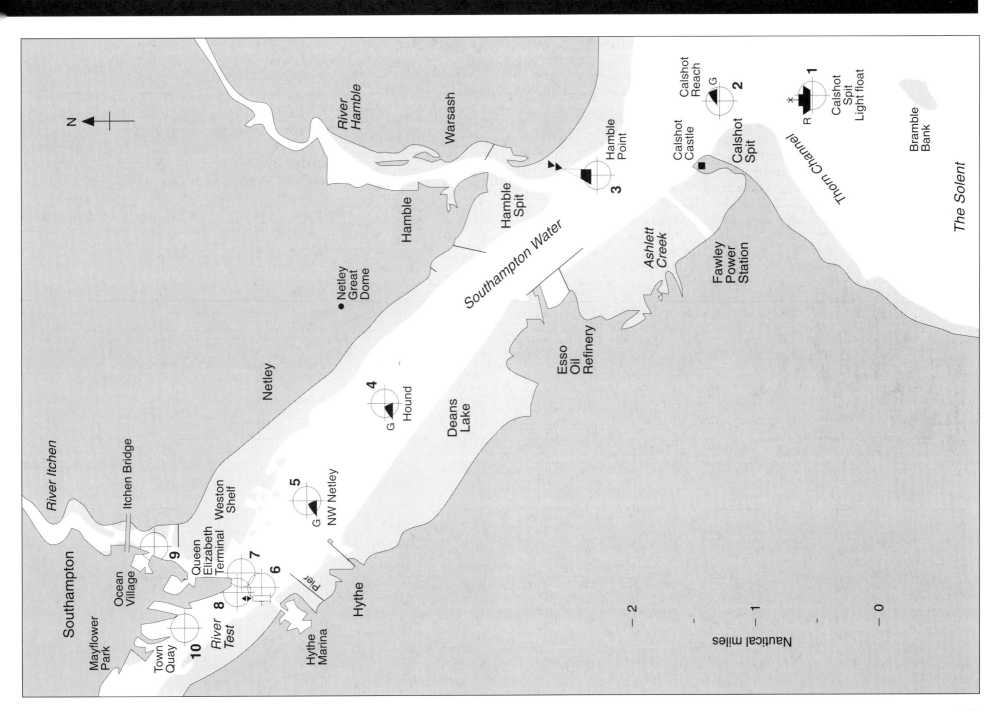

Southampton

River Itchen

Mayflower Park

Ocean Village

Itchen Bridge

9

Town Quay

10

River Test

Queen Elizabeth Terminal

Weston Shelf

7

6

8

Pier

Hythe

Hythe Marina

Netley

5
G
NW Netley

4
G
Hound

Deans Lake

Netley
Great Dome

N

River Hamble

Warsash

Hamble

Hamble Spit

Southampton Water

Esso Oil Refinery

Ashlett Creek

Fawley Power Station

Hamble Point

3

Calshot Reach

G

2

Calshot Castle

Calshot Spit

R
1

Calshot Spit Light float

Thorn Channel

Bramble Bank

The Solent

— 2

— 1

— 0

Nautical miles

WP No	Waypoint name and position	Latitude	Longitude
20-1	Calshot Reach, 50 m SW of Reach green buoy	50°49.00'N	01°17.60'W
20-2	Calshot Spit, 50 m SE of light-float	50°48.29'N	01°17.51'W
20-3	Calshot East, 50 m W of Calshot N-card bell buoy	50°48.39'N	01°17.00'W
20-4	North Channel NW, 1 ca SW of Deck summer yellow buoy	50°48.53'N	01°16.68'W
20-5	North Channel SE, ½ ca NE of East Bramble E-card buoy	50°47.25'N	01°13.41'W
20-6	West Bramble, actual position of W-card buoy	50°47.17'N	01°18.57'W
20-7	Egypt Point, 1½ ca 340°T from Gurnard N-card buoy	50°46.33'N	01°18.83'W
20-8	Cowes approach, 3 ca 255°T from Prince Consort N-card	50°46.31'N	01°17.94'W
20-9	Old Castle Point, ½ M E of Prince Consort N-card	50°46.39'N	01°16.69'W
20-10	SE Ryde Middle, 1 ca S of S-card buoy	50°45.82'N	01°11.98'W
20-11	Wootton Creek entrance, 100 m N of Wootton beacon	50°44.60'N	01°12.00'W
20-12	Ryde Sand clearing, ½ M 160°T from Sturbridge N-card buoy	50°44.83'N	01°07.88'W
20-13	Sturbridge clearing, 1 ca N of N-card buoy	50°45.41'N	01°08.15'W
20-14	No Man's Land, ¼ M N of No Man's Land Fort north edge	50°44.63'N	01°05.60'W
20-15	Horse Sand, 4 ca SW of Horse Sand Fort SW edge	50°44.68'N	01°04.71'W
20-16	Portsmouth approach, 100 m SE of Outer Spit S-card buoy	50°45.50'N	01°05.32'W
20-17	Southsea Castle, ¼ M SW of castle lighthouse	50°46.49'N	01°05.51'W

ESTUARY DANGERS

Refer to Admiralty charts 394, 1905

Bramble Bank

The Bramble Bank is a wide triangular area of shoals, some of which dry, in the three-way junction between the south end of Southampton Water and the north corner of the Solent. The Bramble is well marked and straightforward to circumvent, either by the Thorn Channel from the south-west or the North Channel from the south-east.

However, the main significance of the Bramble for boats is that it concentrates shipping bound in or out of Southampton Water into a narrow fairway – the Thorn Channel – which forces ships to make tight turns off Calshot Spit and off the West Bramble buoy. Yachts should therefore navigate the Thorn

Channel with great care, following any directions given by the harbour control launches and staying, as far as possible, just outside the marked channel on the 'wrong' side of the buoys.

Mother Bank

Between Osborne Bay and Ryde off the north-east side of the Isle of Wight, the south side of the Solent is very shallow with one or two patches that dry at chart datum. This broad shoal area is marked on its north side by several red can buoys and boats straying inside these buoys near low water are prone to be brought up short.

Ryde Sands

Opposite and to the east of Ryde Pier, an extensive shoal area of drying sand and mud stretches north of the Isle of Wight coast for over 1 mile. These flats are marked on their north side by red post beacons more or less opposite the Sturbridge Shoal N-cardinal buoy.

No Man's Land

To the east of Ryde Sands, No Man's Land Fort stands on the edge of the continuing shoal area opposite Nettlestone Point, with an underwater obstruction stretching back south-west towards the Isle of Wight. Strangers should always keep north of No Man's Land, although to the east of the fort you can start nudging back inshore towards St Helen's Fort and the entrance to Bembridge Harbour.

Horse Sand Fort

This north-eastern partner of the two Spithead forts guards the east side of the approach channel for Portsmouth Harbour. Horse Sand Fort stands about 1¾ miles off the Southsea shore and marks the south end of a dangerous submerged barrier across the shallowest part of Horse and Dean Sand. This barrier, a relic of World War II, is marked at intervals by yellow posts with 'X' topmarks. There is a narrow navigable gap through the centre of this barrier, marked by a concrete dolphin and a spar beacon. This passage should only be taken above half-tide, and then only in quiet conditions unless you know the area well.

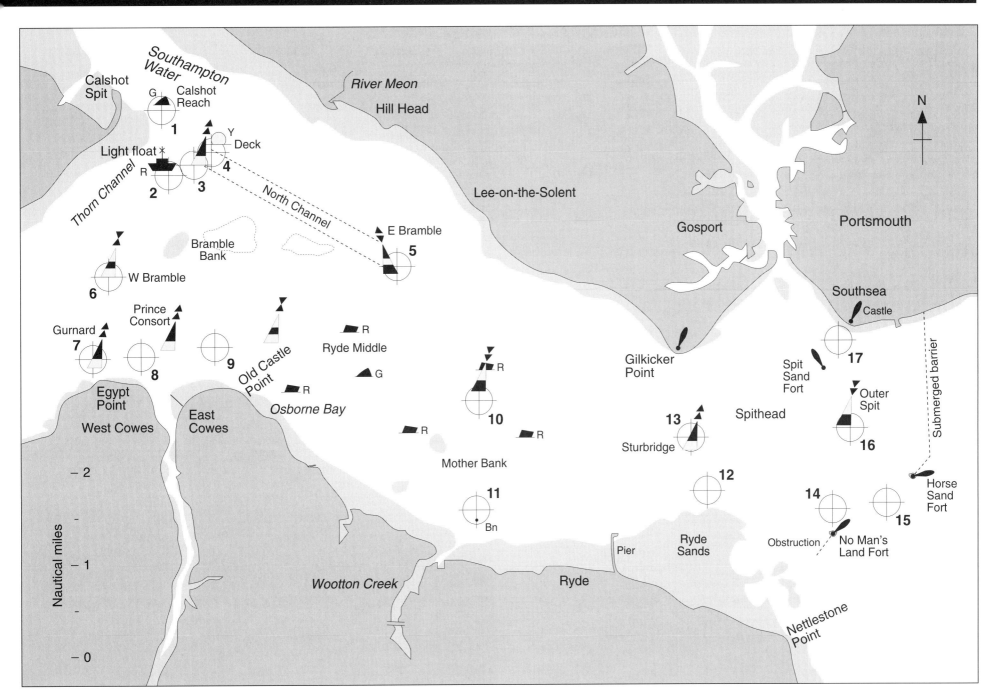

Calshot Spit

Southampton Water

River Meon

Hill Head

G Calshot Reach

1

Y Deck

Light float ✳

4

R

2 **3**

Thorn Channel

North Channel

Lee-on-the-Solent

E Bramble

5

Bramble Bank

W Bramble

6

Gosport

Portsmouth

Prince Consort

Gurnard

7

8

9

Old Castle Point

Ryde Middle R

G

R

Mother Bank

R

R

10

Southsea

Castle

Gilkicker Point

Spit Sand Fort

Spithead

17

Outer Spit

16

Submerged barrier

Egypt Point

West Cowes

East Cowes

Osborne Bay

Sturbridge

13

12

Horse Sand Fort

11

Bn

14

15

Obstruction

No Man's Land Fort

Nautical miles

— 2

— 1

— 0

Pier

Ryde Sands

Wootton Creek

Ryde

Nettlestone Point

N

Isle of Wight – South Coast

WP No	Waypoint name and position	Latitude	Longitude
21-1	Warden clearing, 100 m NW of Warden green bell buoy	50°41.49'N	01°33.52'W
21-2	Mid Shingles, 1½ ca SE of red buoy	50°41.09'N	01°34.42'W
21-3	Needles approach, ½ ca W of Bridge W-card buoy	50°39.59'N	01°36.88'W
21-4	Needles fairway buoy, actual position	50°38.20'N	01°38.90'W
21-5	Freshwater Bay, 4 ca 160°T from conspicuous hotel	50°39.78'N	01°30.40'W
21-6	St Catherine's inner, 1½ M due S of lighthouse	50°33.01'N	01°17.80'W
21-7	St Catherine's outer, 5 M due S of lighthouse	50°29.51'N	01°17.80'W
21-8	Dunnose inner, 2½ M SE of main radar scanner	50°34.42'N	01°08.69'W
21-9	Dunnose outer, 5 M SE of main radar scanner	50°32.70'N	01°05.90'W
21-10	East Solent (west), 2 M W of Nab Tower	50°40.04'N	01°00.20'W
21-11	West Princessa, 1 ca W of W-card buoy	50°40.12'N	01°03.71'W
21-12	Bembridge Ledge, 1 ca E of E-card buoy	50°41.12'N	01°02.55'W
21-13	East Solent (east), 1 M E of Nab Tower	50°40.04'N	00°55.50'W

East Solent approach

Foreland Point, the extreme east tip of the Isle of Wight, has Bembridge Ledge extending ¾ mile due east, with a wide area of drying ledges up to 3 cables offshore on the south-east side. Keep outside the Bembridge Ledge E-cardinal buoy when rounding the Foreland since the Cole Rock, inside the buoy, dries 0.2 metre at chart datum.

COASTAL DANGERS
Refer to Admiralty charts 2045, 2050

The Needles Channel

The Needles Channel is rough with wind over tide, especially in a south-westerly over the ebb, when the North Channel is quieter. In heavy weather, seas can break dangerously between the Needles and Hurst Point. Remember that the tide sets across the Shingles bank, so that the ebb through the Needles will be trying to set you west towards the Shingles.

The Bridge Ledge, which extends westward from the Needles lighthouse for almost 1 mile, has overfalls over it with wind over tide, and is dangerous in heavy onshore weather. In such conditions, you should stay in the Needles Channel entrance between the Bridge W-cardinal buoy and the SW Shingles red buoy.

The North Channel

The North Channel into and out of the Solent can be a quieter and safer passage than the Needles Channel in heavy onshore weather. However, approaching the North Channel under these conditions requires care, partly to stay in the deep water between Christchurch Ledge and the Dolphin, and then to pick up the North Head green buoy without straying too close either to the Shingles bank on the south side or the lee shore on the north side.

St Catherine's Point

Overfalls extend up to 1½ miles south-west and south-east of St Catherine's Point, which are steep with a strong wind over tide and dangerous in gales. In heavy weather, the whole area up to at least 5 miles seaward of St Catherine's Point and Dunnose Head can be dangerously rough, partly because of the uneven seabed south of St Catherine's and partly because of the strong tides around the south of the Isle of Wight.

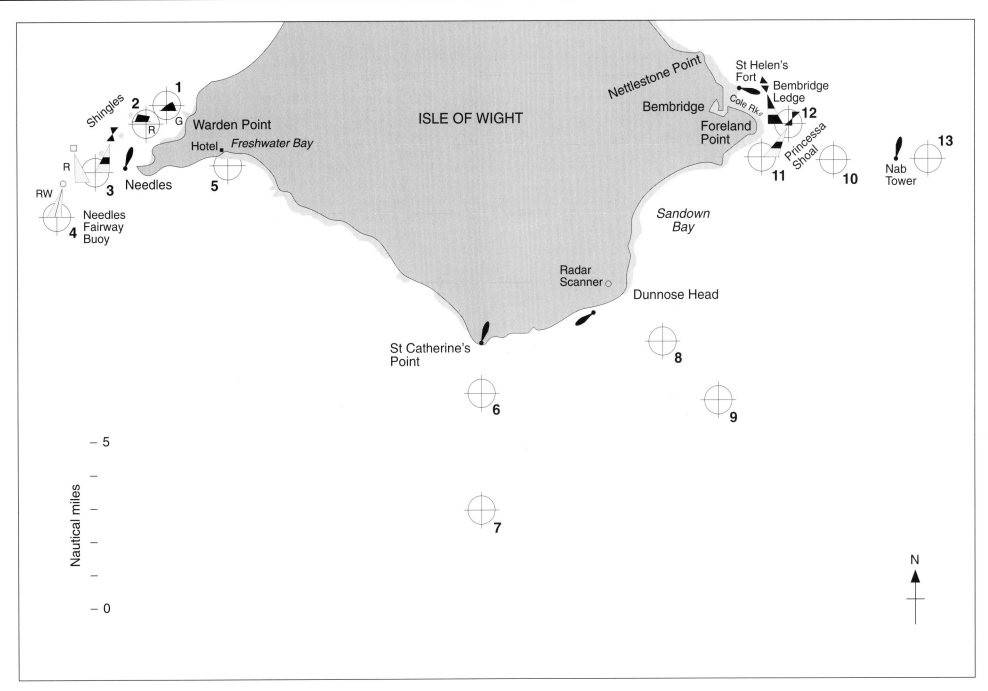

Shingles

1

2
R

G

Warden Point

R

Hotel

Freshwater Bay

ISLE OF WIGHT

Nettlestone Point

St Helen's Fort

Bembridge

Cole Rk

Bembridge Ledge

12

Foreland Point

Princessa Shoal

13

R

3

Needles

5

11

10

Nab Tower

RW

4

Needles Fairway Buoy

Sandown Bay

Radar Scanner

Dunnose Head

8

St Catherine's Point

6

9

Nautical miles

— 5

—

—

—

7

—

— 0

N

Portsmouth to Selsey Bill

WP No	Waypoint name and position	Latitude	Longitude
22-1	Ryde Sand clearing, ½ M 160°T from Sturbridge N-card buoy	50°44.83'N	01°07.88'W
22-2	Sturbridge clearing, 1 ca N of N-card buoy	50°45.41'N	01°08.15'W
22-3	No Man's Land, ¼ M N of No Man's Land Fort north edge	50°44.63'N	01°05.06'W
22-4	Horse Sand, 4 ca SW of Horse Sand Fort SW edge	50°44.68'N	01°04.71'W
22-5	Portsmouth approach, 100 m SE of Outer Spit S-card buoy	50°45.50'N	01°05.32'W
22-6	Southsea Castle, ¼ M SW of castle lighthouse	50°46.49'N	01°05.51'W
22-7	Bembridge approach, 3 ca 025°T from St Helen's Fort	50°42.54'N	01°04.74'W
22-8	Bembridge channel, 2 ca NW from St Helen's Fort	50°42.42'N	01°05.17'W
22-9	St Helen's Road, 3 ca 340°T from lifeboat house	50°41.67'N	01°04.32'W
22-10	Bembridge Ledge, 1 ca E of E-card buoy	50°41.12'N	01°02.55'W
22-11	West Princessa, 1 ca W of W-card buoy	50°40.12'N	01°03.71'W
22-12	East Solent (west), 2 M W of Nab Tower	50°40.04'N	01°00.20'W
22-13	East Solent (east), 1 M E of Nab Tower	50°40.04'N	00°55.50'W
22-14	Langstone approach, 1 M, 190°T from fairway buoy	50°45.30'N	01°01.55'W
22-15	Langstone fairway, actual position of fairway buoy	50°46.28'N	01°01.27'W
22-16	Langstone narrows, 100 m E of QR entrance light	50°47.20'N	01°01.50'W
22-17	Chichester approach, 4 ca 195°T from West Pole beacon	50°45.28'N	00°56.53'W
22-18	Chichester entrance, 50 m E of bar beacon	50°45.88'N	00°56.34'W
22-19	Medmery Bank clearing, 3 M 245°T from Selsey CG Tr	50°42.55'N	00°52.40'W
22-20	Looe Channel west, 1 ca NW of Boulder green buoy	50°41.61'N	00°49.14'W
22-21	Looe Channel east 1 M SE of The Mixon red beacon	50°41.63'N	00°45.08'W
22-22	Selsey anchorage, 1 ca due S of lifeboat house	50°43.45'N	00°46.65'W
22-23	Outer Owers, 1 ca due S of S-card buoy	50°38.64'N	00°41.33'W
22-24	Hooe Bank clearing, 1 ca due S of Owers LANBY	50°37.18'N	00°40.60'W

COASTAL DANGERS
Refer to Admiralty charts 394, 2045, 3418

East Solent approach
Foreland Point, the extreme east tip of the Isle of Wight, has Bembridge Ledge extending ¾ mile due east, with a wide area of drying ledges up to 3 cables offshore on the south-east side. Keep outside the Bembridge Ledge E-cardinal buoy when rounding the Foreland since the Cole Rock, inside the buoy, dries 0.2 metres at chart datum.

Horse Sand Fort
This north-eastern partner of the two Spithead forts guards the east side of the approach channel for Portsmouth Harbour. Horse Sand Fort stands about 1¾ miles off the Southsea shore and marks the south end of a dangerous submerged barrier across the shallowest part of Horse and Dean Sand. This barrier, a relic of World War II, is marked at intervals by yellow posts with 'X' topmarks.

There is a narrow navigable gap through the centre of the barrier, marked by a concrete dolphin and a spar beacon. This passage should only be taken above half-tide, and then only in quiet conditions unless you know the area well.

Selsey Bill
For anyone approaching the Solent from the east along the Sussex coast, the low promontory of Selsey Bill, with its dangerous off-lying banks and shoals, is always an uneasy obstacle before the last clear stretch towards the Spithead forts. If you are making a cross-Channel landfall near the Nab Tower in fresh weather, Selsey is lurking not far to starboard, a nasty lee shore in a south-westerly and barely 7 miles from the Nab.

The main danger area stretches south from Selsey Bill for about 3 miles to the Boulder, Pullar and Middle Ground banks, and southeast for 6 miles to the southern tip of the Outer Owers. The inshore areas of drying rock and sand lie up to 1½ miles from the Bill, from the Mixon off to the SSE, past the Dries and the Grounds to the south-west and then the Streets to the west.

The narrow Looe channel runs between these inner dangers and the outer banks, a useful short-cut round Selsey in daylight and reasonable weather. But tide is a critical factor around the Bill. The streams run strongly through the narrow west end of the Looe and play funny tricks near the banks. Although the Looe channel is easier these days with GPS, you still have to be careful in a summer haze when the buoys can be difficult to pick up and the coast invisible as you go round.

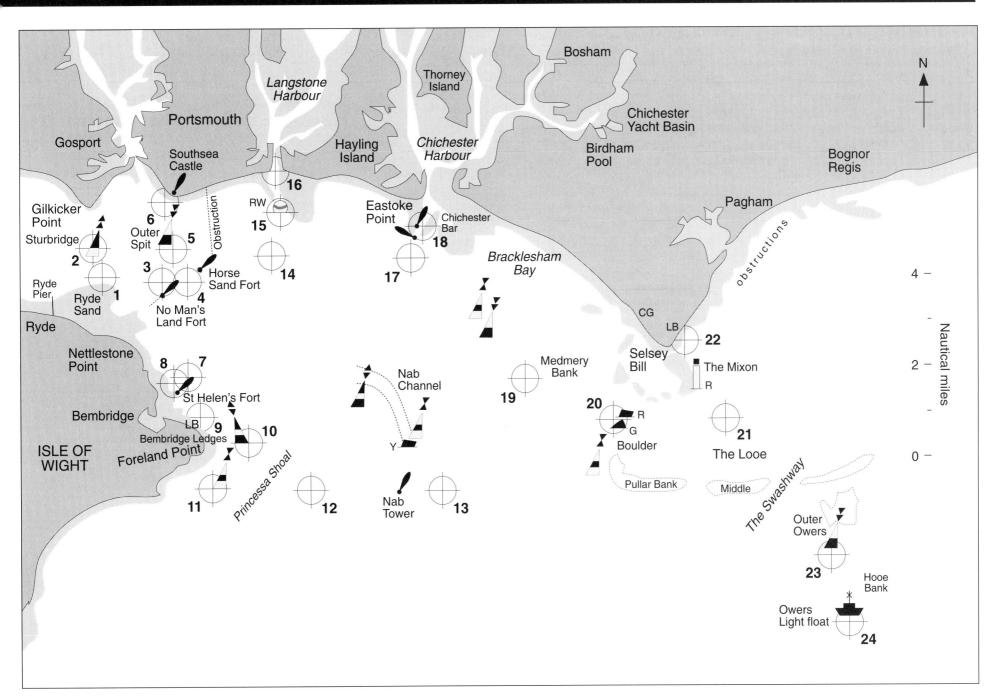

Bosham

Langstone
Harbour

Thorney
Island

Chichester
Yacht Basin

Portsmouth

Gosport

Southsea
Castle

Hayling
Island

*Chichester
Harbour*

Birdham
Pool

Bognor
Regis

Gilkicker
Point

16

Pagham

RW

Eastoke
Point

Chichester
Bar

Sturbridge

15

*Bracklesham
Bay*

6

Outer
Spit

5

18

2

14

3

Horse
Sand Fort

17

4 —

Ryde
Pier

4

No Man's
Land Fort

CG

Nautical miles

Ryde
Sand

1

LB

22

Ryde

The Mixon

Nettlestone
Point

8

7

Selsey
Bill

2 —

Medmery
Bank

R

St Helen's Fort

Nab
Channel

19

Bembridge

LB

9

10

20

R

G

ISLE OF
WIGHT

Bembridge Ledges

Boulder

21

Foreland Point

Y

The Looe

0 —

Princessa Shoal

Pullar Bank

The Swashway

11

12

Nab
Tower

13

Middle

Outer
Owers

23

Hooe
Bank

Owers
Light float

24

WP No	Waypoint name and position	Latitude	Longitude
23-1	Medmery Bank clearing, 3 M 245°T from Selsey CG Tr	50°42.55'N	00°52.40'W
23-2	Looe Channel west, 1 ca NW of Boulder green buoy	50°41.61'N	00°49.14'W
23-3	Looe Channel east 1 M SE of The Mixon red beacon	50°41.63'N	00°45.08'W
23-4	Selsey anchorage, 1 ca due S of lifeboat house	50°43.45'N	00°46.65'W
23-5	Outer Owers, 1 ca due S of S-card buoy	50°38.64'N	00°41.33'W
23-6	Hooe Bank clearing, 1 ca due S of Owers LANBY	50°37.18'N	00°40.60'W
23-7	East Borough Head, ¾ M due N of E-card buoy	50°42.25'N	00°38.84'W
23-8	Littlehampton approach, ½ M S of outer green beacon	50°47.33'N	00°32.29'W
23-9	Littlehampton entrance, 50 m E of tide gauge	50°47.85'N	00°32.33'W
23-10	Shoreham approach, ½ M S of east b/water head	50°49.00'N	00°14.72'W
23-11	Shoreham entrance, 50 m E of west b/water head	50°49.45'N	00°14.74'W
23-12	Brighton entrance, 100 m SE of west b/water head	50°48.42'N	00°06.23'W
23-13	Newhaven approach, 1 M 170°T from west b/water head	50°45.55'N	00°03.90'E
23-14	Newhaven entrance, 100 m E of west b/water head	50°46.52'N	00°03.70'E
23-15	Beachy Head inner, 1½ M due S of lighthouse	50°42.50'N	00°14.60'E
23-16	Beachy Head outer, 5 M due S of lighthouse	50°39.00'N	00°14.60'E

COASTAL DANGERS

Refer to Admiralty charts 536, 1652, 2045

Selsey Bill

For anyone approaching the Solent from the east along the Sussex coast, the low promontory of Selsey Bill, with its dangerous off-lying banks and shoals, is always an uneasy obstacle before the last clear stretch towards the Spithead forts. If you are making a cross-Channel landfall near the Nab Tower in fresh weather, Selsey is lurking not far to starboard, a nasty lee shore in a south-westerly and barely 7 miles from the Nab.

The main danger area stretches south from Selsey Bill for about 3 miles to the Boulder, Pullar and Middle Ground banks, and south-east for 6 miles to the southern tip of the Outer Owers. The inshore areas of drying rock and sand lie up to 1½ miles from the Bill, from The Mixon off to the SSE, past the Dries and the Grounds to the south-west and then the Streets to the west.

The narrow Looe channel runs between these inner dangers and the outer banks, a useful short-cut round Selsey in daylight and reasonable weather. But tide is a critical factor around the Bill. The streams run strongly through the narrow west end of the Looe and play funny tricks near the banks. Although the Looe channel is easier these days with Decca and GPS, you still have to be careful in a summer haze when the buoys can be difficult to pick up and the coast invisible as you go round.

Bognor Spit

For any boats coasting close inshore between Littlehampton and Selsey Bill, the long drying ledge known as Bognor Spit should be given a wide berth. Bognor Spit lies just over 5 miles north-east of the Mixon beacon off Selsey Bill, and it extends about 1 mile offshore.

Pagham Harbour obstructions

A few miles south-west of Bognor Spit are the numerous obstructions of Pagham Harbour, most of which are old concrete caissons which came to grief in the period before the Mulberry Harbours were waiting to be towed across to Normandy before D-Day.

Beachy Head overfalls

The dramatic chalk face of Beachy Head, over 160 metres high with the famous red-and-white striped lighthouse at its foot, has a tidal race extending a good 1 mile offshore. Parts of the coast close inshore near Beachy Head are shallow. Holywell Bank, which extends almost a mile along the shore to the east of Beachy Head, has a least depth of 1.3 metres at chart datum. Closer to the lighthouse, Head Ledge, which almost dries in patches, extends a good ½ mile south of the cliffs.

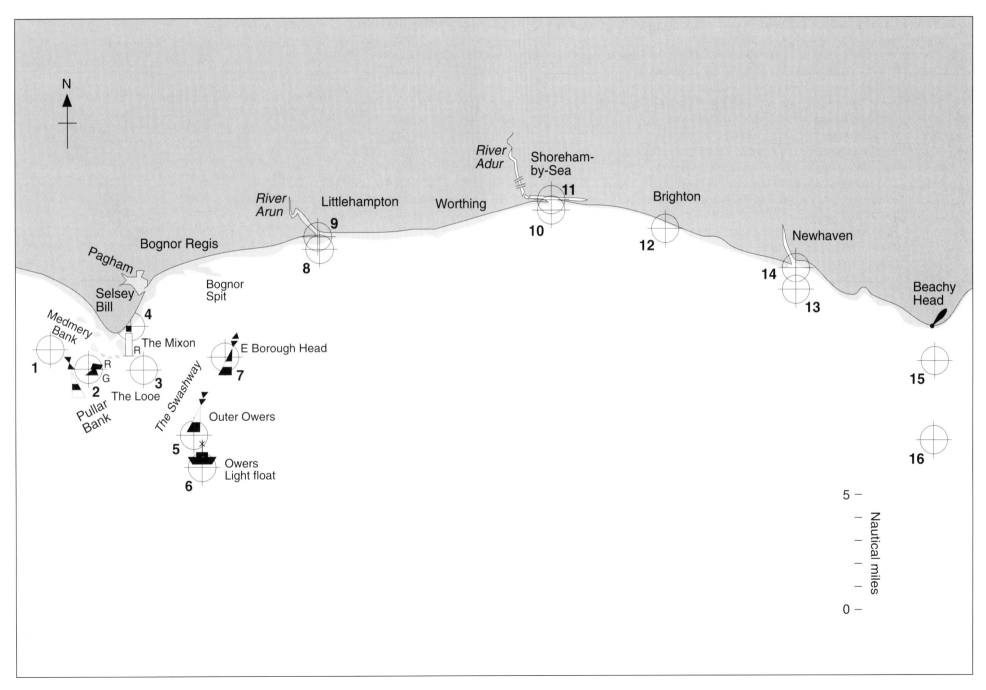

N

River
Adur
Shoreham-
by-Sea
River
Arun
Littlehampton
Worthing
Brighton
11
9
10
Bognor Regis
Newhaven
12
Pagham
8
Bognor
Spit
14
Selsey
Bill
4
Beachy
Head
Medmery
Bank
The Mixon
E Borough Head
13
R
1
R
3
7
G
15
2
The Looe
The Swashway
Pullar
Bank
Outer Owers
5
16
6
Owers
Light float

5 —

Nautical miles

0 —

Beachy Head to Dover Strait

WP No	Waypoint name and position	Latitude	Longitude
24-1	Beachy Head inner, 1½ M due S of lighthouse	50°42.50'N	00°14.60'E
24-2	Beachy Head outer, 5 M due S of lighthouse	50°39.00'N	00°14.60'E
24-3	Royal Sovereign north, midway between tower and red buoy	50°43.80'N	00°26.10'E
24-4	Royal Sovereign south, 1 M due S of tower	50°42.40'N	00°26.18'E
24-5	Royal Sovereign inner, 2.6 M due N of tower	50°46.00'N	00°26.18'E
24-6	Rye fairway, actual position of fairway buoy	50°54.00'N	00°48.12'E
24-7	Dungeness inner, 1 M SE of lighthouse	50°54.04'N	00°59.80'E
24-8	Dungeness outer, 2½ M SE of lighthouse	50°53.00'N	01°01.45'E
24-9	Folkestone approach, 2 ca SE from ferry pierhead	51°04.38'N	01°12.01'E
24-10	Dover west approach, 1½ ca SE of Admiralty pierhead	51°06.45'N	01°19.94'E
24-11	Dover east approach, 1 ca 100°T from E Arm pierhead	51°07.25'N	01°20.87'E
24-12	Varne LANBY, actual position	51°01.25'N	01°24.00'E
24-13	Colbart SW S-card buoy, actual position	50°48.80'N	01°16.55'E
24-14	Colbart N-card buoy, actual position	50°57.44'N	01°23.40'E
24-15	Calais CA6 red approach buoy, actual position	50°58.30'N	01°45.70'E
24-16	Calais entrance, midway between outer pierheads	50°58.37'N	01°50.52'E
24-17	ZC2 yellow buoy off Cap Gris-Nez, actual position	50°53.50'N	01°30.98'E
24-18	Cap Gris-Nez inner, 1½ M NW of lighthouse	50°53.14'N	01°33.40'E
24-19	Bassure de Baas inner, ½ M E of N-card buoy	50°48.50'N	01°33.91'E
24-20	Bassure de Baas outer, 1M W of N-card buoy	50°48.50'N	01°31.59'E
24-21	Boulogne approach, actual position of ZC1 yellow buoy	50°44.88'N	01°27.10'E
24-22	Boulogne entrance, 2 ca NW of south pierhead	50°44.60'N	01°33.92'E
24-23	Le Touquet approach, 1 M 340°T from Mérida W-card buoy	50°33.75'N	01°32.80'E

COASTAL DANGERS

Refer to Admiralty charts 536, 1892, 2451

Beachy Head

The dramatic chalk face of Beachy Head, over 160 metres high with the famous red-and-white striped lighthouse at its foot, has a tidal race extending a good mile offshore. Parts of the coast close inshore near Beachy Head are very shallow. Holywell Bank, which extends almost a mile along the shore to the east of Beachy Head, has a least depth of 1.3 metres at chart datum. Closer to the lighthouse, Head Ledge, which almost dries in patches, extends a good ½ mile south of the cliffs.

Royal Sovereign

The Royal Sovereign shoals, which lie from between 5 and 8 miles east of Beachy Head, represent a very uneven area of seabed and a consequently uneasy stretch of water. Boats on passage between Beachy Head and Dungeness will either pass clear outside the impressive Royal Sovereign light-tower and thus stay in relatively deep and undisturbed water, or they will keep well inshore to the north of the shoals, following the coast past Eastbourne Bay and Pevensey Bay. The Royal Sovereign red buoy lies just under 1 mile north of the tower on the south edge of the Sovereign shoals

Dungeness

The long, low promontory of Dungeness is perhaps the bleakest headland in the English Channel. It is little more than a low shingle bank which is steep-to on its seaward edge. Boats can pass very close, although the ebb tide runs at over 2 knots at springs, kicking up a nasty steep sea if the stream is weather-going.

Le Colbart

This narrow bank lies in mid-Channel, running SSW-NNE some 9 miles opposite Cap Gris-Nez. The shallowest depths range from about 1.5 metres to 4.5 metres at LAT. In quiet weather, most boats can pass over Le Colbart at most tides, but the bank soon becomes dangerous as the wind freshens and the sea builds up.

Calais – Ridens de la Rade

This narrow bank runs WSW-ENE off Calais, forming a partial natural breakwater up to 1 mile offshore. The shallowest depths are about 0.8 metre at LAT ½ mile seaward of Calais breakwaters, with a wider, more shoal area further east which dries 0.1 metre and 0.5 metre at LAT over 1 mile off the hoverport.

In reasonably quiet weather, with sufficient rise of tide, it is safe for boats to cut across Ridens de la Rade, especially when leaving Calais near high water. However, the bank is dangerous in fresh to strong onshore winds, or in fresh north-easterlies or south-westerlies when the tide is weather-going.

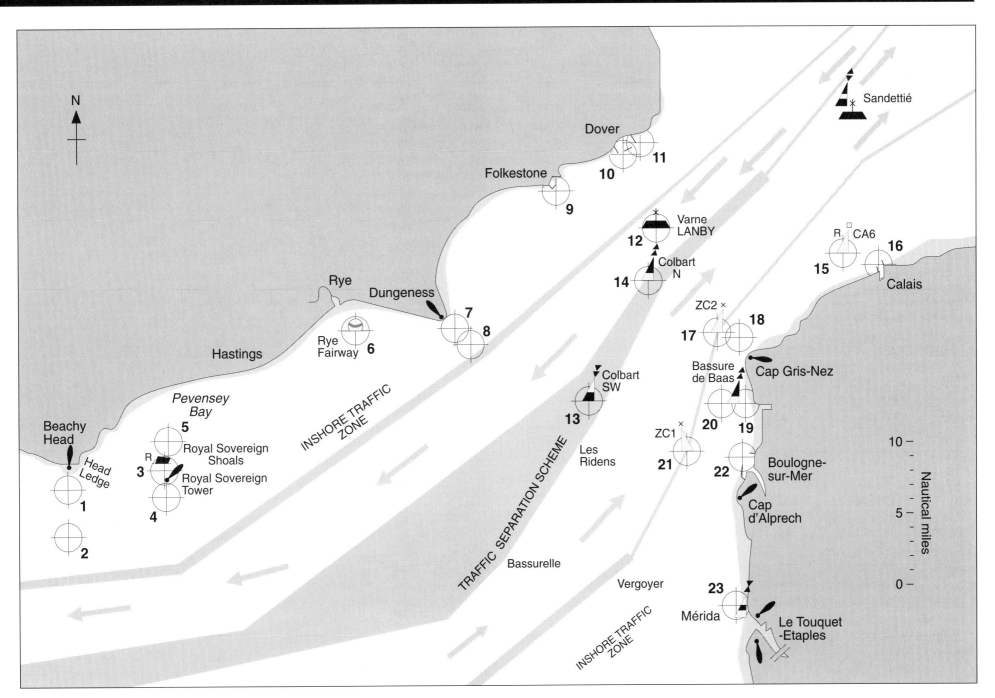

N

Sandettié

Dover

Folkestone

11

10

9

Varne
LANBY

12

Colbart
N

14

R □ CA6

16

15

Calais

Rye

Dungeness

7

8

ZC2 ×

18

17

Rye
Fairway **6**

Hastings

Colbart
SW

Bassure
de Baas

Cap Gris-Nez

13

ZC1 ×

20 **19**

*Pevensey
Bay*

5

INSHORE TRAFFIC ZONE

Les
Ridens

21

22

Boulogne-
sur-Mer

Royal Sovereign
Shoals

R

3

Royal Sovereign
Tower

Beachy
Head

TRAFFIC SEPARATION SCHEME

Cap
d'Alprech

10 –

Head
Ledge

4

Nautical miles

1

5 –

Bassurelle

Vergoyer

23

2

Mérida

Le Touquet
-Etaples

0 –

INSHORE TRAFFIC
ZONE

WP No	Waypoint name and position	Latitude	Longitude
25-1	Dover west approach, 1½ ca SE of Admiralty pierhead	51°06.45'N	01°19.94'E
25-2	Dover east approach, 1 ca 100°T from E Arm pierhead	51°07.25'N	01°20.87'E
25-3	South Goodwin light-float, actual position	51°07.95'N	01°28.59'E
25-4	East Goodwin E-card buoy, actual position	51°16.00'N	01°35.60'E
25-5	Gull Stream South, between S Brake and W Goodwin buoys	51°15.35'N	01°27.17'E
25-6	Gull Stream Mid, between Brake red buoy and NW Goodwin	51°16.83'N	01°28.55'E
25-7	Goodwin Knoll green conical buoy, actual position	51°19.55'N	01°32.30'E
25-8	Ramsgate Quern, 2 cables due E of N-card buoy	51°19.37'N	01°26.52'E
25-9	Ramsgate entrance, midway between outer pierheads	51°19.50'N	01°25.51'E
25-10	North Foreland, 1 mile due E of lighthouse	51°22.46'N	01°28.40'E
25-11	Elbow N-card buoy, actual position	51°23.20'N	01°31.68'E

COASTAL DANGERS

Refer to Admiralty charts 1828, 323

Goodwin Sands

The Goodwins are probably the most notorious dangers in the English Channel, extensive drying sands lying up to 7 miles offshore between Ramsgate and South Foreland. The Goodwins should be avoided in all circumstances, and are well marked on their east, north and south sides.

The well-used channel between the Goodwins and the Kent coast is partly sheltered by the banks in onshore winds. The wide, southern entrance to this channel lies between South Foreland and the South Goodwin light-float. Working north, you need to pick up Goodwin Fork S-cardinal buoy and then the narrow gate between South Brake red buoy and West Goodwin green buoy. From this gate, you can make good north true for 4 miles, passing safely east of Brake Sand, until you join the Ramsgate entrance channel.

Gull Stream is a buoyed channel running SW-NE for just over 5 miles between the West Goodwin buoy and the north entrance between Gull E-cardinal buoy and Goodwin Knoll green buoy.

Brake Sand

The Brake is a nasty area of banks stretching from ½ mile to nearly 4 miles south of Ramsgate entrance. The shallowest, drying area is about 2½ miles south of Ramsgate. Making between Quern N-cardinal buoy and the gateway formed by South Brake red buoy and West Goodwin green, boats should leave the Brake safely to the west. Alternatively, pass inside Brake Sand via the Ramsgate Channel, using B1 and B2 green conical buoys to clear the west edge of the shoals.

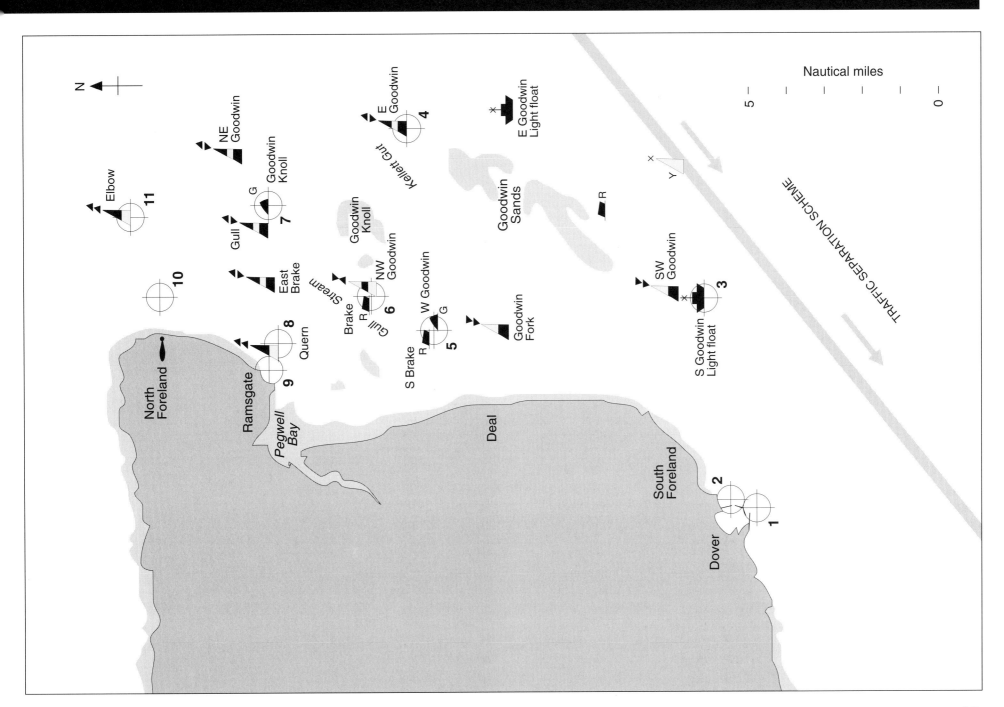

North Foreland

Ramsgate

Pegwell Bay

Deal

South Foreland

Dover

Quern **8**

9

10

Elbow **11**

NE Goodwin

Goodwin Knoll G **7**

Gull

East Brake

Stream

Gull

Brake R

NW Goodwin **6**

Goodwin Knoll

W Goodwin G **5**

S Brake R

Goodwin Fork

Kellett Gut

E Goodwin **4**

Goodwin Sands

E Goodwin Light float ✳

Y ✕

R

SW Goodwin

S Goodwin Light float ✳ **3**

R

2

1

TRAFFIC SEPARATION SCHEME

N

Nautical miles

5

0

Calais and Cap Gris-Nez

WP No	Waypoint name and position	Latitude	Longitude
26-1	Ruytingen SW green buoy, actual position	51°04.98'N	01°46.87'E
26-2	Calais entrance, midway between outer pierheads	50°58.37'N	01°50.52'E
26-3	Calais CA10 buoy, actual position	50°58.59'N	01°50.00'E
26-4	Calais CA6 red approach buoy, actual position	50°58.30'N	01°45.70'E
26-5	CA4 W-card buoy, actual position	50°58.94'N	01°45.19'E
26-6	Les Quénocs clearing, 2 ca NW of CA3 green buoy	50°56.97'N	01°41.00'E
26-7	La Barrière inner, 1 ca SE of CA1 green buoy	50°55.67'N	01°39.00'E
26-8	La Barrière outer, ¼ M NW of Abbeville W-card buoy	50°56.05'N	01°37.34'E
26-9	ZC2 yellow buoy off Cap Gris-Nez, actual position	50°53.50'N	01°30.98'E
26-10	Cap Gris-Nez inner, 1½ M NW of lighthouse	50°53.14'N	01°33.40'E

COASTAL DANGERS

Refer to Admiralty charts 1351, 1892

Ridens de la Rade

This narrow bank runs WSW-ENE off Calais, forming a partial natural breakwater up to a mile offshore. The shallowest depths are about 0.8 metres at LAT ½ mile seaward of Calais breakwaters, with a wider, more shoal area further east over a mile off the hoverport.

In reasonably quiet weather, with sufficient rise of tide, it is safe for boats to cut across Ridens de la Rade, especially when leaving Calais near high water. However, the bank is dangerous in fresh to strong onshore winds, or in fresh north-easterlies or south-westerlies when the tide is weather-going.

Ferry traffic

More than natural coastal dangers, the greatest threat to yachts in the Dover Strait is posed by the almost continuous and rapid movement of cross-Channel ferries. The Strait is one of the busiest seaways in the world, with shipping movements monitored by the Channel Navigation Information Service run by Dover Coastguard and the French 'Crossma' station at Cap Gris-Nez.

Shipping lanes

It is a legal requirement that you cross the Dover Strait shipping lanes at *right-angles*, regardless of what the tide happens to be doing. Low-powered vessels and sailing yachts should not make allowance for the tidal stream while crossing if, by so doing, they will not have a heading nearly at right-angles to the traffic flow.

For most craft, therefore, the enforced strategy will be one of dashing across the 10-mile-wide shipping lanes as quickly as possible while keeping careful track of the effect of the tide. Because of the powerful streams in the Dover Strait – up to 3½–4 knots at top of springs – it is best to time your departure so that the overall effect of the tide works in your favour.

Cap Blanc-Nez

About 6 miles WSW of Calais entrance, various shoal patches lie up to 1½ miles seaward of Cap Blanc-Nez, a prominent rise in the cliffs some 130 metres high. Le Rouge Riden bank has a minimum depth of 1.3 metres, and a shallow wreck, with only 0.2 metres over it, lies only about ¼ mile inside CA3 (Les Quénocs) green buoy. Yachts should stay outside a line between this buoy and Cap Gris-Nez, to avoid La Barrière shoals and Banc à la Ligne.

Banc à la Ligne

The shallow Banc à la Ligne extends within a couple of miles north-east of Cap Gris-Nez, with depths in parts only just above chart datum. Boats making between Cap Gris-Nez and Calais need to stay outside CA1 green buoy and CA3 (Les Quénocs) green buoy.

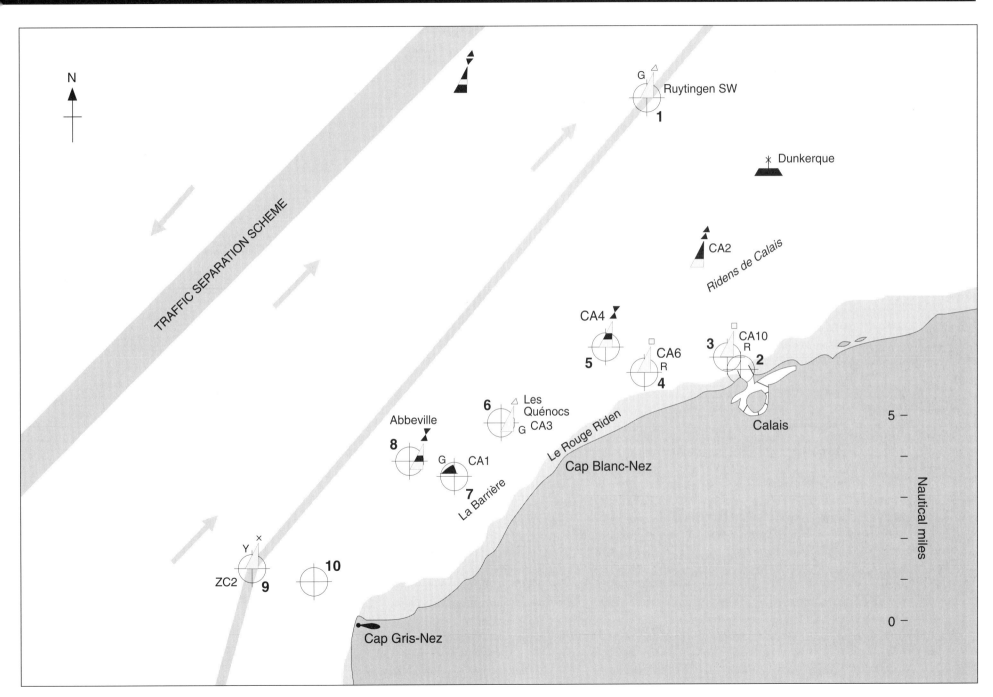

N

TRAFFIC SEPARATION SCHEME

G △
Ruytingen SW
1

✳ Dunkerque

CA2
Ridens de Calais

CA4
CA10
R
3
CA6
R
2
5
4
Calais

6
Les
Quénocs
G CA3
Le Rouge Riden
Abbeville
Cap Blanc-Nez
8
G CA1
7
La Barrière

Y ✕
ZC2
9
10

5 —

Nautical miles

—

—

—

0 —

Cap Gris-Nez

Boulogne to Dieppe

WP No	Waypoint name and position	Latitude	Longitude
27-1	Boulogne approach, actual position of ZC1 yellow buoy	50°44.88'N	01°27.10'E
27-2	Boulogne entrance, 2 ca NW of south pierhead	50°44.60'N	01°33.92'E
27-3	Vergoyer North, actual position of N-card buoy	50°39.64'N	01°22.31'E
27-4	Le Touquet approach, 1 M 340°T from Mérida W-card buoy	50°33.75'N	01°32.80'E
27-5	Bassurelle, actual position of red TSS buoy	50°32.70'N	00°57.80'E
27-6	Somme approach, 1½ ca due N of AT-SO N-card buoy	50°14.10'N	01°28.60'E
27-7	Somme entrance, midway between S1 and S2 channel buoys	50°13.92'N	01°30.00'E
27-8	Le Tréport approach, ½ M NW of west pierhead	50°04.29'N	01°21.67'E
27-9	Le Tréport entrance, midway between pierheads	50°03.93'N	01°22.26'E
27-10	Dieppe approach, 1 M NW of west pierhead light	49°56.91'N	01°03.96'E
27-11	Dieppe entrance, 50 m due E of west pierhead light	49°56.20'N	01°05.10'E
27-12	Roches d'Ailly, ½ M due N of N-card buoy	49°56.88'N	00°56.80'E

COASTAL DANGERS

Refer to Admiralty charts 438, 2147, 2451

Le Colbart

This narrow bank lies in mid-Channel, running SSW-NNE some 9 miles off the French coast opposite Cap Gris-Nez. The shallowest depths range from about 1½ metres to 4½ metres at LAT. In quiet weather, most boats can pass over Le Colbart at most tides, but the bank soon becomes dangerous as the wind freshens and the sea builds up.

Bassure de Baas

This narrow bank, not quite 3 miles long, lies 2-3 miles off the French coast not far north of Boulogne. The north tip is marked by Bassure de Baas N-cardinal bell buoy. Although there is plenty of water for boats over most of the bank, a shallow wreck, with only 1 metre over it, lies about 6 cables south of the buoy.

Le Touquet approaches

The shallow Baie d'Étaples and the estuary of La Cranche river mostly dry for up to a mile offshore and boats should only approach in quiet weather near high water. The buoyed channel runs fairly close along the north shore of the estuary and is approached opposite Pointe de Lornel. About 1½ miles south-west of Pointe de Lornel, right in the middle of the estuary, Mérida W-cardinal buoy marks a shallow wreck which just dries at chart datum.

Baie de Somme approaches

The approaches to the Somme estuary dry for a considerable distance offshore, in fact for just over 3 miles WNW of Pointe du Hourdel. Yachts should only approach in quiet weather and in the last 2 hours before high water. The buoyed channel, which is liable to change, winds into the estuary from a position just north of the outer 'AT-SO' N-cardinal buoy, then leading between S1 green and S2 red buoys.

Note that various submerged obstructions, some with barely 1 metre over them and some almost drying at chart datum, lie up to 2 miles offshore between 4 and 8 miles south of the outer Somme N-cardinal buoy. These obstructions should be given a wide berth if you are coasting between the Somme and Le Tréport or Dieppe.

Dieppe approaches

The approaches to Dieppe are largely straightforward, but are rough in heavy weather because of the uneven seabed and relatively shallow depths. The Berneval W-cardinal buoy, just over 7 miles north of Dieppe entrance, marks a wreck with 2½ metres over it.

Pointe d'Ailly

This prominent headland, 5 miles west of Dieppe entrance, is fringed by the drying Roches d'Ailly for nearly ½ mile offshore. There are also several wrecks lurking off the headland, up to 1½ miles offshore. The shallowest wreck has only 1.2 metres over it and is marked on its seaward side by Roches d'Ailly N-cardinal whistle buoy; boats on passage round Pointe d'Ailly should keep outside this buoy.

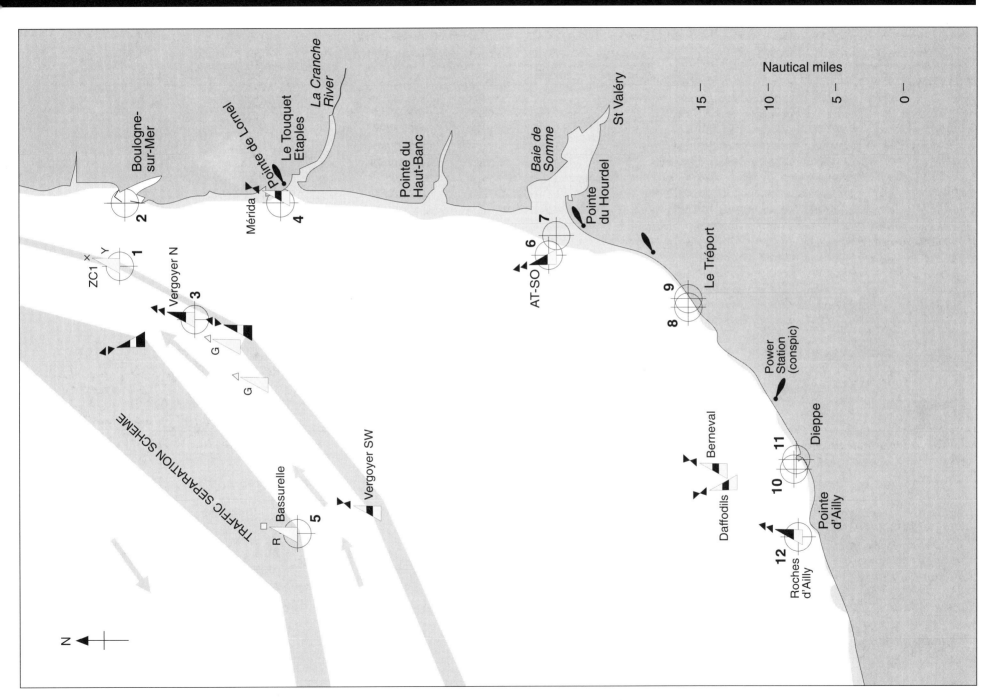

Nautical miles

15 —

10 —

5 —

0 —

Boulogne-
sur-Mer

Pointe de Lornel

Mérida

Le Touquet
Etaples

*La Cranche
River*

Pointe du
Haut-Banc

*Baie de
Somme*

St Valéry

Pointe
du Hourdel

ZC1
Y

Vergoyer N

AT-SO

Le Tréport

Power
Station
(conspic)

TRAFFIC SEPARATION SCHEME

Vergoyer SW

R Bassurelle

Berneval

Dieppe

Daffodils

Pointe
d'Ailly

Roches
d'Ailly

G

G

N

2

1

4

3

5

7

6

9

8

11

10

12

WP No	Waypoint name and position	Latitude	Longitude
28-1	Dieppe approach, 1 M NW of west pierhead light	49°56.91'N	01°03.96'E
28-2	Dieppe entrance, 50 m due E of west pierhead light	49°56.20'N	01°05.10'E
28-3	Roches d'Ailly, ½ M due N of N-card buoy	49°56.88'N	00°56.80'E
28-4	St Valéry-en-Caux approach, 1 M due N of west pierhead	49°53.45'N	00°42.60'E
28-5	St Valéry-en-Caux entrance, midway between pierheads	49°52.43'N	00°42.56'E
28-6	Paluel clearing, ¼ M due N of Paluel N-card buoy	49°52.48'N	00°38.11'E
28-7	Pointe Fagnet clearing, ¾ M NW of signal station	49°46.63'N	00°21.43'E
28-8	Fécamp approach, 1 M due W of north pierhead	49°45.99'N	00°20.32'E
28-9	Fécamp entrance, midway between pierheads	49°45.97'N	00°21.88'E
28-10	Étretat clearing, 1½ M NW of Aiguille d'Étretat	49°43.55'N	00°10.02'E
28-11	Cap d'Antifer outer, 2½ M NW of lighthouse	49°42.80'N	00°07.29'E
28-12	Cap d'Antifer inner, 1 M NW of lighthouse	49°41.77'N	00°08.92'E

COASTAL DANGER

Refer to Admiralty charts 2147, 2451, 2146

Dieppe approaches

The approaches to Dieppe are largely straight-forward, but are rough in heavy weather because of the uneven seabed and relatively shallow depths. The Berneval W-cardinal buoy, just over 7 miles north of Dieppe entrance, marks a wreck with 2½ metres over it.

Pointe d'Ailly

This prominent headland, 5 miles west of Dieppe entrance, is fringed by the drying Roches d'Ailly for nearly ½ mile offshore. There are also several wrecks lurking off the headland, up to 1½ miles offshore. The shallowest wreck has only 1.2 metres over it and is marked on its seaward side by Roches d'Ailly N-cardinal whistle buoy; boats on passage round Pointe d'Ailly should keep outside this buoy.

Approaches to Fécamp

The approaches and entrance to Fécamp are mostly straightforward, but boats coming along the coast from the east should give Pointe Fagnet a wide berth as they come round to line up for Fécamp pierheads. This sheer chalk headland, just north east of Fécamp entrance, is fringed with rocks for 2 cables offshore.

Port du Havre-Antifer

The huge deepwater port of Havre-Antifer lies just over 1 mile south of Cap d'Antifer. The massive main breakwater extends nearly 1½ miles offshore and the deep buoyed approach channel leads in from the north-west from the A7 and A8 buoys 12 miles offshore.

Boats should avoid the Havre-Antifer approach channel if possible, or else cross it at right-angles as quickly as possible. Vessels coasting between Fécamp and Le Havre should give the Havre-Antifer breakwater a good 1 mile berth, both on account of shipping and to avoid the possibility of being set down on to the breakwater by the tide.

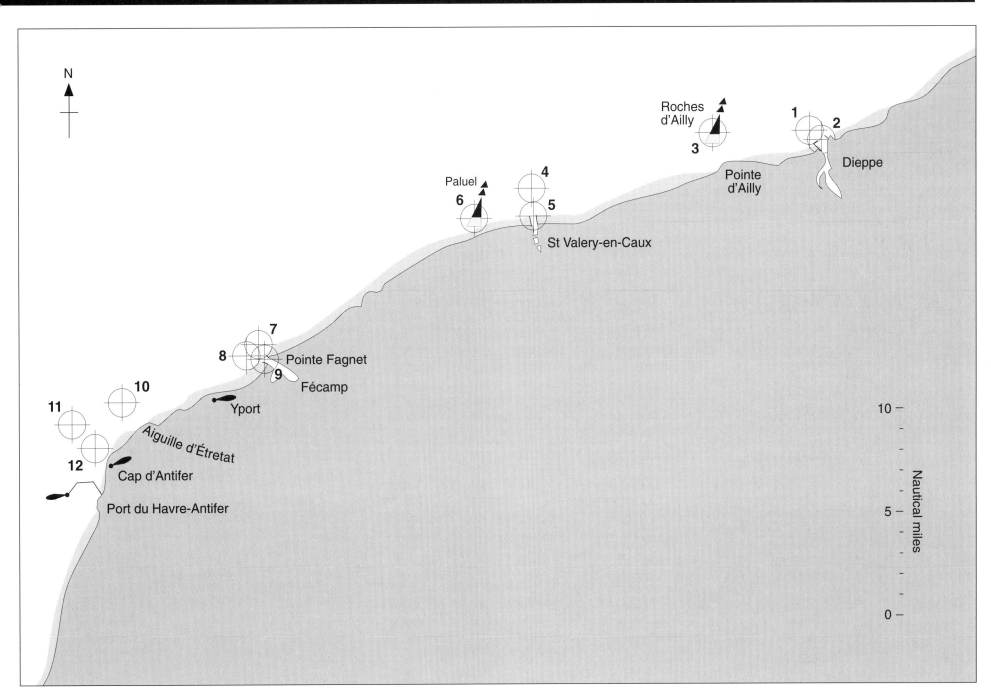

N

Roches
d'Ailly

1 **2**
Dieppe

3

Pointe
d'Ailly

Paluel **4**

6 **5**

St Valery-en-Caux

7

8 Pointe Fagnet

9 Fécamp

10

Yport

11

Aiguille d'Étretat

12

Cap d'Antifer

Port du Havre-Antifer

Nautical miles

10 —

5 —

0 —

Cap d'Antifer to Honfleur

WP No	Waypoint name and position	Latitude	Longitude
29-1	Cap d'Antifer outer, 2½ M NW of lighthouse	49°42.80'N	00°07.29'E
29-2	Cap d'Antifer inner, 1 M NW of lighthouse	49°41.77'N	00°08.92'E
29-3	Le Havre outer approach, between LH3 and LH4 buoys	49°31.03'N	00°03.85'W
29-4	Le Havre inner approach, 2 M 245°T of Cap de la Hève LH	49°29.98'N	00°01.50'E
29-5	Le Havre entrance, on leading line between pierheads	49°29.18'N	00°05.49'E
29-6	Seine outer, ½ M W of Chenal de Rouen No 4 red buoy	49°27.05'N	00°01.82'E
29-7	Ratier NW, 1 ca NW of Ratier green buoy	49°26.91'N	00°02.43'E
29-8	Seine inner, between Nos 9 and 10 channel buoys	49°26.07'N	00°06.37'E
29-9	Honfleur approach, 1 ca N of Honfleur channel mouth	49°25.84'N	00°13.95'E
29-10	Ratelets, 2 ca due W of W-card buoy	49°25.35'N	00°01.50'E
29-11	Deauville outer, on leading line, 1 M from outer green beacon	49°23.29'N	00°03.42'E
29-12	Deauville inner, 50 m 060°T from outer green beacon	49°22.45'N	00°04.22'E

COASTAL DANGERS

Refer to Admiralty charts 2146, 2613

Port du Havre-Antifer

The huge deepwater port of Havre-Antifer lies just over 1 mile south of Cap d'Antifer. The massive main breakwater extends nearly 1½ miles offshore and the deep buoyed approach channel leads in from the north-west from the A7 and A8 buoys 12 miles offshore.

Boats should avoid the Havre-Antifer approach channel if possible, or else cross it at right-angles as quickly as possible. Vessels coasting between Fécamp and Le Havre should give the Havre-Antifer breakwater a good 1 mile berth, both on account of shipping and to avoid the possibility of being set down on to the breakwater by the tide.

Cap de la Hève

Just north of Le Havre approaches, the area off Cap de la Hève is littered with various wrecks and their corresponding buoys. Most of these present no danger to yachts, except perhaps the wreck with only 2.8 metres over it, just over 4 miles WNW of Cap de la Hève lighthouse, which is marked on its north side by a N-cardinal buoy. Boats approaching Le Havre from the north can therefore keep fairly close in round Cap de la Hève, a mile or so offshore, aiming to join the buoyed entrance channel at the LH11 and LH12 pair of buoys.

Le Havre approaches

Le Havre is fairly straightforward to approach navigationally, the main danger being posed by shipping coming in and out, especially at night. Boats following the main buoyed channel into Le Havre should stay just outside the line of the buoys as far as LH11 and LH12. Thereafter you need to keep inside the buoys to avoid Banc de l'Éclat on the north side and the wide shoals of the outer Seine estuary on the south side.

Approaches to La Seine

Like all the estuaries of the great French rivers, the Seine is littered with sandbanks and can be uncomfortable to enter or leave in fresh onshore winds. The approaches are well buoyed though, because large ships go right up to Rouen, some 70 miles inland.

Tidal streams in the Seine estuary can be strong and boats need to time their entrance or exit carefully. If you are bound for Honfleur, about half-flood is a good time to enter the Chenal de Rouen at the Ratier NW green buoy. Turning into Honfleur can be tricky, as the tide runs strongly past the entrance with some nasty swirls and back-eddies. If you round up into the stream to take the sails down, do this well before reaching the narrow gap or you could be swept past.

Approaches to Deauville-Trouville

The approaches to Deauville-Trouville are shallow, especially on the north side where the Banc de Trouville extends well offshore beyond a direct line between Les Ratelets W-cardinal buoy and Deauville-Trouville entrance. Strangers should only approach Deauville-Trouville in quiet weather above half-flood. The approach is dangerous in strong onshore winds.

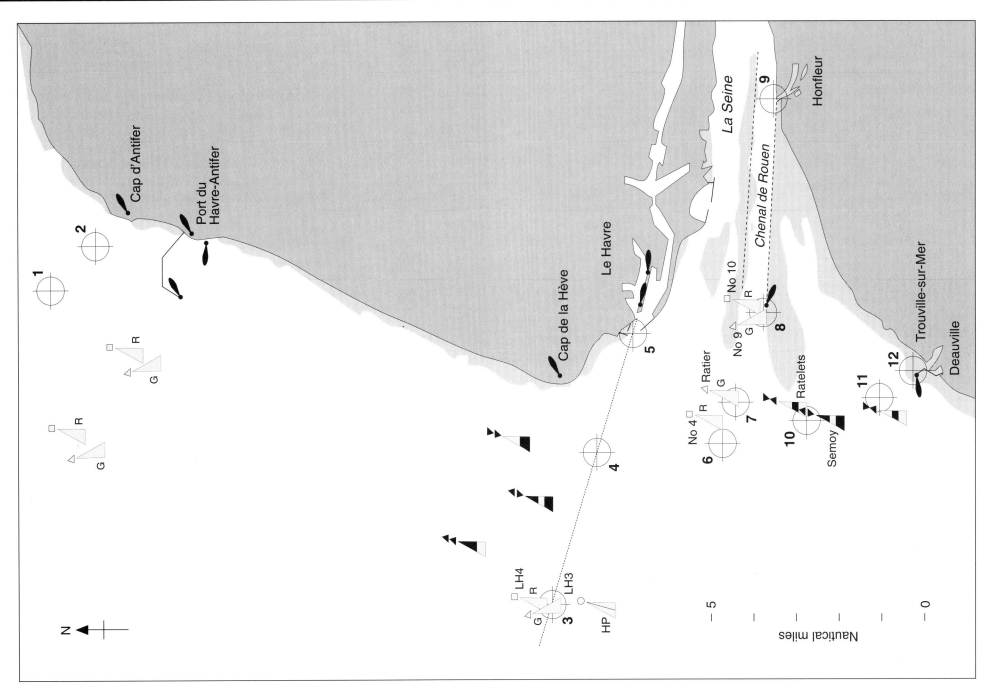

N

Cap d'Antifer

2

1

Port du
Havre-Antifer

R
G

R
G

Cap de la Hève

Le Havre

5

La Seine

9

Honfleur

R

No 10

No 9

G

8

Chenal de Rouen

Ratier

R
G

7

4

No 4

R

G

6

Ratelets

10

Semoy

11

12

Trouville-sur-Mer

Deauville

LH4
R
G
LH3

3

HP

— 5

— 0

Nautical miles

71

La Seine to Ouistreham

WP No	Waypoint name and position	Latitude	Longitude
30-1	LHA, ½ M due N of Le Havre lightfloat	49°31.93'N	00°09.78'W
30-2	Le Havre outer approach, between LH3 and LH4 buoys	49°31.03'N	00°03.85'W
30-3	Le Havre inner approach, 2 M 245°T from Cap de la Hève LH	49°29.98'N	00°01.50'E
30-4	Le Havre entrance, on leading line between pierheads	49°29.18'N	00°05.49'E
30-5	RNA fairway buoy, actual position	49°28.69'N	00°05.43'W
30-6	Seine outer, ½ M W of Chenal de Rouen No 4 red buoy	49°27.05'N	00°01.82'E
30-7	Ratier NW, 1 ca NW of Ratier green buoy	49°26.91'N	00°02.43'E
30-8	Seine inner, between Nos 9 and 10 channel buoys	49°26.07'N	00°06.37'E
30-9	Honfleur approach, 1 ca N of Honfleur channel mouth	49°25.84'N	00°13.95'E
30-10	Ratelets, 2 ca due W of W-card buoy	49°25.35'N	00°01.50'E
30-11	Deauville outer, on leading line, 1 M from outer green beacon	49°23.29'N	00°03.42'E
30-12	Deauville inner, 50 m 060°T from outer green beacon	49°22.45'N	00°04.22'E
30-13	Dives approach, 1½ M 338°T from leading lighthouse	49°19.24'N	00°06.01'W
30-14	Dives entrance, on leading line, close E of No 7 green buoy	49°17.98'N	00°05.22'W
30-15	Ouistreham outer, 2 ca E of E-cardinal buoy on leading line	49°20.48'N	00°14.43'W
30-16	Ouistreham entrance, between outer light beacons	49°18.08'N	00°14.61'W

COASTAL DANGERS
Refer to Admiralty charts 2146, 2613

Cap de la Hève
Just north of Le Havre approaches, the area off Cap de la Hève is littered with various wrecks and their corresponding buoys. Most of these present no danger to yachts, except perhaps the wreck with only 2.8 metres over it, just over 4 miles WNW of Cap de la Hève lighthouse, which is marked on its north side by a N-cardinal buoy. Boats approaching Le Havre from the north can therefore keep fairly close in round Cap de la Hève, a mile or so offshore, aiming to join the buoyed entrance channel at the LH11 and LH12 pair of buoys.

Le Havre approaches
Le Havre is fairly straightforward to approach navigationally, the main danger being posed by

shipping coming in and out, especially at night. Boats following the main buoyed channel into Le Havre should stay just outside the line of the buoys as far as LH11 and LH12. Thereafter you need to keep inside the buoys to avoid Banc de l'Éclat on the north side and the wide shoals of the outer Seine estuary on the south side.

Approaches to La Seine
Like all the estuaries of the great French rivers, the Seine is littered with sandbanks and can be uncomfortable to enter or leave in fresh onshore winds. The approaches are well buoyed though, because large ships go right up to Rouen, some 70 miles inland.

Tidal streams in the Seine estuary can be strong and boats need to time their entrance or exit carefully. If you are bound for Honfleur, about half-flood is a good time to enter the

Chenal de Rouen at the Ratier NW green buoy. Turning into Honfleur can be tricky, as the tide runs strongly past the entrance with some nasty swirls and back-eddies. If you round up into the stream to take the sails down, do this well before reaching the narrow gap or you could be swept past.

Approaches to Deauville-Trouville
The approaches to Deauville-Trouville are shallow, especially on the north side where the Banc de Trouville extends well offshore beyond a direct line between Les Ratelets W-cardinal buoy and Deauville-Trouville entrance. Strangers should only approach Deauville-Trouville in quiet weather above half-flood. The approach is dangerous in strong onshore winds.

Approaches to Dives-sur-Mer
The approaches to Dives are shallow, with banks drying for a good ¾ mile offshore. Strangers should only approach in the last 2 hours before high water. The lock gate into Port Guillaume is normally open for about 3 hours each side of local high water.

Approaches to Ouistreham
The outer approaches to Ouistreham are shallow, although the buoyed channel is dredged for the ferries and can be entered at any state of tide from a position just east of Ouistreham E-cardinal buoy. The approaches to Ouistreham are rough-going in strong onshore winds, when you need to be sure of your position if closing the coast.

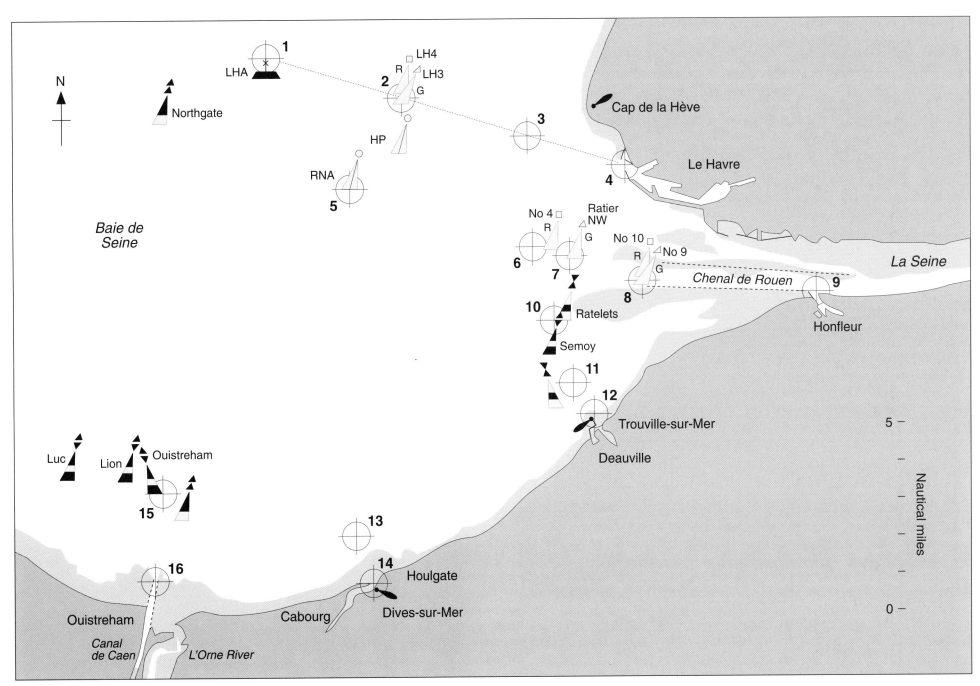

N

Northgate

LHA **1**

2 LH4
R □ LH3
G △

HP

3

Cap de la Hève

Le Havre

La Seine

RNA

4

5

Baie de
Seine

No 4 □ Ratier
R   NW △

No 10 □ No 9
R   G △

6

7

8

Chenal de Rouen

9

Honfleur

10 Ratelets

Semoy

11

12

Trouville-sur-Mer

Deauville

5 —

Luc
Lion   Ouistreham

15

13

16

14 Houlgate

Cabourg   Dives-sur-Mer

Ouistreham

Canal
de Caen   L'Orne River

Nautical miles

0 —

Ouistreham to Port-en-Bessin

WP No	Waypoint name and position	Latitude	Longitude
31-1	Ouistreham outer, 2 ca E of E-card buoy on leading line	49°20.48'N	00°14.43'W
31-2	Ouistreham entrance, between outer light beacons	49°18.08'N	00°14.61'W
31-3	Essarts de Langrune, 1 ca due N of N-card buoy	49°22.73'N	00°21.22'W
31-4	Plateau du Calvados, 3 M N of Courseulles E pierhead	49°23.32'N	00°27.32'W
31-5	Courseulles fairway buoy, actual position	49°21.34'N	00°27.60'W
31-6	Courseulles approach, 7 ca 018°T from E pierhead	49°20.98'N	00°26.98'W
31-7	Courseulles entrance, 25 m E of outer green beacon	49°20.48'N	00°27.26'W
31-8	Arromanches clearing, ½ M N of Roseberry E-card buoy	49°23.68'N	00°36.11'W
31-9	Port-en-Bessin outer, 2 M 024°T from W pierhead	49°23.00'N	00°44.10'W

COASTAL DANGERS

Refer to Admiralty charts 2613, 1349, 2136

Approaches to Ouistreham

The outer approaches to Ouistreham are shallow, although the buoyed channel is dredged for the ferries and can be entered at any state of tide from a position just east of Ouistreham E-cardinal buoy. The approaches to Ouistreham are rough-going in strong onshore winds, when you need to be sure of your position if closing the coast.

Les Essarts de Langrune

A broad rocky plateau, Les Essarts de Langrune, stretches along the Normandy coast for 4 miles east of Courseulles-sur-Mer and the shoals extend up to 2 miles offshore. Drying rocks lurk up to 1½ miles offshore and the plateau is marked on its north-east side by Essarts de Langrune N-cardinal bell buoy. Boats coasting between Ouistreham and Courseulles should pass outside, or at least close to this buoy.

About midway between Ouistreham E-cardinal buoy and Essarts de Langrune N-cardinal, the Luc E-cardinal buoy guards the east side of a wreck, parts of which dry 2.9 metres at LAT. Yachts should pass well outside the Luc buoy.

Plateau du Calvados

Opposite and to the west of Courseulles-sur-Mer, the Plateau du Calvados is an even broader area of drying rocks and shoals, extending about 7 miles along the coast and up to 2 miles offshore. This shoal area, which is well-littered with wrecks, is not marked directly by buoys. Boats coasting past Courseulles in either direction should stay 2½–3 miles offshore, preferably outside a direct line between Essarts de Langrune N-cardinal and Roseberry E-cardinal buoys.

Arromanches and the Mulberry harbour

Some 6 miles west of Courseulles-sur-Mer, the still substantial remains of the famous wartime 'Mulberry harbour' conceived by Winston Churchill provide a dramatic reminder of the Normandy landings which helped turn the tide of the war. The area is littered with wrecks, the outer of which, the *Roseberry*, lies nearly 2¾ miles offshore with 2.2 metres over it, marked on its east side by Roseberry E-cardinal buoy. Further inshore, just opposite Arromanches, the *Harpagas* wreck has only 0.3 metres over it and is also marked on its east side by an E-cardinal buoy.

The numerous caissons of the Mulberry harbour lie off Arromanches just inside the Rochers du Calvados, still forming a partially enclosing breakwater 3 miles long. Yachts can enter the Mulberry harbour in quiet weather, passing between a red and a green buoy which mark a gap in the caissons just under 1 mile SSE of Harpagas E-cardinal buoy. Care must be taken once inside the Mulberry harbour, where there are also drying obstructions and wrecks. Unless the weather is very calm, stay well clear of this whole area when coasting past, keeping outside the Roseberry E-cardinal buoy.

Approaches to Port-en-Bessin

The approaches to the fishing harbour of Port-en-Bessin are straightforward, but the shore dries out on either side of the harbour as far out as the two outer breakwater heads. Boats should keep a good ½ mile offshore until opposite the entrance.

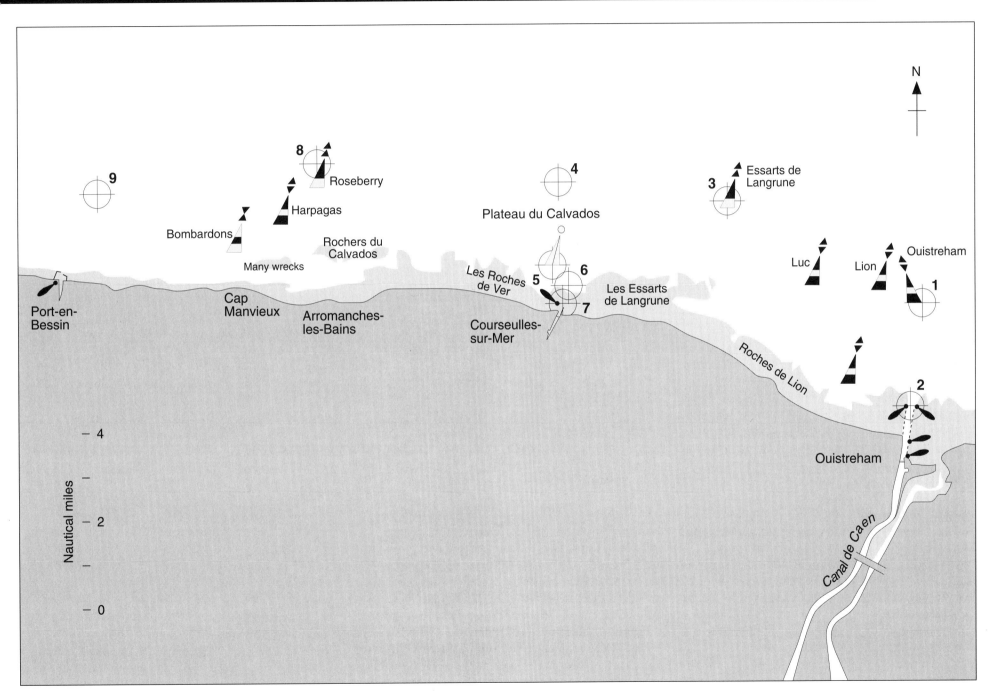

9

8

Roseberry

Harpagas

Bombardons

Rochers du
Calvados

Many wrecks

4

Plateau du Calvados

3 Essarts de
Langrune

Luc   Lion   Ouistreham

Les Roches **5 6**
de Ver

7

Les Essarts
de Langrune

1

Port-en-
Bessin

Cap
Manvieux

Arromanches-
les-Bains

Courseulles-
sur-Mer

Roches de Lion

2

Ouistreham

N

Nautical miles

— 4

— 2

— 0

Canal de Caen

Port-en-Bessin to Carentan

WP No	Waypoint name and position	Latitude	Longitude
32-1	Port-en-Bessin outer, 2 M 024°T from W pierhead	49°23.00'N	00°44.10'W
32-2	Omaha clearing, 6 ca 020°T from middle N-card buoy	49°23.84'N	00°51.50'W
32-3	Broadsword clearing, ¾ M N of Broadsword E-card buoy	49°26.20'N	00°52.68'W
32-4	St Pierre du Mont, 1¼ M due N of 39 m spot height	49°24.79'N	00°57.23'W
32-5	Cardonnet E-card buoy, actual position	49°26.95'N	01°01.00'W
32-6	Grandcamp No 3, ¼ M due N of No 3 N-card buoy	49°25.23'N	01°03.61'W
32-7	Grandcamp outer, on leading line 2¾ M 326°T from pierheads	49°25.77'N	01°05.20'W
32-8	Grandcamp entrance, between outer pierheads	49°23.51'N	01°02.80'W
32-9	Isigny outer, ¼ M NE of Isigny N-card buoy	49°24.57'N	01°06.00'W
32-10	Isigny approach, 2¼ M 352°T from Pte du Grouin beacons	49°23.71'N	01°07.57'W
32-11	Isigny entrance, between Pte du Grouin beacons	49°21.49'N	01°07.07'W
32-12	Carentan C1 fairway buoy, actual position	49°25.30'N	01°07.18'W
32-13	Carentan outer, between No 1 and No 2 entrance buoys	49°24.20'N	01°08.45'W
32-14	Carentan entrance, between outer training wall beacons	49°21.96'N	01°09.81'W

COASTAL DANGERS
Refer to Admiralty chart 2613, 2135

Approaches to Port-en-Bessin
The approaches to the fishing harbour of Port-en-Bessin are straightforward, but the shore dries out on either side of the harbour as far out as the two outer breakwater heads. Yachts should keep a good ½ mile offshore until opposite the entrance.

Omaha Beach
Between 3 and 6 miles west of Port-en-Bessin, the famous Omaha Beach is still encumbered with numerous wrecks and obstructions for a good ¾ mile offshore. Three N-cardinal buoys guard these dangers, and yachts should stay outside these buoys when coasting between Port-en-Bessin and Grandcamp-Maisy.

Broadsword wreck
This wreck, with 2.4 metres over it, lies 2½ miles offshore opposite the west end of Omaha Beach, marked on its east side by the Broadsword E-cardinal buoy.

Les Roches de Grandcamp
This wide drying plateau fringes the coast for nearly 5 miles opposite Grandcamp-Maisy, from near Pointe du Hoc in the east to the Isigny entrance channel in the west. Les Roches de Grandcamp extend up to 1½ miles offshore and are guarded by three N-cardinal buoys. Grandcamp-Maisy harbour can be approached for 2 hours each side of local high water, from a fairway position between No 3 and No 5 N-cardinal buoys.

Approaches to Carentan
The Baie du Grand Vey, which forms the outer approaches to Carentan and Isigny, is a broad expanse of mostly drying sand. Two buoyed channels – the Passe de Carentan and Passe d'Isigny – lead across these shoals and can be negotiated for about 2 hours each side of high water, although strangers bound for Carentan should aim to arrive off the C1 fairway buoy an hour before local high water or just before.

Banc du Cardonnet
This long narrow bank lies about 4 miles offshore opposite the Baie du Grand Vey, and extends for about 6 miles parallel to the coast between Iles St-Marcouf and the Est du Cardonnet E-cardinal buoy. The bank itself has plenty of water over it for boats, but is best avoided on account of the numerous wrecks which lie along it, of rather uncertain depth.

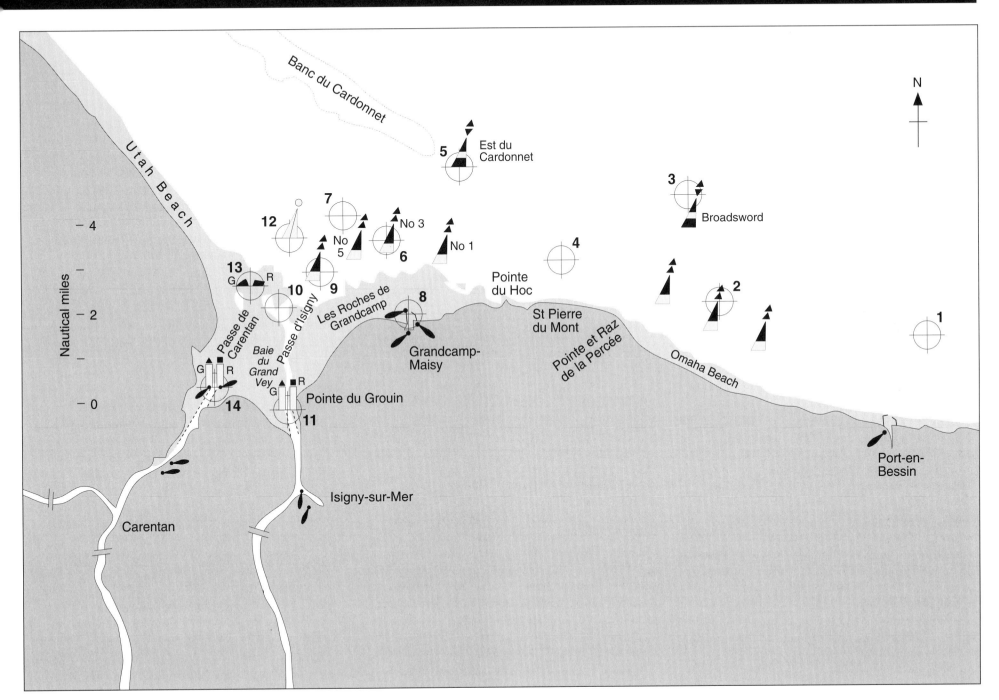

Banc du Cardonnet

N

Utah Beach

5 Est du
Cardonnet

3
Broadsword

7

12

No 3

No 5
6
No 1

4

2

13
G R

10

9

Les Roches de
Grandcamp

Pointe
du Hoc

Nautical miles

— 4

— 2

— 0

Passe de Carentan

Baie
du
Grand
Vey

Passe d'Isigny

8

Grandcamp-
Maisy

St Pierre
du Mont

Pointe et Raz
de la Percée

Omaha Beach

1

G R

G R

Pointe du Grouin

14

11

Isigny-sur-Mer

Port-en-
Bessin

Carentan

Carentan to St Vaast-la-Hougue

WP No	Waypoint name and position	Latitude	Longitude
33-1	Cardonnet E-card buoy, actual position	49°26.95'N	01°01.00'W
33-2	Grandcamp No 3, ¼ M due N of No 3 N-card buoy	49°25.23'N	01°03.61'W
33-3	Grandcamp outer, on leading line 2¾ M 326°T from pierheads	49°25.77'N	01°05.20'W
33-4	Grandcamp entrance, between outer pierheads	49°23.51'N	01°02.80'W
33-5	Isigny outer, ¼ M NE of Isigny N-card buoy	49°24.57'N	01°06.00'W
33-6	Carentan C1 fairway buoy, actual position	49°25.30'N	01°07.18'W
33-7	Carentan outer, between No 1 and No 2 entrance buoys	49°24.20'N	01°08.45'W
33-8	Cardonnet west clearing, 3¼ M due W of E-card buoy	49°26.95'N	01°06.04'W
33-9	Cardonnet north, ¾ M N of Norfalk E-card buoy	49°29.58'N	01°03.40'W
33-10	St Marcouf west, 2 ca W of St Marcouf W-card buoy	49°29.79'N	01°12.20'W
33-11	St Marcouf NE, ½ M NE of Ile du Large lighthouse	49°30.36'N	01°08.07'W
33-12	St Floxel E-card buoy, actual position	49°30.72'N	01°13.70'W
33-13	St Vaast E approach, 2¼ M 150°T from Pte de Saire LH	49°34.45'N	01°11.97'W
33-14	St Vaast Passe du Nord, on leading line ¾ M S of Fort L'Ilet	49°34.36'N	01°14.43'W
33-15	St Vaast entrance, 1½ ca due E of outer pierhead	49°35.23'N	01°15.10'W
33-16	St Vaast NE approach, 1½ M E of Pointe de Saire LH	49°36.44'N	01°11.36'W

COASTAL DANGERS
Refer to Admiralty charts 2135, 1349

Approaches to Carentan
The Baie du Grand Vey, which forms the outer approaches to Carentan and Isigny, is a broad expanse of mostly drying sand. Two buoyed channels – the Passe de Carentan and Passe d'Isigny – lead across these shoals and can be negotiated for about 2 hours each side of high water, although strangers bound for Carentan should aim to arrive off the C1 fairway buoy an hour before local high water or just before.

Utah Beach
The Utah Beach stretches north-west from the west side of Baie du Grand Vey, marked at its south-east end by the prominent American monument. Various wrecks, some awash at chart datum, still lie over 1 mile offshore. Boats following the Normandy coast between Carentan and St Vaast-la-Hougue should therefore keep just outside a direct line between Carentan 'C1' red-and-white fairway buoy and St Floxel E-cardinal buoy.

Banc du Cardonnet
This long narrow bank lies about 4 miles offshore opposite the Baie du Grand Vey, and extends for about six miles parallel to the coast between Iles St-Marcouf and the Est du Cardonnet E-cardinal buoy. The bank itself has plenty of water over it for boats, but is best avoided on account of the numerous wrecks which lie along it, of rather uncertain depth.

Iles St-Marcouf
These two small islands lie about 4 miles north of Utah Beach, more or less in the middle of the long line of banks which curves parallel to the shore between St Vaast and the Est du Cardonnet E-cardinal buoy. Iles St-Marcouf are fairly steep-to and in quiet weather you can anchor off the south-west side of the north island, Ile du Large, for lunch. The south island, Ile de Terre, is a bird sanctuary and landing is prohibited.

The banks north-west of Iles St-Marcouf are shoal with numerous wrecks and should be avoided. It is safe to cross the Banc du Cardonnet for up to 1½ miles south-east of Iles St-Marcouf, but further south-east the Cardonnet bank is littered with wrecks with uncertain depths over them.

Roches St Floxel
5 miles south of St Vaast, some rocky ledges known as Roches St Floxel jut out from the coast for almost 1 mile. The extremity of these dangers is marked by St Floxel E-cardinal buoy.

Approaches to St Vaast-la-Hougue
The approaches to St Vaast, although rather rocky, are well marked and quite straightforward by day or night. Coming from the north round Pointe de Saire, you have to stay well out to the east to clear the rocky dangers east and south of Ile de Tatihou before turning west to follow the Passe du Nord south of two S-cardinal buoys and into the Petite Rade.

Coming from the south-east outside Iles St-Marcouf and the banks, you would normally keep a good mile north-east of Iles St-Marcouf and join the Passe du Nord once clear to the north of Banc de la Rade. Coming from the south inside Iles St-Marcouf and the banks, you would normally approach St Vaast from a position close east of St Floxel E-cardinal buoy.

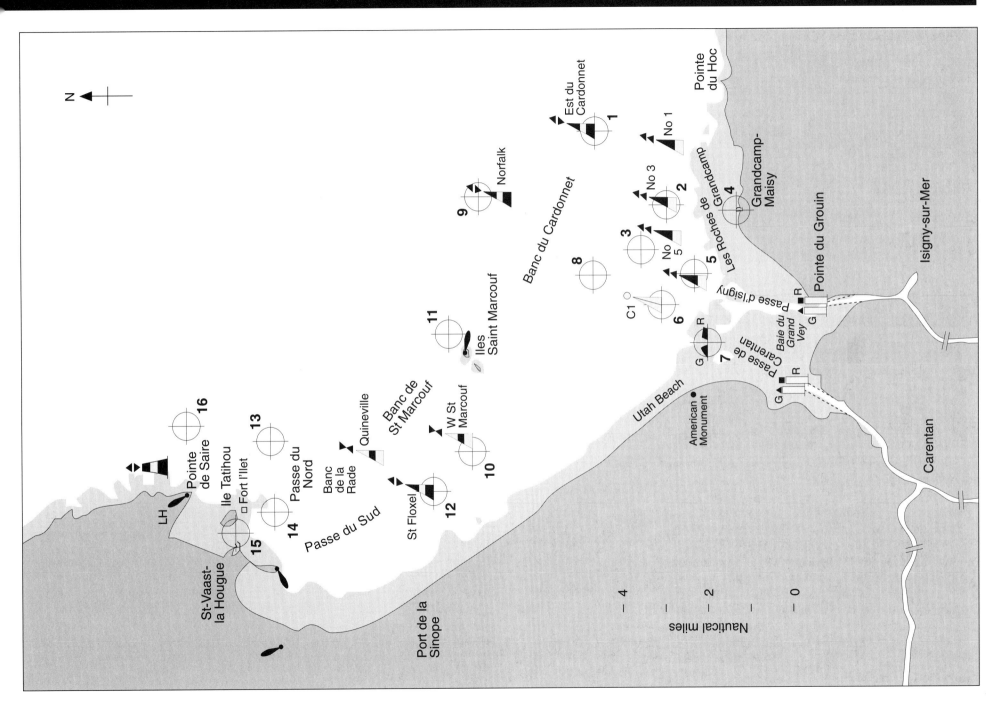

N

Est du
Cardonnet **1**

No 1

No 3 **2**

Norfalk

9

Banc du Cardonnet

No 5 **3**

8

Les Roches de Grandcamp

Grandcamp
4 Maisy

Pointe
du Hoc

5

C1

6

Passe d'Isigny

R

G

Pointe du Grouin

Isigny-sur-Mer

11

Iles
Saint Marcouf

Banc du Cardonnet

G R

7

Passe de
Carentan

Baie du
Grand
Vey

R

G

Banc de
St Marcouf

Quineville

W St
Marcouf

10

Utah Beach

American
Monument

Carentan

16

Pointe
de Saire

13

Ile Tatihou

Fort l'Ilet

Banc
de la
Rade

Passe du
Nord

14

St Floxel

12

Passe du Sud

LH

St-Vaast-
la Hougue

15

Port de la
Sinope

4

2

0

Nautical miles

WP No	Waypoint name and position	Latitude	Longitude
34-1	St Vaast NE approach, 1½ M E of Pointe de Saire LH	49°36.44'N	01°11.36'W
34-2	St Vaast E approach 2¼ M 150°T of Pointe de Saire LH	49°34.45'N	01°11.97'W
34-3	St Vaast Passe du Nord, on leading line ¾ M S of Fort L'Ilet	49°34.36'N	01°14.43'W
34-4	St Vaast entrance, 1½ ca due E of outer pierhead	49°35.23'N	01°15.10'W
34-5	Barfleur north clearing, 4 M due N of lighthouse	49°45.84'N	01°15.87'W
34-6	Barfleur east clearing, 4 M due E of lighthouse	49°41.84'N	01°09.64'W
34-7	Barfleur inner, 3 M 063°T from lighthouse on leading line	49°43.22'N	01°11.68'W
34-8	Barfleur approach, 1¼ M 040°T from b/water hd on leading line	49°41.33'N	01°14.15'W
34-9	Barfleur entrance, b/water head actual position	49°40.38'N	01°15.39'W
34-10	Basse du Rénier, ½ M due N of N-card buoy	49°45.40'N	01°22.02'W
34-11	La Pierre Noire, 1 ca due N of W-card buoy	49°43.70'N	01°28.98'W
34-12	Port Lévi approach, ¾ M due W of Fort Lévi	49°41.48'N	01°29.70'W
34-13	Port Lévi anchorage, 1½ ca due W of S pierhead	49°41.28'N	01°28.64'W

COASTAL DANGERS

Refer to Admiralty charts 2135, 1349, 1106

Approaches to St Vaast-la-Hougue

The approaches to St Vaast, although rather rocky, are well marked and quite straightforward by day or night. Coming from the north round Pointe de Saire, you have to stay well out to the east to clear the rocky dangers east and south of Ile de Tatihou before turning west to follow the Passe du Nord south of two S-cardinal buoys and into the Petite Rade.

Coming from the south-east outside Iles St-Marcouf and the banks, you would normally keep a good mile north-east of Iles St-Marcouf and join the Passe du Nord once clear to the north of Banc de la Rade. Coming from the south inside Iles St-Marcouf and the banks, you would normally approach St Vaast from a position close east of St Floxel E-cardinal buoy.

Pointe de Barfleur

A significant tidal race extends 3–4 miles east and north-east from Pointe de Barfleur, with heavy breaking seas when the stream is weather-going, especially at springs. Give the Barfleur Race a wide berth or, better still, round Pointe de Barfleur at slack water.

Pointe de Barfleur is a low rocky promontory on both its north and east sides and, even at slack water, should be given a generous offing as you go round. On the north side, the Banc de St Pierre and the Plateau des Équets extend for more than 1½ miles offshore and are marked on their north-west corner by Les Équets N-cardinal buoy.

Basse du Rénier

Between Pointe de Barfleur and Cap Lévi, numerous rocky dangers extend up to 2 miles offshore. Les Équets N-cardinal buoy marks the north-west extremity of Banc de St Pierre and the Plateau des Équets and the Basse du Rénier N-cardinal buoy marks the most outlying dangers. La Pierre Noire W-cardinal buoy, not quite 2 miles north of Cap Lévi, serves as a corner mark for the westernmost of the dangers along this stretch of coast.

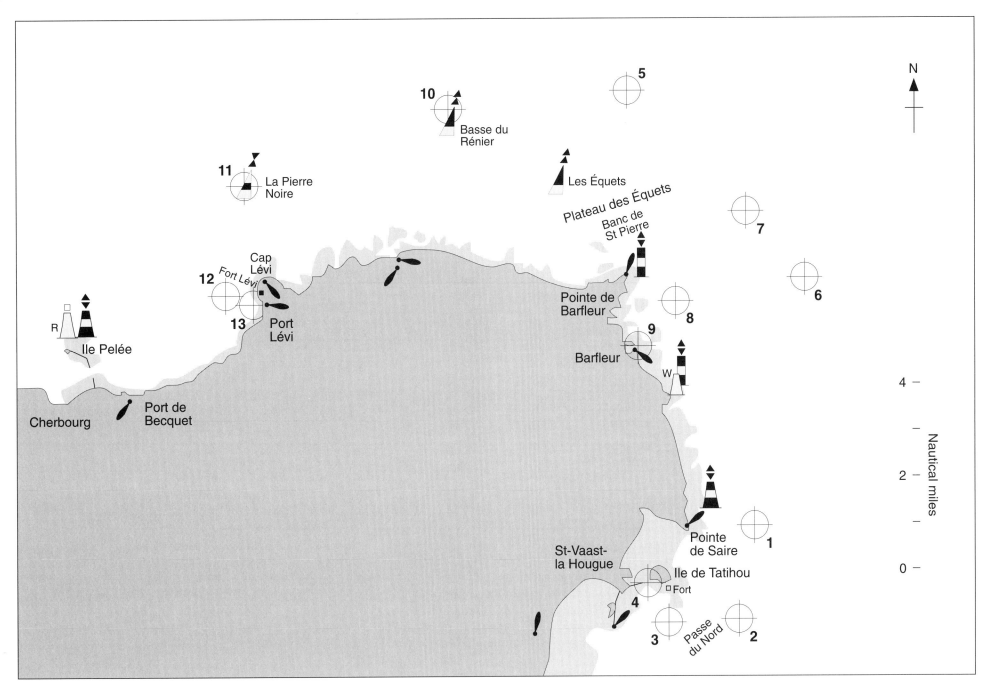

N

5

10 Basse du Rénier

Les Équets

11 La Pierre Noire

Plateau des Équets

Banc de St Pierre

7

Cap Lévi

12 Fort Lévi

6

Pointe de Barfleur

13 Port Lévi

8

R

9

Ile Pelée

Barfleur

W

Cherbourg

Port de Becquet

4 —

2 —

Pointe de Saire **1**

St-Vaast-la Hougue

Ile de Tatihou

0 —

Fort

Nautical miles

4

3 Passe du Nord **2**

WP No	Waypoint name and position	Latitude	Longitude
35-1	La Pierre Noire, 1 ca due N of W-card buoy	49°43.70'N	01°28.98'W
35-2	Port Lévi approach, ¾ M due W of Fort Lévi	49°41.48'N	01°29.70'W
35-3	Port Lévi anchorage, 1½ ca due W of S pierhead	49°41.28'N	01°28.64'W
35-4	Cherbourg East, ¼ M NE of Fort de l'Est	49°40.53'N	01°35.57'W
35-5	Cherbourg West, 1½ ca W of Fort de l'Ouest	49°40.51'N	01°39.01'W
35-6	CH1 fairway buoy, actual position	49°43.30'N	01°42.10'W
35-7	Raz de Bannes, 6 ca N of N-card beacon tower	49°41.99'N	01°44.41'W
35-8	Omonville east approach, 1 M 077°T from leading light	49°42.52'N	01°48.59'W
35-9	Omonville entrance, 1½ ca E of Le Tunard green beacon tower	49°42.38'N	01°49.50'W
35-10	Basse Bréfort, 2 ca N of N-card buoy	49°43.90'N	01°51.03'W

COASTAL DANGERS

Refer to Admiralty charts 1106, 2602

Cap Lévi

Rocks and rocky banks extend for nearly 1¾ miles north of Cap Lévi. The most seaward danger of significance to boats is La Pierre Noire Rock, with 2.2 metres over it, which lies about 1¼ miles north of Cap Lévi. La Pierre Noire is guarded by a W-cardinal buoy, which acts as a corner mark for the westernmost of the extensive area of offshore dangers between Pointe de Barfleur and Cap Lévi.

Ile Pelée

On the east side of Cherbourg east entrance, an area of drying reefs extends seawards from the east fort for 3 cables. This plateau is guarded on its north edge by Ile Pelée red beacon tower and an E-cardinal beacon tower, but it is important not to confuse these two towers if approaching Cherbourg east entrance in poor visibility.

Ferry traffic

Cherbourg is a busy cross-Channel ferry port and care must be taken to keep clear of shipping when entering or leaving either the east or west entrance.

Raz de Bannes

Just over 3 miles west of Cherbourg west entrance, an area of drying rocky ledges juts 6 cables offshore opposite the village and beach of Urville. These dangers are marked on their north edge by the Raz de Bannes N-cardinal beacon tower. Just under ½ mile WNW of this tower is an isolated rock with only 1 metre over it at chart datum.

Pointe de Jardeheu

About 8 miles WNW of Cherbourg west entrance, just beyond the pleasant harbour of Omonville-la-Rogue, the promontory of Pointe de Jardeheu is fringed by drying rocks on both sides and just over ½ mile seaward. The extremity of these dangers is marked by the Basse Bréfort N-cardinal whistle buoy, which most boats leave fairly close to the south on their way between Cherbourg and Cap de la Hague.

If leaving Omonville for Cap de la Hague, you need to make a positive circle around Les Tataquets, Basse de Moitié and La Coque Rocks before steering to pass outside the Basse Bréfort buoy, making due allowance for the west-going tide on the way.

Inshore Eddy

A west-going eddy runs close inshore between Cherbourg and Cap de la Hague, starting about three hours before HW Dover off Cherbourg and much earlier further west. By taking advantage of this eddy, it is possible to carry a fair stream from Cherbourg either to St Peter Port, or direct to St Helier via Corbière Point.

Cap de la Hague is just over 14 miles from Cherbourg west entrance, so most yachts bound for Guernsey or Jersey would be aiming to pass Cherbourg Fort de l'Ouest 2½–3 hours before slack water in the Race ie at around 3½ hours before HW Dover.

Yachts making for Alderney from Cherbourg should leave up to an hour earlier and then hold well up to the north when crossing between Cap de la Hague and the north-east corner of Alderney. You need to be skirting the north end of the Race during the last of the north-going run and then the brief period of slack, to avoid being sucked south of Alderney by the new south-west-going stream in the Race.

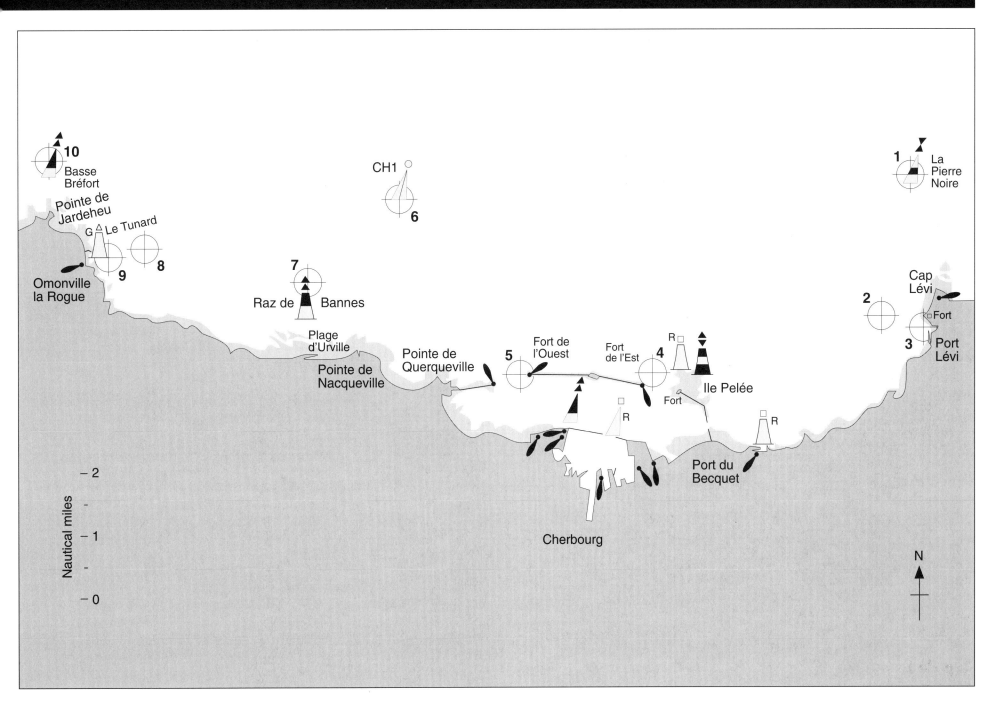

La Pierre Noire **1**

Cap Lévi

2

Port Lévi **3**

Fort

Basse Bréfort **10**

Pointe de Jardeheu

G △ Le Tunard

Omonville la Rogue

9 **8**

CH1

6

7

Raz de ▮ Bannes

Plage d'Urville

Pointe de Nacqueville

Pointe de Querqueville

Fort de l'Ouest **5**

Fort de l'Est **4**

R □

Fort

Ile Pelée

R □

R

Port du Becquet

R

Cherbourg

Nautical miles

− 2

−

− 1

−

− 0

N

WP No	Waypoint name and position	Latitude	Longitude
36-1	Omonville east approach, 1 M 077°T from leading light	49°42.52'N	01°48.59'W
36-2	Omonville entrance, 1½ ca E of Le Tunard green beacon tower	49°42.38'N	01°49.50'W
36-3	Basse Bréfort, 2 ca N of N-card buoy	49°43.90'N	01°51.03'W
36-4	Cap de la Hague, 8 ca due N of La Plate tower	49°44.82'N	01°55.65'W
36-5	Alderney Race, 4 M E of Alderney LH	49°43.81'N	02°03.58'W
36-6	Braye Harbour, 6½ ca N of Château à L'Étoc LH	49°44.65'N	02°10.55'W
36-7	The Swinge, ¾ M due W of Fort Clonque	49°42.87'N	02°15.03'W
36-8	Swinge South approach, 1½ M 214°T from Les Étacs west edge	49°41.09'N	02°15.70'W
36-9	Alderney Race South, 3½ M S of old Telegraph Tower	49°38.83'N	02°13.20'W
36-10	Jobourg clearing, 3½ M SW of Nez de Jobourg	49°37.90'N	02°00.23'W
36-11	Diélette NW offing, 3.2 M 326°T from N power station tower	49°34.97'N	01°55.52'W
36-12	Diélette entrance, 2 ca 320°T from Jetée Ouest light	49°33.39'N	01°51.93'W

COASTAL DANGERS

Refer to Admiralty charts 60, 1106, 3653

Pointe de Jardeheu

About 8 miles WNW of Cherbourg west entrance, just beyond the pleasant harbour of Omonville-la-Rogue, the promontory of Pointe de Jardeheu is fringed by drying rocks on both sides and just over ½ mile seaward. The extremity of these dangers is marked by the Basse Bréfort N-cardinal whistle buoy, which most boats leave fairly close to the south on their way between Cherbourg and Cap de la Hague.

If leaving Omonville for Cap de la Hague, you need to make a positive circle around Les Tataquets, Basse de Moitié and La Coque Rocks before steering to pass outside the Basse Bréfort buoy, making due allowance for the west-going tide on the way.

Cap de la Hague

This rather bleak promontory, right at the north-west tip of the Cherbourg peninsula, is an important psychological gateway between the Normandy coast and the more rugged cruising grounds of Brittany and the Channel Islands. Cap de la Hague, together with Quénard Point at the east tip of Alderney, forms the famous tidal gateway of the Alderney Race.

Cap de la Hague is fringed with drying rocks on its north and west sides. On the Channel side, the dangers extend nearly ¾ mile north-west of the blockhouse on Cap de la Hague. La Plate N-cardinal beacon tower, standing not quite ½ mile offshore, should itself be cleared by a good ½ mile to be sure of avoiding Petite Grune (dries 0.6 metres) and La Grande Grune (with only 1.3 metres over it) as you round Cap de la Hague.

On the west side of Cap de la Hague, La Foraine drying reefs extend a good 6 cables beyond Gros du Raz lighthouse, and are marked on their west side by La Foraine W-cardinal whistle buoy. Boats bound for Diélette, Carteret marina or direct for Jersey, should aim to pass a couple of miles *west* of Cap de la Hague – that is, something over half a mile west of La Foraine buoy.

Nez de Jobourg

3 miles south of Cap de la Hague, the promontory of Nez de Jobourg has dangerous rocks lurking almost 1 mile to the WNW, ½ mile to the west and (Les Calenfriers and Les Huquets de Jobourg) 1½ miles to the south. This far north-west tip of Normandy needs a wide berth if you are heading south from the Alderney Race towards Diélette, Carteret marina or direct for Jersey.

The Alderney Race

Streams are powerful in the Alderney Race, with areas of heavy overfalls, especially with a weather-going tide. Spring rates reach 5–6 knots through most of the Race, but 8–9 knots locally.

Alderney, Braye Harbour approach

East of Braye harbour entrance, the Grois Rocks and Boués Briées extend up to ¼ mile north and NNE of Château à L'Étoc Point. On the west side of Braye harbour entrance, avoid the old submerged breakwater which extends about 3 cables north-east of the existing breakwater.

The Swinge

The Swinge channel, between Alderney and Burhou, can kick up savage overfalls with even a light wind over the tide. Spring rates can exceed 6–7 knots and the Swinge should be taken as near to slack water as possible – that is, at around half-tide (up or down) at Braye Harbour.

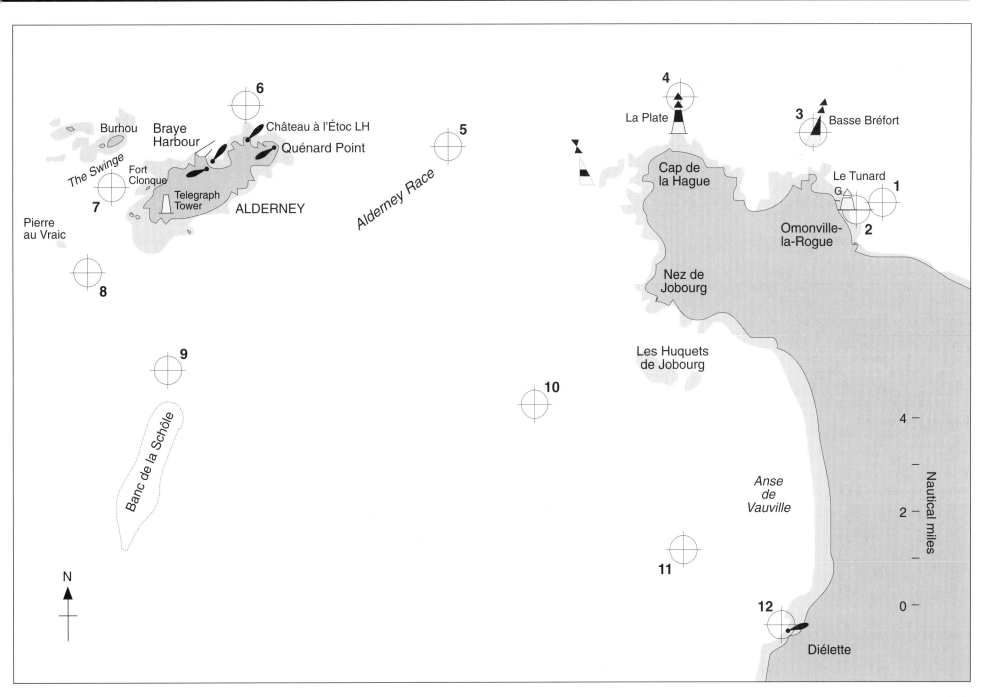

Burhou

Braye
Harbour

Château à l'Étoc LH

6

Quénard Point

5

The Swinge

Fort
Clonque

Telegraph
Tower

ALDERNEY

Alderney Race

7

Pierre
au Vraic

8

9

Banc de la Schôle

10

La Plate

4

3

Basse Bréfort

Cap de
la Hague

Le Tunard

G

1

2

Omonville-
la-Rogue

Nez de
Jobourg

Les Huquets
de Jobourg

Anse
de
Vauville

4 —

—

2 —

Nautical miles

11

—

0 —

12

Diélette

N

WP No	Waypoint name and position	Latitude	Longitude
37-1	Jobourg clearing, 3½ M SW of Nez de Jobourg	49°37.90'N	02°00.23'W
37-2	Diélette NW offing, 3.2 M 326°T from N power station tower	49°34.97'N	01°55.52'W
37-3	Diélette entrance, 2 ca 320°T from Jetée Ouest light	49°33.39'N	01°51.93'W
37-4	Flamanville clearing, 2½ M W of power station towers	49°32.26'N	01°56.65'W
37-5	Les Trois Grunes, ¼ M due W of W-card buoy	49°21.88'N	01°55.50'W
37-5A	Les Trois Grunes north clearing, 6 ca due N of buoy	49°22.48'N	01°55.11'W
37-5B	Les Trois Grunes south clearing, 6 ca due S of buoy	49°21.28'N	01°55.11'W
37-6	Cap de Carteret, ¾ M SW of lighthouse	49°21.94'N	01°49.15'W
37-7	Carteret approach, 1 M 190°T from west pierhead	49°21.20'N	01°47.57'W
37-8	Carteret entrance, 2 ca due S of east pierhead beacon	49°22.03'N	01°47.22'W
37-9	Portbail approach, 2 ca SE of RW fairway buoy	49°18.31'N	01°44.43'W
37-10	Déroute N outer, 5 M 230°T from Cap de Carteret lighthouse	49°19.24'N	01°54.25'W
37-11	Déroute N inner, 8 ca E of Écrevière S-card buoy	49°15.33'N	01°50.85'W
37-12	Écrevière, ¼ M due S of Écrevière S-card buoy	49°15.08'N	01°52.08'W
37-13	Les Écrehou approach, 1½ M 202°T from Bigorne Rock	49°15.80'N	01°55.69'W
37-14	Les Dirouilles West, 2¼ M NE of Sorel Point N tip	49°17.34'N	02°07.10'W
37-15	Les Écrehou SW, 1½ M NE of La Coupe Point (Jersey)	49°15.12'N	01°59.78'W

COASTAL DANGERS

Refer to Admiralty charts 3653, 3655

Diélette approach

This stretch of coast is a lee shore in westerlies or north-westerlies, so it is not prudent to run for Diélette in fresh to strong winds from this quarter. There are drying dangers just off the coast within ¾ mile either side of Diélette harbour, so choose your spot with care if anchoring outside the harbour. Diélette has an attractive marina with a half-tide sill.

Flamanville to Carteret

Parts of the coast between Cap de Flamanville and Cap de Carteret are shallow to within a mile of the shore. The Chausée des Cagnes juts out seawards for 3 cables not far south-east of Cap de Flamanville. Pointe du Rozel, about 3 miles SSE of Cap de Flamanville, has drying ledges and shoal patches extending offshore for a radius of almost a mile. Further south, towards Cap de Carteret, the drying plateau known as Roches du Rit extends for nearly ¾ mile offshore opposite Les Dunes d'Hatainville, with shoal water reaching out another ½ mile.

Between P du Rozel and Roches du Rit, the Banc de Surtainville has shoal patches extending from 1½–2½ miles offshore. The shallowest patch, Basse Bihard with two metres over it, lies about 2½ miles S-W of P du Rozel.

Approaches to Carteret

The approaches to Carteret are shallow and therefore rough-going in fresh onshore winds. Strangers should not, in any event, close the coast near Carteret except within a couple of hours of high water.

Plateau des Trois-Grunes

This small rocky plateau, parts of which dry up to 1.6 metres, lies about 3½ miles west of Cap de Carteret and is marked on its west side by Les Trois Grunes W-cardinal buoy.

Banks between Les Écrehou and the mainland

There are various banks and shoals strung out between the French mainland and the rocky plateau of rocks and islets known as Les Écrehou. Close south-east of Les Écrehou, the Écrevière Bank dries up to 2.3 metres and stretches SSE from L'Écrevière Rock for nearly 1½ miles. The tip of this bank is marked by a S-cardinal buoy. There is then a deep channel, about 1½ miles wide, between the east side of Les Écrehou and the Basses de Taillepied shoals, parts of which have less than a metre over them, with a rocky patch drying 0.7 metres near the north-west tip of the shoal area.

Basses de Taillepied are about 5 miles offshore, and there are more shoals between Taillepied and the mainland, parts of which dry or almost dry at chart datum. These banks merge into the coastal shoals off Portbail, a small drying harbour which should only be approached near high water.

Les Écrehou

This fascinating plateau of reefs and islets can be visited in quiet weather, but pilotage around Les Écrehou needs great care, especially as the tides are very strong in this area. Strangers should approach from the SSW, using the waypoints given in this directory and following the advice of a reliable pilot book. A good time to arrive is around half-ebb, when there is plenty of water in the approach channel but enough of the key rocks exposed to make them clearly visible.

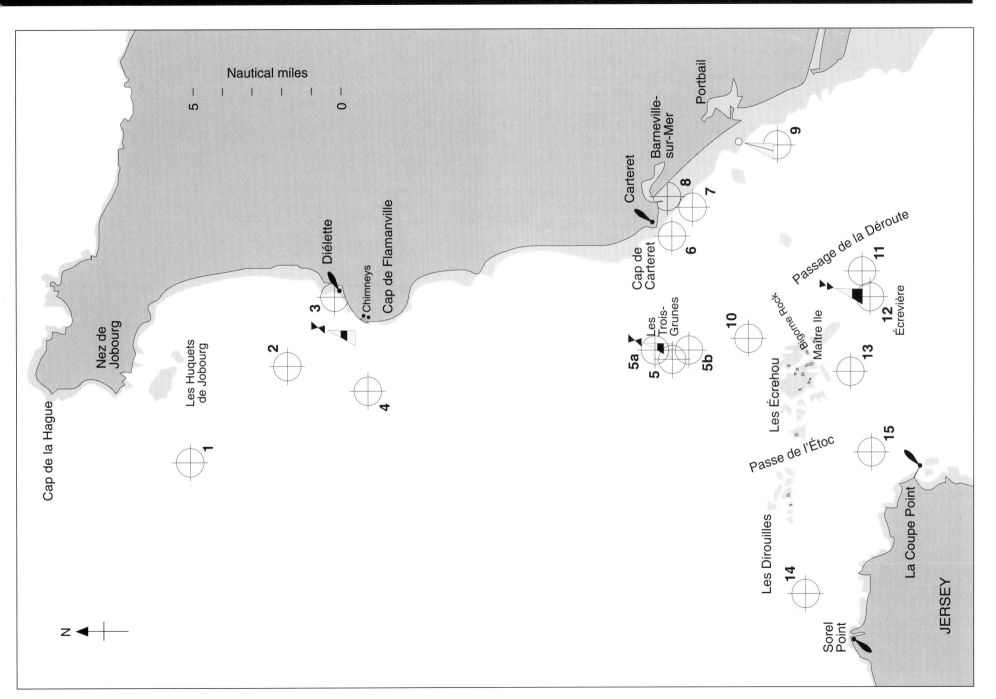

Nautical miles

5 · · · · · 0

N

Cap de la Hague

Nez de Jobourg

Les Huquets de Jobourg

Diélette

Chimneys

Cap de Flamanville

Carteret

Barneville-sur-Mer

Portbail

Cap de Carteret

Passage de la Déroute

Écrevière

Les Trois-Grunes

Bigorne Rock

Maître Ile

Les Écrehou

Passe de l'Étoc

Les Dirouilles

Sorel Point

La Coupe Point

JERSEY

1
2
3
4
5
5a
5b
6
7
8
9
10
11
12
13
14
15

Alderney Race to Guernsey

WP No	Waypoint name and position	Latitude	Longitude
38-1	Cap de la Hague, 8 ca due N of La Plate tower	49°44.82'N	01°55.65'W
38-2	Alderney Race, 4 M E of Alderney lighthouse	49°43.81'N	02°03.58'W
38-3	Braye Hr, 6½ ca N of Château à L'Étoc lighthouse	49°44.65'N	02°10.55'W
38-4	The Swinge, ¾ M due W of Fort Clonque	49°42.87'N	02°15.03'W
38-5	Swinge South approach, 1½ M 214°T from Les Étacs west edge	49°41.09'N	02°15.70'W
38-6	Casquets, 1¾ M due W of lighthouse	49°43.38'N	02°25.24'W
38-7	Alderney Race South, 3½ M S of old Telegraph Tower	49°38.83'N	02°13.20'W
38-8	Jobourg clearing, 3½ M SW of Nez de Jobourg	49°37.90'N	02°00.23'W
38-9	Diélette NW offing, 3.2 M 326°T from N power station tower	49°34.97'N	01°55.52'W
38-10	Diélette entrance, 2 ca 320°T from Jetée Ouest light	49°33.39'N	01°51.93'W
38-11	Schôle Bank East, 10 M due S of Quénard Point lighthouse	49°33.81'N	02°09.77'W
38-12	East Sark, ½ M due E of Blanchard E-card buoy	49°25.42'N	02°16.57'W
38-13	Little Russel North, 6 ca ENE Platte Fougère lighthouse	49°31.14'N	02°28.22'W
38-14	Roustel, 1 ca due W of BW tower	49°29.29'N	02°28.88'W
38-15	St Peter Port, 1 ca ENE of Castle pierhead	49°27.41'N	02°31.20'W
38-16	Little Russel South, 6 ca ESE St Martin's LH	49°25.16'N	02°30.75'W
38-17	Big Russel North, 2 M E of Grande Amfroque beacons	49°30.61'N	02°21.44'W
38-18	Big Russel South, 1 M E of Lower Heads S-card buoy	49°25.89'N	02°26.93'W
38-19	Sark, Havre Gosselin, 1½ ca due S of Les Dents Rocks	49°25.48'N	02°23.62'W
38-20	Guernsey south coast, 1½ M S of Corbière tower	49°23.78'N	02°37.07'W
38-21	Les Hanois, 2 M due W of lighthouse	49°26.16'N	02°45.16'W
38-22	Lower Heads south clearing, 1 ca due S of S-card buoy	49°25.80'N	02°28.46'W
38-23	Sark north clearing, ½ M due N of Bec du Nez light	49°27.65'N	02°22.08'W
38-24	Little Sark west clearing, 8½ ca 222°T from Les Dents	49°25.00'N	02°24.49'W
38-25	Sark south clearing, 9 ca 230°T from S tip of L'Étac	49°23.54'N	02°23.00'W

COASTAL DANGERS

Refer to Admiralty charts 60, 807, 808, 3653, 3654

Alderney Race

Streams are powerful in the Alderney Race, with areas of heavy overfalls especially on a weather-going tide. Spring rates reach 5–6 knots through most of the Race, but 8–9 knots locally.

The Swinge

The Swinge channel, between Alderney and Burhou, can kick up savage overfalls with even a light wind over the tide. Spring rates can reach 6–7 knots and the Swinge should be taken as near slack water as possible, at around half-tide (up or down) at Braye Harbour.

The Casquets

Although the main island of the Casquets is comparatively steep-to and can be passed within ½ mile on its west side, the whole area around these reefs is notorious for strong tides, patches of overfalls and an uneasy swell. Strangers on passage are advised to leave Casquets lighthouse a good 1½–2 miles to the east.

Herm Island

Herm is surrounded by wide expanses of drying rocks. Approaching the Little Russel from Alderney, be sure you are well north of Platte Boue and Boufresse, the most north-easterly (and unmarked) out-lying dangers.

Guernsey North Coast

Along the north-west coast of Guernsey, between Les Hanois and Platte Fougère, dangers extend up to 2 miles offshore. In poor visibility, be sure you are approaching either safely west of Les Hanois or east of Platte Fougère.

Les Hanois

The rocks off the south-west tip of Guernsey extend 1¾ miles WNW of Pleinmont Point, over ½ mile seaward of the lighthouse. Give this corner a safe berth, particularly when rounding from the N and especially if the tide is N-E going as you approach Les Hanois.

Guernsey South Coast

Guernsey's south coast is relatively steep-to, but the west end has several patches – notably Les Kaines (drying 1.2 metres) and Les Lieuses (drying 4–5 metres) – which lie nearly ½ mile offshore. Give these dangers a wide berth at half-tide or below.

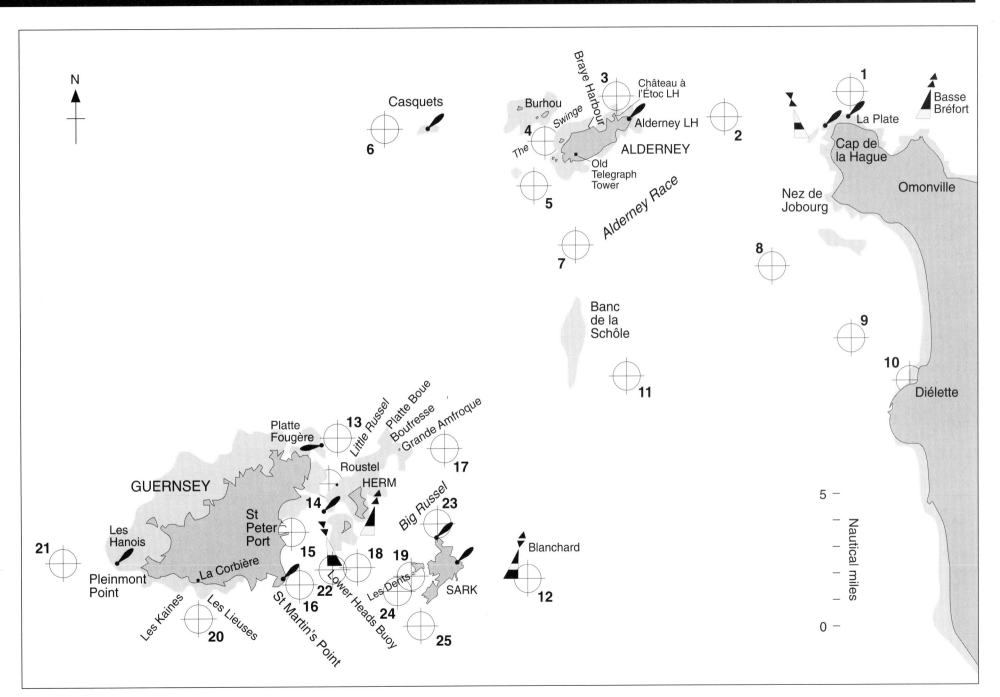

N

Casquets

6

Burhou

Braye Harbour

3 Château à
l'Étoc LH

Swinge

Alderney LH

4

The

5

Old
Telegraph
Tower

ALDERNEY

2

1

La Plate

Basse
Bréfort

Cap de
la Hague

Nez de
Jobourg

Omonville

7

Alderney Race

8

Banc
de la
Schôle

9

10

Diélette

11

Platte
Fougère

13

Little Russel

Platte Boue

Boufresse

Grande Amfroque

17

GUERNSEY

Roustel

HERM

14

Big Russel

23

Blanchard

12

Les
Hanois

St
Peter
Port

15

18

19

21

La Corbière

Lower Heads Buoy

Les Dents

SARK

Pleinmont
Point

22

16

St Martin's Point

24

5 —

Nautical miles

Les Kaines

Les Lieuses

20

25

0 —

WP No	Waypoint name and position	Latitude	Longitude
39-1	Little Russel North, 6 ca ENE Platte Fougère lighthouse	49°31.14'N	02°28.22'W
39-2	Roustel, 1 ca due W of BW tower	49°29.29'N	02°28.88'W
39-3	St Peter Port, 1 ca ENE of Castle pierhead	49°27.41'N	02°31.20'W
39-4	Little Russel South, 6 ca ESE St Martin's lighthouse	49°25.16'N	02°30.75'W
39-5	Big Russel North, 2 M E of Grande Amfroque beacons	49°30.61'N	02°21.44'W
39-6	Big Russel South, 1 M E of Lower Heads buoy	49°25.89'N	02°26.93'W
39-7	Guernsey south coast, 1½ M S of Corbière tower	49°23.78'N	02°37.07'W
39-8	Les Hanois, 2 M due W of lighthouse	49°26.16'N	02°45.16'W
39-9	East Sark, ½ M due E of Blanchard E-card buoy	49°25.42'N	02°16.57'W
39-10	Les Dirouilles West, 2¼ M NE of Sorel Point N tip	49°17.34'N	02°07.10'W
39-11	Les Écrehou SW, 1½ M NE of La Coupe Point (Jersey)	49°15.12'N	01°59.78'W
39-12	Desormes, 1 ca due W of W-card buoy	49°19.01'N	02°18.08'W
39-13	La Corbière, 1.2 M due W of lighthouse	49°10.85'N	02°16.79'W
39-14	Noirmont Point, 2 ca due S of lighthouse	49°09.76'N	02°10.01'W
39-15	St Helier, 2¼ ca 200°T from Platte beacon	49°10.00'N	02°07.38'W
39-16	Roches Douvres West, 3 M WNW of lighthouse	49°07.80'N	02°52.79'W
39-17	Roches Douvres East, 3½ M due E of lighthouse	49°06.48'N	02°43.34'W
39-18	Lower Heads south clearing, 1 ca due S of S-card buoy	49°25.80'N	02°28.46'W
39-19	Sark south clearing, 9 ca 230°T from S tip of L'Étac	49°23.54'N	02°23.00'W
39-20	Les Trois Grunes north clearing, 6 ca due N of buoy	49°22.48'N	01°55.11'W
39-21	Les Trois Grunes, ¼ M due west of W-card buoy	49°21.88'N	01°55.50'W
39-22	Les Trois Grunes south clearing, 6 ca due S of buoy	49°21.28'N	01°55.11'W

COASTAL DANGERS

Refer to Admiralty charts 2669, 3654, 3655

Guernsey North Coast

See page 88.

Les Hanois

The rocks off the south-west tip of Guernsey extend 1¾ miles WNW of Pleinmont Point, more than ½ mile seaward of the lighthouse. Give this corner a safe berth, particularly when rounding from the north and if the tide is north-east going as you approach Les Hanois.

Guernsey South Coast

See page 88.

Herm

The island of Herm is surrounded by large expanses of drying rocks. Approaching the north end of the Little Russel channel from the direction of Alderney, be sure you are well north of Platte Boue and Boufresse.

Sark

There are many off-lying rocks around Sark, especially on the north-east side between Bec du Nez and Creux Harbour, and off the south and west coasts of Little Sark. The streams round Sark can be strong, up to 4 or 5 knots at springs off the east and west coasts, up to 6 knots in the Goulet between Creux Harbour and Les Burons Rocks, and up to 7 knots in the Gouliot Passage between Brecqhou and the west coast. Night navigation around Sark is not advisable.

Jersey North Coast

Approaching Jersey from northward, especially direct from the Alderney Race, avoid the Paternosters which lie 2–3 miles offshore between Grosnez Point and Sorel Point. Further east, from 3–5 miles off the NE corner of Jersey, are Les Dirouilles plateau and the numerous reefs around Les Écrehou islands.

La Corbière Point

Drying rocks lurk up to ½ mile west and WNW of La Corbière. Rounding the point from the north to line up for the Western Passage to St Helier, stay at least ¾ mile west of the lighthouse until you have passed nicely south of it and cleared these dangers.

Roches Douvres

The Roches Douvres plateau is about 2 miles across from west to east and 1½ miles from north to south. The tides set strongly in this area, especially between Roches Douvres and Plateau de Barnouic. It is important to pass both these areas of rocks a safe distance off, preferably keeping 'down-tide' of the dangers. The clearing waypoints in this directory have been set with this in mind.

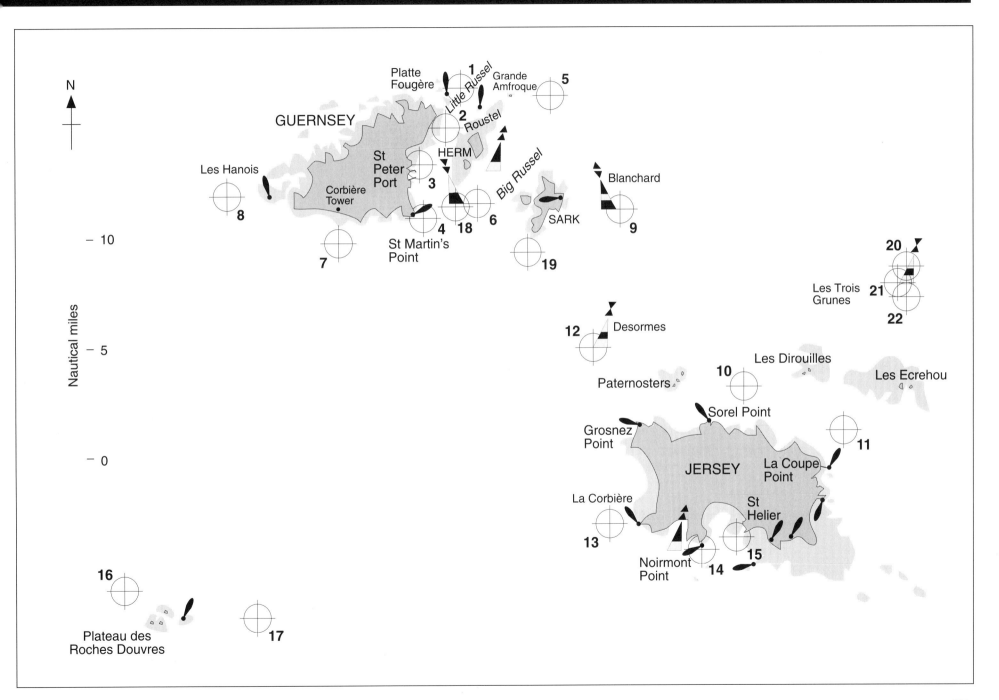

N

Nautical miles

— 10

— 5

— 0

GUERNSEY

Platte
Fougère

1 Little Russel

Grande
Amfroque

5

2 Roustel

HERM

Big Russel

St
Peter
Port

3

Les Hanois

Corbière
Tower

8

4 **18**

6

St Martin's
Point

7

Blanchard

SARK

9

19

20

Les Trois
Grunes

21

22

12 Desormes

Les Dirouilles

10

Les Ecrehou

Paternosters

Sorel Point

Grosnez
Point

11

JERSEY

La Coupe
Point

La Corbière

St
Helier

13

Noirmont
Point

14

15

16

17

Plateau des
Roches Douvres

Jersey including Les Écrehou

WP No	Waypoint name and position	Latitude	Longitude
40-1	Déroute N outer, 5 M 230°T from Cap de Carteret lighthouse	49°19.24'N	01°54.25'W
40-2	Déroute N inner, 8 ca E of Écrevière S-card buoy	49°15.33'N	01°50.85'W
40-3	Écrevière, ¼ M due S of Écrevière S-card buoy	49°15.08'N	01°52.08'W
40-4	Les Écrehou approach, 1½ M 202°T from Bigorne rock	49°15.80'N	01°55.69'W
40-5	Les Dirouilles West, 2¼ M NE of Sorel Point N tip	49°17.34'N	02°07.10'W
40-6	Les Écrehou SW, 1½ M NE of La Coupe Point, Jersey	49°15.12'N	01°59.78'W
40-7	Desormes West, 1 ca W of Desormes W-card buoy	49°19.01'N	02°18.08'W
40-8	Plemont Point, ¾ M NE of headland NE tip	49°16.22'N	02°12.69'W
40-9	Grosnez West, 3½ M due W of Grosnez Point lighthouse	49°15.54'N	02°20.10'W
40-10	La Corbière West, 1.2 M due W of lighthouse	49°10.85'N	02°16.79'W
40-11	La Corbière SW, 2½ M SW of lighthouse on leading line	49°09.07'N	02°17.69'W
40-12	La Corbière South, 1 M due S of lighthouse	49°09.85'N	02°14.93'W
40-13	Noirmont Point, 2 ca due S of lighthouse	49°09.76'N	02°10.01'W
40-14	St Helier entrance, 2¼ ca 200°T from Platte beacon	49°10.00'N	02°07.38'W
40-15	East Passage outer, 2 ca S of Demie de Pas beacon	49°08.86'N	02°06.08'W
40-16	Canger Rock West, ½ M NW of W-card buoy	49°07.77'N	02°00.85'W
40-17	Frouquier Aubert, ¾ M due S of S-card buoy	49°05.40'N	01°58.77'W
40-18	Violet SW, 6 ca WSW of Violet fairway buoy	49°07.62'N	01°57.93'W
40-19	Violet North, 8½ ca 353°T from Violet fairway buoy	49°08.71'N	01°57.20'W
40-20	Gorey SE, 1.6 M 118°T from Gorey pierhead	49°11.10'N	01°59.10'W
40-21	Gorey NE outer, 1¾ M 050°T from Mont Orgueil	49°13.13'N	01°59.02'W
40-22	Gorey NE inner, 7 ca 050°T from Mont Orgueil	49°12.48'N	02°00.22'W

COASTAL DANGERS

Refer to Admiralty charts 1136, 1138, 3655

Pierres de Lecq

This plateau of drying and above-water rocks, also known as the Paternosters, lies between 1½ and 3 miles off the west end of Jersey's north coast, between Grosnez Point and Sorel Point. The plateau is about 1¼ miles across and represents a particular danger for boats arriving off the north-west corner of Jersey direct from the Alderney Race, or for vessels coasting inshore around Jersey. The Desormes W-cardinal buoy

lies just over 3 miles WNW of Pierres de Lecq.

Further east, from 3 to 5 miles off the north-east corner of Jersey, are Les Dirouilles plateau and the numerous reefs around Les Écrehou islands.

Jersey West Coast

Rocky shoals extend up to a mile seaward of Jersey's west coast and boats should keep well off St Ouen Bay when approaching Corbière Point from the north, or when bound northwards having rounded Corbière. The Rigdon Bank, a couple of miles south-east of Grosnez Point, should be avoided except in quiet weather. The Rigdon has only 3 metres over it

at chart datum and any swell can break heavily over these shoals in even a moderate onshore wind.

La Corbière

Drying rocks lurk up to ½ mile W and WNW of La Corbière. Rounding the point from the north to line up for the Western Passage to St Helier, stay at least ¾ mile W of the lighthouse until you have passed nicely south of it and cleared these dangers.

Approaches to St Helier

There are numerous drying rocks off the south coast of Jersey, through or inside which lead the various approach passages to St Helier. The Western Passage is the main 'big-ship' channel to St Helier, leading close along Jersey's south-west coast inside the off-lying dangers. Arriving from the east and south, most boats use the Eastern Passage which leads between the Hinguette Rocks and the coastal dangers north of the Demie de Pas beacon tower.

Violet Bank

This vast area of drying rocks lies off the south-east corner of Jersey, extending south-east from La Rocque Point for over 3 miles. Although the Violet Bank looks pretty horrific on a chart, the dangers are reasonably compact on the south side, and the passage between St Helier and Gorey via the Violet Channel is fairly straightforward in reasonable visibility. Perhaps the greatest care is needed when on passage between St Helier and Granville, when the various drying dangers extending south-eastwards beyond the Violet Bank need to be left well clear to the north.

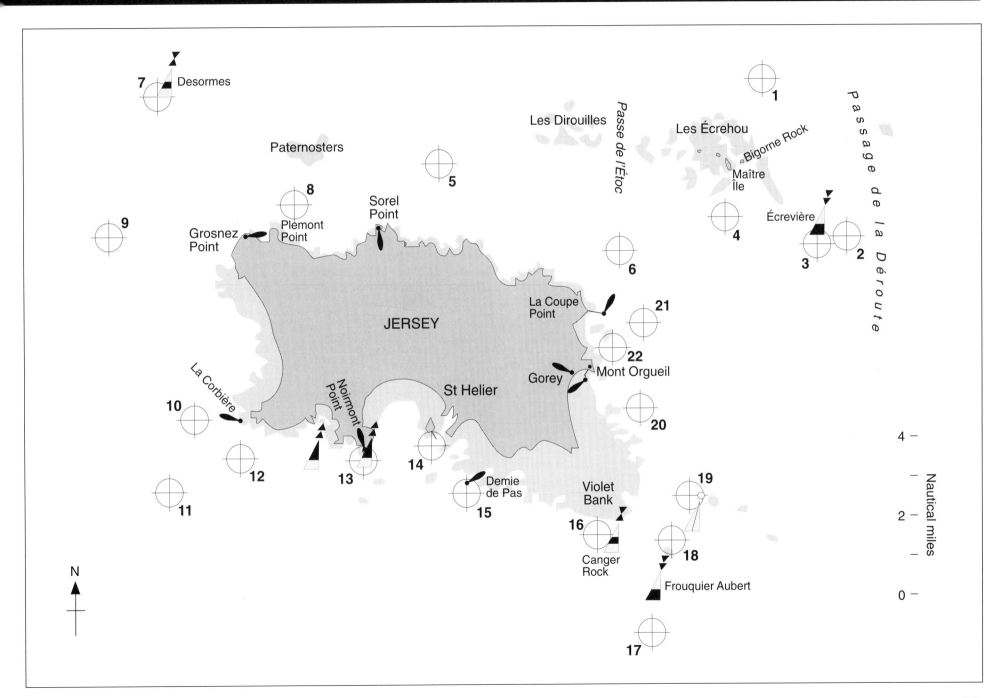

7 Desormes

Les Dirouilles

Paternosters

Passe de l'Étoc

Les Écrehou

Bigorne Rock

1

Maître Île

Passage de la Déroute

8

5

9

Sorel Point

Plémont Point

Grosnez Point

Écrevière

4

6

3

2

La Coupe Point

21

JERSEY

22

Mont Orgueil

La Corbière

Noirmont Point

Gorey

St Helier

20

10

12

13

14

Demie de Pas

19

Violet Bank

11

15

16

18

Canger Rock

17

Frouquier Aubert

N

4 —

Nautical miles

2 —

0 —

WP No	Waypoint name and position	Latitude	Longitude
40-1	Déroute N outer, 5 M 230°T from Cap de Carteret L/H	49°19.24'N	01°54.25'W
40-2	Déroute N inner, 8 ca E of Écrevière S-card buoy	49°15.33'N	01°50.85'W
40-3	Écrevière, ¼ M due S of Écrevière S-card buoy	49°15.08'N	01°52.08'W
40-4	Les Écrehou approach, 1½ M 202°T from Bigorne rock	49°15.80'N	01°55.69'W
40-5	Les Dirouilles West, 2¼ M NE of Sorel Point N tip	49°17.34'N	02°07.10'W
40-6	Les Écrehou SW, 1½ M NE of La Coupe Point, Jersey	49°15.12'N	01°59.78'W
40-7	Desormes West, 1 ca W of Desormes W-card buoy	49°19.01'N	02°18.08'W
40-8	Plemont Point, ¾ M NE of headland NE tip	49°16.22'N	02°12.69'W
40-9	Grosnez West, 3½ M due W of Grosnez Point lighthouse	49°15.54'N	02°20.10'W
40-10	La Corbière West, 1.2 M due W of lighthouse	49°10.85'N	02°16.79'W
40-11	La Corbière SW, 2½ M SW of lighthouse on leading line	49°09.07'N	02°17.69'W
40-12	La Corbière South, 1 M due S of lighthouse	49°09.85'N	02°14.93'W
40-13	Noirmont Point, 2 ca due S of lighthouse	49°09.76'N	02°10.01'W
40-14	St Helier entrance, 2¼ ca 200°T from Platte beacon	49°10.00'N	02°07.38'W
40-15	East Passage outer, 2 ca S of Demie de Pas beacon	49°08.86'N	02°06.08'W
40-16	Canger Rock West, ½ M NW of W-card buoy	49°07.77'N	02°00.85'W
40-17	Frouquier Aubert, ¾ M due S of S-card buoy	49°05.40'N	01°58.77'W
40-18	Violet SW, 6 ca WSW of Violet fairway buoy	49°07.62'N	01°57.93'W
40-19	Violet North, 8½ ca 353°T from Violet fairway buoy	49°08.71'N	01°57.20'W
40-20	Gorey SE, 1.6 M 118°T from Gorey pierhead	49°11.10'N	01°59.10'W
40-21	Gorey NE outer, 1¾ M 050°T from Mont Orgueil	49°13.13'N	01°59.02'W
40-22	Gorey NE inner, 7 ca 050°T from Mont Orgueil	49°12.48'N	02°00.22'W

waypoints given in this directory and following the advice of a reliable pilot book.

A good time to arrive is around half-ebb, when there is plenty of water in the approach channel but enough of the key rocks exposed to make them clearly visible. The visitors' buoys off Gorey offer a convenient point of departure for a day trip to Les Écrehou. GPS has made it much simpler and safer to visit intriguing rocky corners such as the anchorage south of Marmotière island.

Jersey East Coast

The east side of the Violet Bank extends eastwards for up to 2 miles off La Rocque Point, with drying dangers extending north to Grouville Bay and the south-east approaches to Gorey. The seaward side of these dangers is marked by various spar beacons, but care must be taken that these are not confused. Out-lying reefs also extend east and south-east of the Violet fairway buoy and their beacons must be identified with care as you come through the Violet Channel.

Various drying rocks, some marked by beacons, litter the east approaches to Gorey. Just over 1 mile seaward of Gorey harbour, parts of the Banc du Château have less than 1 metre over them, and the shallowest part of the Middle Bank has only 0.4 metres at chart datum. There are numerous rocks off and in St Catherine Bay, just north of Gorey, which becomes significant below half-tide.

Les Écrehou

This fascinating plateau of reefs and islets can be visited in quiet weather, but pilotage around Les Écrehou needs great care, especially as the tides are very strong in this area. Strangers should approach from the SSW, using the

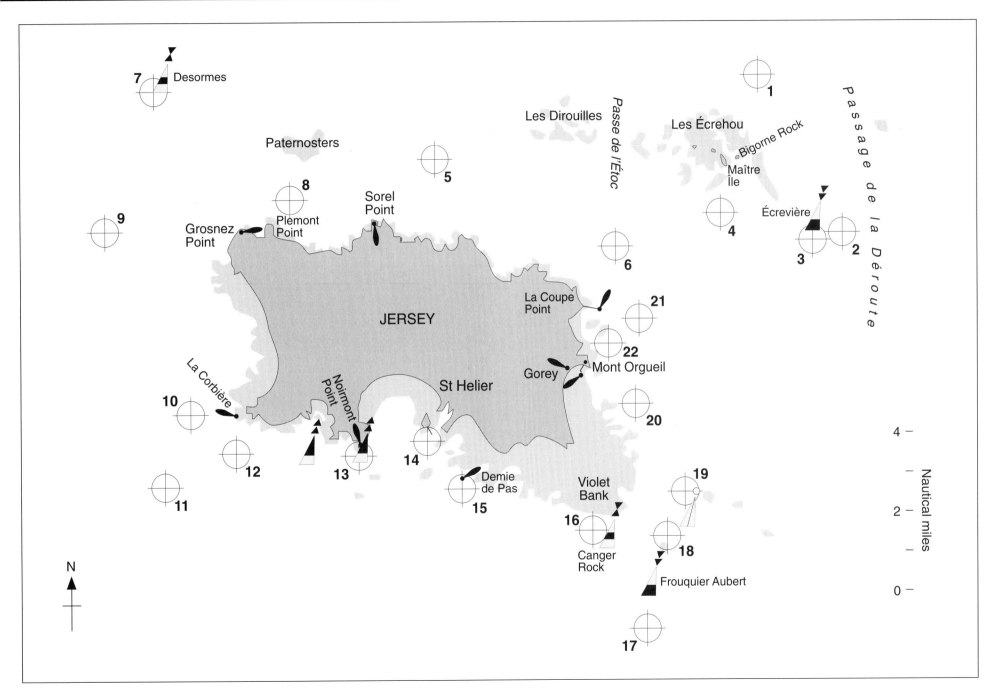

7 Desormes

Les Dirouilles

Passe de l'Étoc

Les Écrehou

Bigorne Rock

Passage de la Déroute

1

Paternosters

Maître Île

Écrevière

5

8

Sorel Point

4

3   2

Plémont Point

Grosnez Point

9

6

La Coupe Point

21

JERSEY

22

Mont Orgueil

La Corbière

Gorey

Noirmont Point

St Helier

10

20

14

12

13

Demie de Pas

15

Violet Bank

19

16

11

18

Canger Rock

17

Frouquier Aubert

N

Nautical miles

4 —

2 —

0 —

Jersey to Plateau des Minquiers and Chausey

WP No	Waypoint name and position	Latitude	Longitude
41-1	La Corbière West, 1.2 M due W of lighthouse	49°10.85'N	02°16.79'W
41-2	La Corbière SW, 2½ M SW of lighthouse on leading line	49°09.07'N	02°17.69'W
41-3	La Corbière South, 1 M due S of lighthouse	49°09.85'N	02°14.93'W
41-4	Noirmont Point, 2 ca due S of lighthouse	49°09.76'N	02°10.01'W
41-5	St Helier entrance, 2¼ ca 200°T from Platte beacon	49°10.00'N	02°07.38'W
41-6	East Passage outer, 2 ca S of Demie de Pas beacon	49°08.86'N	02°06.08'W
41-7	Canger Rock West, ½ M NW of W-card buoy	49°07.77'N	02°00.85'W
41-8	Frouquier Aubert, ¾ M due S of S-card buoy	49°05.40'N	01°58.77'W
41-9	Violet SW, 6 ca WSW of Violet fairway buoy	49°07.62'N	01°57.93'W
41-10	Violet North, 8½ ca 353°T from Violet fairway buoy	49°08.71'N	01°57.20'W
41-11	Gorey SE, 1.6 M 118°T from Gorey pierhead	49°11.10'N	01°59.10'W
41-12	Gorey NE outer, 1¾ M 050°T from Mont Orgueil	49°13.13'N	01°59.02'W
41-13	Gorey NE inner, 7 ca 050°T from Mont Orgueil	49°12.48'N	02°00.22'W
41-14	Les Minquiers Demie de Vascelin buoy, actual position	49°00.88'N	02°05.09'W
41-15	N Minquiers N-card buoy, actual position	49°01.70'N	02°00.50'W
41-16	NE Minquiers, 1 ca 060°T from E-card buoy	49°00.98'N	01°55.05'W
41-17	Les Ardentes NE, ¾ M NE of Ardentes E-card buoy	48°58.37'N	01°50.73'W
41-18	Les Ardentes W, 1.8 M W of Ardentes E-card buoy	48°57.83'N	01°54.28'W
41-19	Chausey N approach, 2 M 336°T from L'Enseigne beacon	48°55.55'N	01°51.50'W
41-20	Chausey N entrance, 1 M 336°T from L'Enseigne beacon	48°54.64'N	01°50.89'W
41-21	L'État clearing, 7 ca NE of L'État BW beacon	48°55.23'N	01°45.38'W
41-22	Chausey NE clearing, 6 ca NE of Canuettes E-card beacon tr	48°54.53'N	01°43.52'W
41-23	Chausey East, midway between Anvers and Le Founet buoys	48°53.62'N	01°41.55'W
41-24	Pointe du Roc NW, 1¼ M 297°T from lighthouse	48°50.70'N	01°38.38'W
41-25	St Germain-sur-Ay offing, 4½ M W of Le Cabot BRB beacon	49°12.28'N	01°43.95'W
41-26	Basse Jourdan E, 1 ca E of Basse Jourdan E-card buoy	49°06.90'N	01°43.89'W
41-27	Le Sénéquet clearing, 2½ M W of Le Sénéquet lighthouse	49°05.55'N	01°43.48'W
41-28	Les Nattes clearing, ¾ M W of Les Nattes buoy	49°03.59'N	01°42.92'W
41-29	La Catheue East, 8 ca E of La Catheue buoy	48°57.88'N	01°40.74'W
41-30	Anvers East, 6 ca E of Anvers E-card buoy	48°53.92'N	01°39.93'W
41-31	Chausey S approach, 1 M 152°T from La Crabière-Est beacon	48°51.65'N	01°48.62'W
41-32	Chausey S entrance, ½ M 152°T from La Crabière-Est beacon	48°52.09'N	01°48.98'W
41-33	Chausey SW, ¾ M SW of La Cancalaise S-card beacon	48°51.47'N	01°51.88'W
41-34	Chausey W, 2.8 M 260°T from L'Enseigne BW beacon	48°53.27'N	01°54.46'W
41-35	SE Minquiers, 2 ca SE of SE Minquiers E-card buoy	48°53.36'N	01°59.78'W
41-36	S Minquiers, 2 ca S of S Minquiers S-card buoy	48°52.94'N	02°10.00'W
41-37	SW Minquiers W-card buoy, actual position	48°54.40'N	02°19.32'W
41-38	NW Minquiers N-card buoy, actual position	48°59.70'N	02°20.50'W

COASTAL DANGERS
Refer to Admiralty charts 3655, 3656

La Corbière
Drying rocks lurk up to ½ mile W and WNW of La Corbière. Rounding the point from the north to line up for the Western Passage to St Helier, stay at least ¾ mile W of the lighthouse until you have passed nicely south of it.

Approaches to St Helier
There are numerous drying rocks off the south coast of Jersey, through or inside which lead the various approach passages to St Helier. The Western Passage is the main 'big-ship' channel to St Helier, leading close along Jersey's south-west coast inside the off-lying dangers. Arriving from the east and south, most boats use the Eastern Passage which leads between the Hinguette rocks and the coastal dangers north of the Demie de Pas beacon tower.

Violet Bank
This vast area of drying rocks lies off the south-east corner of Jersey, extending south-east from La Rocque Point for over 3 miles. Although the Violet Bank looks pretty horrific on a chart, the dangers are reasonably compact on the south side and the passage between St Helier and Gorey via the Violet Channel is fairly straightforward in reasonable visibility.

Perhaps the greatest care is needed when on passage between St Helier and Granville or Iles Chausey, when the various drying dangers extending south-eastwards beyond the Violet Bank need to be left well clear to the north.

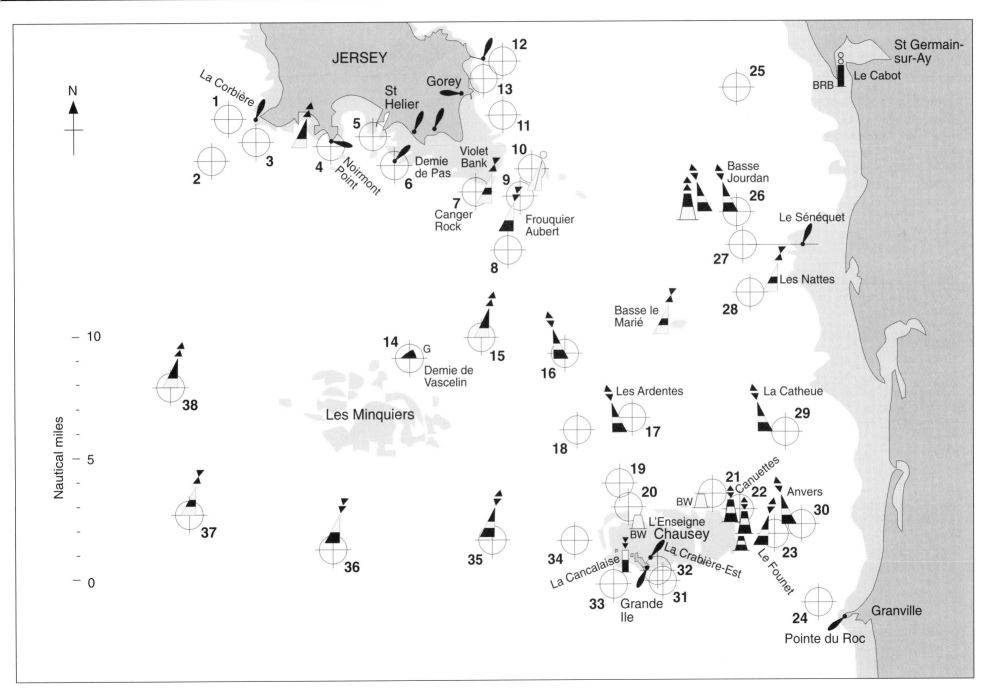

JERSEY

N

La Corbière

1

12

Gorey

13

St
Helier

11

5

Noirmont
Point

Demie
de Pas

Violet
Bank

10

3

4

6

7

Canger
Rock

9

2

Frouquier
Aubert

8

Nautical miles

14

Demie de
Vascelin

G

15

Basse le
Marié

Les Minquiers

16

— 10

38

Les Ardentes

17

La Catheue

29

18

19

21 Canuettes

— 5

20

BW

22 Anvers

30

L'Enseigne

37

BW Chausey

23

La Crabière-Est

Le Founet

34

35

36

La Cancalaise

32

— 0

33 Grande
Ile

31

24

Pointe du Roc

Granville

25

St Germain-
sur-Ay

BRB Le Cabot

Basse
Jourdan

26

Le Sénéquet

27

Les Nattes

28

WP No	Waypoint name and position	Latitude	Longitude
41-1	La Corbière West, 1.2 M due W of lighthouse	49°10.85'N	02°16.79'W
41-2	La Corbière SW, 2½ M SW of lighthouse on leading line	49°09.07'N	02°17.69'W
41-3	La Corbière South, 1 M due S of lighthouse	49°09.85'N	02°14.93'W
41-4	Noirmont Point, 2 ca due S of lighthouse	49°09.76'N	02°10.01'W
41-5	St Helier entrance, 2¼ ca 200°T from Platte beacon	49°10.00'N	02°07.38'W
41-6	East Passage outer, 2 ca S of Demie de Pas beacon	49°08.86'N	02°06.08'W
41-7	Canger Rock West, ½ M NW of W-card buoy	49°07.77'N	02°00.85'W
41-8	Frouquier Aubert, ¾ M due S of S-card buoy	49°05.40'N	01°58.77'W
41-9	Violet SW, 6 ca WSW of Violet fairway buoy	49°07.62'N	01°57.93'W
41-10	Violet North, 8½ ca 353°T from Violet fairway buoy	49°08.71'N	01°57.20'W
41-11	Gorey SE, 1.6 M 118°T from Gorey pierhead	49°11.10'N	01°59.10'W
41-12	Gorey NE outer, 1¾ M 050°T from Mont Orgueil	49°13.13'N	01°59.02'W
41-13	Gorey NE inner, 7 ca 050°T from Mont Orgueil	49°12.48'N	02°00.22'W
41-14	Les Minquiers Demie de Vascelin buoy, actual position	49°00.88'N	02°05.09'W
41-15	N Minquiers N-card buoy, actual position	49°01.70'N	02°00.50'W
41-16	NE Minquiers, 1 ca 060°T from E-card buoy	49°00.98'N	01°55.05'W
41-17	Les Ardentes NE, ¾ M NE of Ardentes E-card buoy	48°58.37'N	01°50.73'W
41-18	Les Ardentes W, 1.8 M W of Ardentes E-card buoy	48°57.83'N	01°54.28'W
41-19	Chausey N approach, 2 M 336°T from L'Enseigne beacon	48°55.55'N	01°51.50'W
41-20	Chausey N entrance, 1 M 336°T from L'Enseigne beacon	48°54.64'N	01°50.89'W
41-21	L'État clearing, 7 ca NE of L'État BW beacon	48°55.23'N	01°45.38'W
41-22	Chausey NE clearing, 6 ca NE of Canuettes E-card beacon tr	48°54.53'N	01°43.52'W
41-23	Chausey East, midway between Anvers and Le Founet buoys	48°53.62'N	01°41.55'W
41-24	Pointe du Roc NW, 1¼ M 297°T from lighthouse	48°50.70'N	01°38.38'W
41-25	St Germain-sur-Ay offing, 4½ M W of Le Cabot BRB beacon	49°12.28'N	01°43.95'W
41-26	Basse Jourdan E, 1 ca E of Basse Jourdan E-card buoy	49°06.90'N	01°43.89'W
41-27	Le Sénéquet clearing, 2½ M W of Le Sénéquet lighthouse	49°05.55'N	01°43.48'W
41-28	Les Nattes clearing, ¾ M W of Les Nattes buoy	49°03.59'N	01°42.92'W
41-29	La Catheue East, 8 ca E of La Catheue buoy	48°57.88'N	01°40.74'W
41-30	Anvers East, 6 ca E of Anvers E-card buoy	48°53.92'N	01°39.93'W
41-31	Chausey S approach, 1 M 152°T from La Crabière-Est beacon	48°51.65'N	01°48.62'W
41-32	Chausey S entrance, ½ M 152°T from La Crabière-Est beacon	48°52.09'N	01°48.98'W
41-33	Chausey SW, ¾ M SW of La Cancalaise S-card beacon	48°51.47'N	01°51.88'W
41-34	Chausey W, 2.8 M 260°T from L'Enseigne BW beacon	48°53.27'N	01°54.46'W
41-35	SE Minquiers, 2 ca SE of SE Minquiers E-card buoy	48°53.36'N	01°59.78'W
41-36	S Minquiers, 2 ca S of S Minquiers S-card buoy	48°52.94'N	02°10.00'W
41-37	SW Minquiers W-card buoy, actual position	48°54.40'N	02°19.32'W
41-38	NW Minquiers N-card buoy, actual position	48°59.70'N	02°20.50'W

Plateau des Minquiers

This notorious plateau of reefs, islets and banks lies about 10 miles south of Jersey. The total extent of the Minquiers is almost as large as Jersey itself, with the main drying areas of sand and rock comprising some 25 square miles. The edges of the plateau are guarded by cardinal buoys, and the only outcrop large enough to count as a real island is Maitresse Ile, near the eastern edge of the reefs. Strangers passing around Plateau des Minquiers, either west or east-about, should stay outside the area bounded by the six main cardinal buoys.

Iles Chausey

This compact plateau of reefs and islets lies about 20 miles south-east of Jersey. The Chausey plateau is just over 6 miles wide from east to west and 3 miles from north to south.

The limit of dangers is mostly fairly obvious and steep-to, but you should be careful to keep a safe offing when skirting the west side of Chausey, perhaps *en route* between St Helier and the south entrance to Chausey Sound.

Les Ardentes

This rather nasty reef lies just over 3 miles south-east of the NE Minquiers E-cardinal buoy and a similar distance north of the Chausey plateau. Les Ardentes is covered most of the time, drying 2.1 metres at chart datum, but needs watching below half tide. The reef is marked on its east side by an E-cardinal buoy.

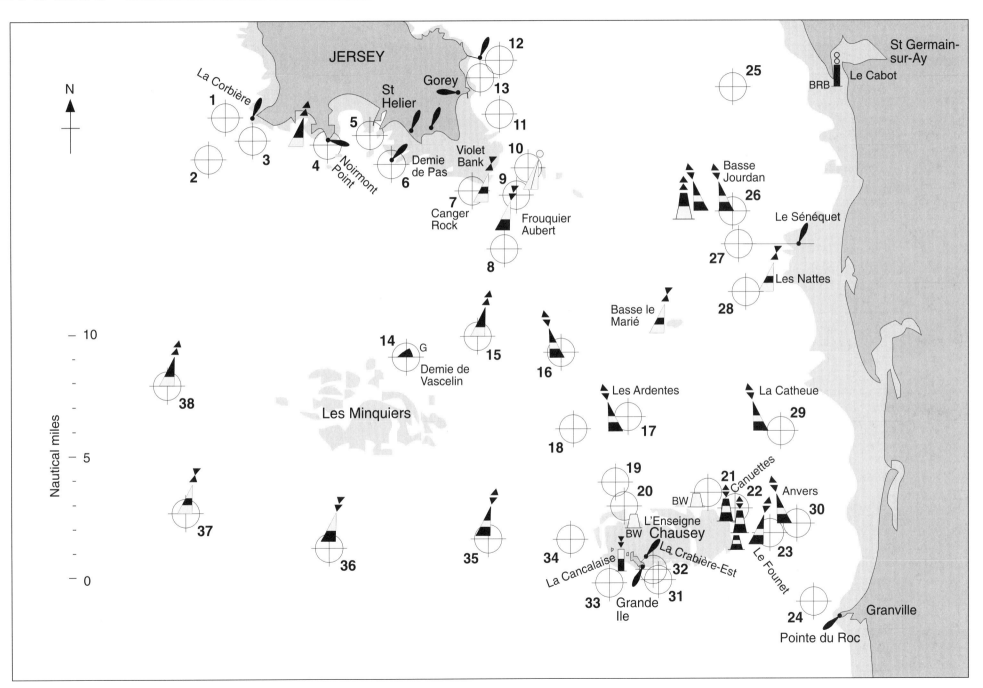

N

JERSEY

La Corbière

1

St
Helier

Gorey

12

13

25

St Germain-
sur-Ay

BRB   Le Cabot

3

5

11

2

4

Noirmont
Point

Demie
de Pas

6

Violet
Bank

10

9

Basse
Jourdan

26

7

Canger
Rock

Frouquier
Aubert

8

Le Sénéquet

27

Les Nattes

28

Basse le
Marié

14

G

Demie de
Vascelin

15

16

Nautical miles

— 10

38

Les Minquiers

Les Ardentes

17

La Catheue

29

— 5

18

19

Canuettes

21

22

Anvers

30

20

BW

37

L'Enseigne
BW   Chausey

23

Le Founet

34

36

35

La Cancalaise

La Crabière-Est

32

31

33

Grande
Ile

24

Granville

Pointe du Roc

99

WP No	Waypoint name and position	Latitude	Longitude
42-1	Pointe du Roc NW, 1¼ M 297°T from lighthouse	48°50.70'N	01°38.38'W
42-2	Granville approach, 7 ca 210°T from Pointe du Roc lighthouse	48°49.52'N	01°37.23'W
42-3	Granville marina approach, 100 m S of Jetée Ouest pierhead	48°49.87'N	01°36.15'W
42-4	Le Videcoq clearing, 2 ca S of Videcoq W-card buoy	48°49.50'N	01°42.02'W
42-5	Pierre d'Herpin E, 1.3 M E of Pierre d'Herpin lighthouse	48°43.83'N	01°46.84'W
42-6	La Fille clearing, 2 ca N of La Fille N-cardinal buoy	48°44.40'N	01°48.39'W
42-7	Le Grand Ruet, ¼ M NE of Herpin islet	48°43.50'N	01°49.48'W
42-8	Vieille Rivière N, between Ruet and Grande Bunouze buoys	48°43.31'N	01°50.47'W
42-9	Pointe Chatry, ¼ M E of headland	48°41.86'N	01°50.25'W
42-10	Cancale N approach, 2 ca NW of Ile des Rimains N tip	48°41.21'N	01°49.75'W
42-11	Chenal de la Bigne outer, 1.3 M N of Pointe du Meinga	48°43.51'N	01°56.15'W
42-12	Rochefort clearing, ½ M N of W-card beacon tower	48°43.40'N	01°58.17'W
42-13	Petits Pointus outer, 1 M 035°T from St Servantine buoy	48°42.81'N	02°00.02'W
42-14	Grande Conchée outer, 1½ M 015°T from La Conchée fort	48°42.52'N	02°01.98'W
42-15	La Petite Porte outer, 150 m NE of fairway buoy	48°41.48'N	02°07.11'W
42-16	La Petite Porte inner, 3 ca 310°T from Le Grand Jardin	48°40.45'N	02°05.24'W
42-17	La Grande Porte outer, 75 m SW of No 2 red buoy	48°40.23'N	02°07.52'W
42-18	Le Grand Jardin West, 250 m W of Le Grand Jardin	48°40.27'N	02°05.10'W
42-19	Le Buron, 100 m NE of Le Buron green tower	48°39.42'N	02°03.53'W
42-20	St Malo entrance, 125 m SW of main north pierhead	48°38.53'N	02°01.92'W

COASTAL DANGERS

Refer to Admiralty charts 3659, 2700

Approaches to Granville

The approaches to Granville are shallow and rough in strong westerlies or south-westerlies, although the area is sheltered from any long fetch by Iles Chausey and Plateau des Minquiers to the WNW and by the mainland coast to the south-west.

Coastal shoals extend several miles seaward of Granville, both north and south of Pointe du Roc. The shallowest areas lie up to 3 miles SSW of Granville, with drying patches on the Banc de Tombelaine and further seaward. Strangers should only approach Granville within two hours of local high water.

Baie du Mont St Michel

This wide shallow bay starts to open up half-a-dozen miles south of Granville, a hostile area of powerful tides and drying sands. The prominent Mont St Michel, down in the south-east corner of the bay, is a rather eerie landmark as you cruise south-west from Granville. The Baie du Mont St Michel is best given a wide berth by boats, except for the north-west corner where the attractive drying harbour at Cancale or the anchorages a mile or two north of the harbour are straightforward enough to visit.

Approaches to Cancale

There are various dangers as you approach Cancale from the north or north-east, but most are safely covered above half tide. In Le Grand Ruet channel, between Pierre d'Herpin lighthouse and Herpin islet, the Basse du Milieu rock only has 1.1 metres over it at chart datum. There are also overfalls and whirlpools in this channel during the strongest hours of the tide. About 3 cables NNW of Pointe du Grouin, the Grande Bunouze Rock (dries 1.6 metres) is marked on its seaward side by a N-cardinal buoy.

In the Grande Rade de Cancale, between Ile des Landes and Ile des Rimains, the Banc de Chatry has only 0.4 metres over it at chart datum. There is also a drying rock off the small headland ½ mile SSE of Pointe Chatry.

Les Tintiaux

West of Pointe du Grouin, between Cancale and St Malo, various drying reefs lie up to 1 mile north of the coast. The most extensive are Les Tintiaux Rocks, up to ½ mile north and a mile north-east of Pointe du Meinga. About 1½ miles west of Les Tintiaux, the Rochefort rocks are marked by a W-cardinal beacon tower.

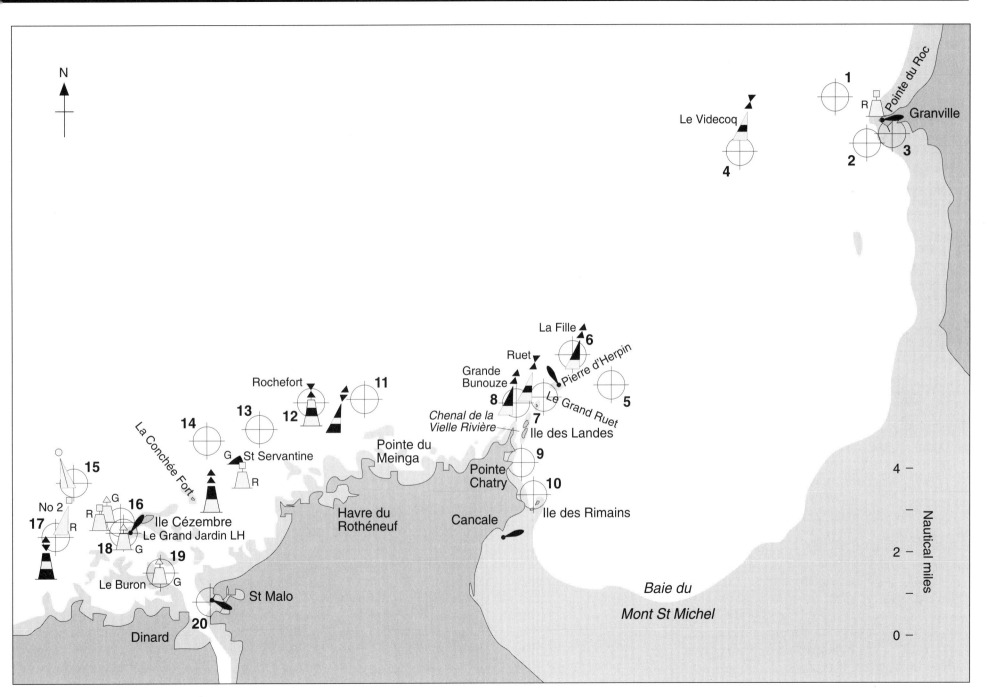

N

1

R Pointe du Roc

Granville

Le Videcoq

4

2   **3**

La Fille ▲
Ruet ▼   **6**
Grande   Pierre d'Herpin
Bunouze   ▲
8   Le Grand Ruet
7   **5**
Chenal de la
Vielle Rivière   Ile des Landes

Rochefort   **11**
13
14   **12**

Pointe du
Meinga

G St Servantine   **9**

R   Pointe
Chatry   **10**

La Conchée Fort

15   Cancale   Ile des Rimains

No 2
17 R G **16**   Havre du
R   Rothéneuf

Ile Cézembre
18 G Le Grand Jardin LH

19
Le Buron G

St Malo

20

Dinard   Baie du
Mont St Michel

4 —

Nautical miles

2 —

0 —

WP No	Waypoint name and position	Latitude	Longitude
43-1	Chenal de la Bigne outer, 1.3 M N of Pointe du Meinga	48°43.51'N	01°56.15'W
43-2	Basse Rochefort, 110 m SE of E-card buoy	48°42.65'N	01°57.30'W
43-3	Chenal de la Bigne inner, 100 m E of La Bigne green beacon	48°41.72'N	01°58.56'W
43-4	Les Létruns, 75 m SE of Les Létruns green buoy	48°40.79'N	02°00.42'W
43-5	Le Grand Bey, 7 ca 007°T from Le Grand Bey fort	48°39.91'N	02°01.82'W
43-6	Le Petit Bey, 4 ca 003°T from Le Petit Bey fort	48°39.63'N	02°02.20'W
43-7	Rochefort clearing, ½ M N of W-card beacon tower	48°43.40'N	01°58.17'W
43-8	Petits Pointus outer, 1 M 035°T from St Servantine buoy	48°42.81'N	02°00.02'W
43-9	St Servantine, ¼ M E of St Servantine green buoy	48°41.98'N	02°00.52'W
43-10	Grande Conchée outer, 1½ M 015°T from La Conchée fort	48°42.52'N	02°01.98'W
43-11	Grande Conchée inner, 3 ca E of La Conchée fort	48°41.07'N	02°02.12'W
43-12	Rade de St Malo, ½ M 123°T from Le Buron green tower	48°39.10'N	02°02.90'W
43-13	La Petite Porte outer, 150 m NE of fairway buoy	48°41.48'N	02°07.11'W
43-14	La Petite Porte inner, 3 ca 310°T from Le Grand Jardin	48°40.45'N	02°05.24'W
43-15	Le Grand Jardin West, 250 m W of Le Grand Jardin	48°40.27'N	02°05.10'W
43-16	Le Buron, 100 m NE of Le Buron green tower	48°39.42'N	02°03.53'W
43-17	St Malo entrance, 125 m SW of main north pierhead	48°38.53'N	02°01.92'W
43-18	Banchenou, ¼ M N of Banchenou green buoy	48°40.76'N	02°11.42'W
43-19	Vieux Banc NE, 300m NE of Vieux Banc N-card buoy	48°42.63'N	02°09.18'W
43-20	Vieux Banc SW, 2 ca SW of Vieux Banc W-card buoy	48°41.78'N	02°10.34'W
43-21	La Grande Porte outer, 75 m SW of No 2 red buoy	48°40.23'N	02°07.52'W
43-22	La Grande Porte inner, 1.4 ca N of Boujaron green beacon	48°40.25'N	02°06.04'W
43-23	Le Décollé outer, 600 m SW of No 2 red buoy	48°40.04'N	02°07.83'W
43-24	Le Décollé inner, ½ M 314°T from Grand Genillet W beacon	48°39.08'N	02°06.33'W

COASTAL DANGERS

Refer to Admiralty charts 3659, 2700

Strong tides

There are strong tides in the outer approaches to St Malo, especially at springs during the middle hours of the flood. Even navigators of fast motor boats need to allow for this when arriving off St Malo, especially as the mainland and Ile de Cézembre may be visible from some distance offshore in clear visibility. It is important not to become complacent about your arrival as soon as the outer marks have been spotted, because the view from offshore can change drastically with a strong cross-tide.

East approaches to St Malo

The eastern approach channels to St Malo cut between numerous drying dangers within the area bounded by Pointe du Meinga, Rochefort beacon tower, Ile de Cézembre and Le Grand Bey and Petit Bey forts. The two main channels – Chenal de la Grande Conchée and Chenal des Petits Pointus – are straightforward in reason-able visibility and at least two hours above low water.

The important outer marks when approaching St Malo from the east are Ile de Cézembre itself, La Grande Conchée fort and its outer above-water rocks, the St Servantine green buoy and Rochefort W-cardinal beacon tower.

The shallowest parts of the east approach channels are at their inner ends, where they converge to the north and north-west of Le Grand Bey and Le Petit Bey forts. Patches of this area almost dry at chart datum, although at ordinary low springs you can reckon on about 1.2 metres least depth in calm conditions. There is plenty of rise of tide over these inner shallows within 3½–4 hours of local high water.

West approaches to St Malo

There are numerous reefs and islets to the west and south-west of Ile de Cézembre, although the outer dangers are well marked by beacon towers and buoys. The two main west approach channels – Chenal de la Grande Porte and Chenal de la Petite Porte – converge and meet just west of Le Grand Jardin lighthouse, which stands not quite ½ mile south-west of Ile de Cézembre. From here, the wide buoyed fairway leads south-east for just over 2½ miles towards St Malo harbour entrance.

The outer mark for Chenal de la Petite Porte is the St Malo fairway buoy, about 2 miles north-west of Le Grand Jardin lighthouse. The outer mark for Chenal de la Grande Porte is the No 2 red whistle buoy, about 1¾ miles west of Le Grand Jardin.

Le Vieux Banc shoals and drying rock lie about 1¾ miles WNW of the St Malo fairway buoy, marked by a N-cardinal and a W-cardinal buoy. Be careful not to confuse these buoys in poor visibility, especially near low water.

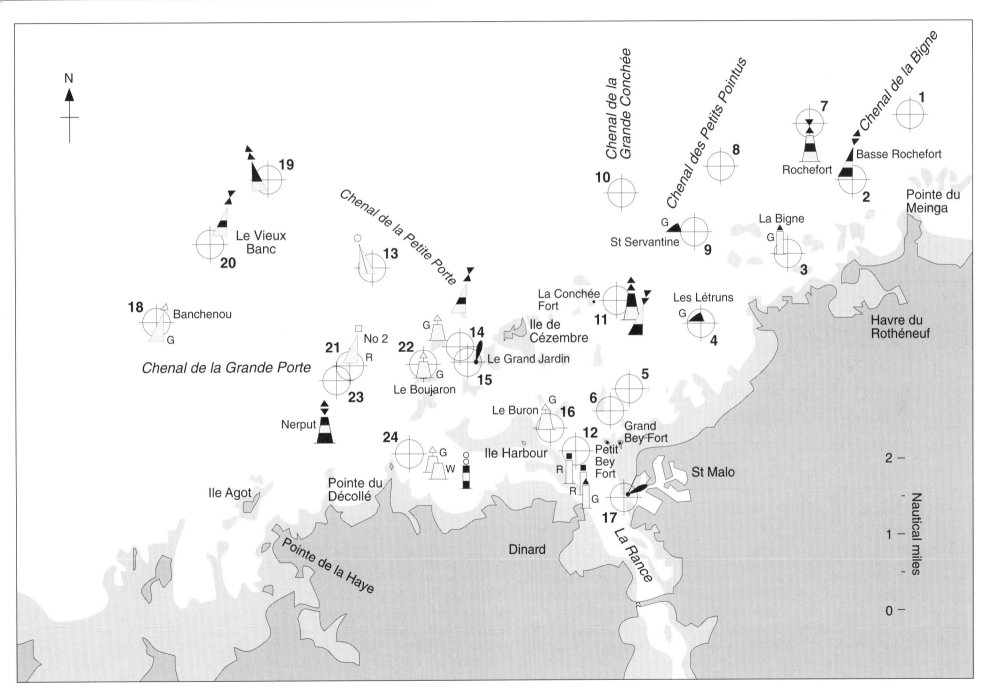

WP No	Waypoint name and position	Latitude	Longitude
44-1	Vieux Banc NE, 300 m NE of Vieux Banc N-card buoy	48°42.63'N	02°09.18'W
44-2	Vieux Banc SW, 2 ca SW of Vieux Banc W-card buoy	48°41.78'N	02°10.34'W
44-3	Banchenou, ¼ M N of Banchenou green buoy	48°40.76'N	02°11.42'W
44-4	Les Bourdinots W, 3½ ca W of Bourdinots E-card buoy	48°39.07'N	02°13.91'W
44-5	Les Bourdinots E, ¼ M E of Bourdinots E-card buoy	48°39.07'N	02°13.04'W
44-6	St Cast entrance, 100 m SE of N pierhead	48°38.43'N	02°14.47'W
44-7	Pointe de la Garde, 2 ca E of Pointe de la Garde N tip	48°37.61'N	02°13.91'W
44-8	Pointe de la Latte clearing, 6 ca NE of La Latte fort	48°40.60'N	02°16.33'W
44-9	Cap Fréhel N clearing, ¾ M N of Cap Fréhel lighthouse	48°41.86'N	02°19.04'W
44-10	Cap Fréhel W, 1 M W of Cap Fréhel N tip	48°41.36'N	02°20.57'W
44-11	Roches d'Erquy N clearing, 4 M N of Cap d'Erquy N tip	48°42.80'N	02°29.18'W
44-12	Les Justières, 4 ca 170°T from S-card buoy	48°40.23'N	02°26.28'W
44-13	Chenal d'Erquy SW, 3 ca NW of Cap d'Erquy	48°39.01'N	02°29.50'W
44-14	Roches d'Erquy W clearing, 1¼ M 260°T from Landas buoy	48°41.31'N	02°33.09'W
44-15	Erquy NW approach outer, 1 M 317°T from L'Evette beacon	48°39.30'N	02°32.40'W
44-16	Erquy NW approach inner, 9 ca 295°T from outer mole head	48°38.50'N	02°29.82'W
44-17	Erquy W approach outer, 7 ca 219°T from L'Evette beacon	48°38.03'N	02°32.06'W
44-18	Erquy W approach inner 1 M 268°T from outer mole head	48°38.09'N	02°30.10'W

COASTAL DANGERS

Refer to Admiralty charts 3659, 3672, 3674

Les Bourdinots

This small drying reef lies 7 cables north-east of Pointe de St Cast, marked on its north-east edge by an E-cardinal buoy. Pointe de St Cast itself is fringed by drying ledges for about ¼ mile on its north and north-east sides.

Pointe de la Latte

Basse de la Latte Rock, with only 0.7 metres over it, lies 3 cables north of the fort on Pointe de la Latte. Basse Raymonde, which dries 2.7 metres, lies about 4 cables WNW of the fort. These rocks are only a practical danger if you are coast-hopping near low water.

Cap Fréhel

A long narrow bank, known as Banc de l'Etendrée, extends for nearly 1 mile just east of Cap Fréhel. Depths over the bank change from time to time, but the shallowest part has about 1½ metres over it at chart datum. At the far west end of this bank, just 4 cables east of Cap Fréhel lighthouse, Roche de l'Etendrée dries 3.9 metres and should be given a clear berth when rounding Fréhel.

Roches d'Erquy

An extensive area of drying and above-water rocks lies up to 2½ miles offshore to the north and north-east of Cap d'Erquy. Rohinet, 6 metres high, is the most obvious above-water rock near high water, but the reefs around Le Grand Pourier become prominent as the tide falls away.

There is a navigable channel, known as Chenal d'Erquy, between these rocks and the shore, passing south of Les Justières and Basses du Courant S-cardinal buoys. The north-west corner of Roches d'Erquy is marked by Les Landas N-cardinal buoy. The north-east corner is unmarked, except by reference to Les Justières S-cardinal buoy.

Plateau des Portes d'Erquy

This fairly compact plateau of drying and underwater rocks, not quite ¾ mile wide from west to east, lies about 1¼ miles west of Cap d'Erquy and is marked on its north-east edge by L'Evette N-cardinal beacon tower.

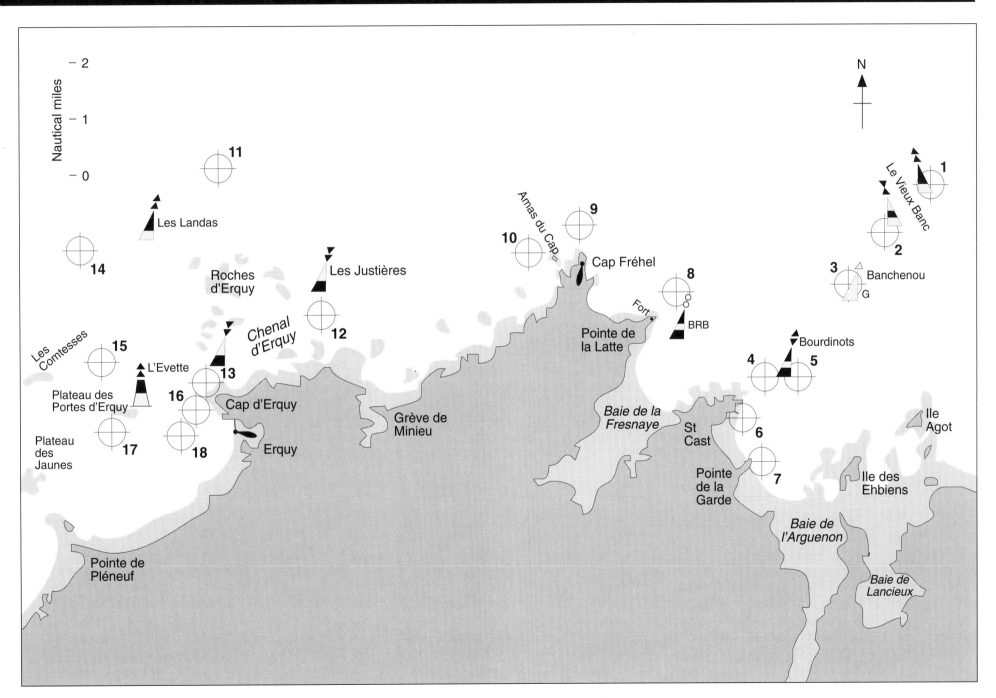

Nautical miles

2

1

0

N

11

Les Landas

14

Roches
d'Erquy

Les Justières

Chenal
d'Erquy

12

Les
Comtesses

15

L'Evette

13

16

Cap d'Erquy

Plateau des
Portes d'Erquy

Plateau
des
Jaunes

17

18

Erquy

Grève de
Minieu

Pointe de
Pléneuf

Amas du Cap

Cap Fréhel

10

9

Fort

Pointe de
la Latte

8

BRB

Baie de la
Fresnaye

St
Cast

Pointe
de la
Garde

6

7

Baie de
l'Arguenon

Baie de
Lancieux

Le Vieux Banc

1

2

3

Banchenou

G

Bourdinots

4

5

Ile Agot

Ile des
Ehbiens

WP No	Waypoint name and position	Latitude	Longitude
45-1	Roches d'Erquy N clearing, 4 M N of Cap d'Erquy N tip	48°42.80'N	02°29.18'W
45-2	Petit Léjon N, 1.4 M N of W-card buoy	48°43.27'N	02°37.48'W
45-3	Petit Léjon S, 1 M S of W-card buoy	48°40.87'N	02°37.48'W
45-4	Roches d'Erquy W clearing, 1¼ M 260°T from Landas buoy	48°41.31'N	02°33.09'W
45-5	Rohein W clearing, 1 M W of Rohein W-card tower	48°38.88'N	02°39.19'W
45-6	Rohein S clearing, 9 ca S of Rohein W-card tower	48°37.98'N	02°37.68'W
45-7	Chenal d'Erquy SW, 3 ca NW of Cap d'Erquy N tip	48°39.01'N	02°29.50'W
45-8	Erquy NW approach outer, 1 M 317°T from L'Evette beacon	48°39.30'N	02°32.40'W
45-9	Erquy NW approach inner, 9 ca 295°T of outer mole head	48°38.50'N	02°29.82'W
45-10	Erquy W approach outer, 7 ca 219°T from L'Evette beacon	48°38.03'N	02°32.06'W
45-11	Erquy W approach inner 1 M 268°T from outer mole head	48°38.09'N	02°30.10'W
45-12	Les Jaunes north, 1 M S of Les Comtesses main rock	48°37.98'N	02°34.37'W
45-13	Petit Bignon west, 1 M W of W-card beacon	48°36.92'N	02°36.45'W
45-14	Dahouet approach, 1 ca NE of Dahouet N-card buoy	48°35.35'N	02°35.18'W
45-15	Dahouet entrance, 200 m NW of La Petite Muette tower	48°34.99'N	02°34.32'W
45-16	Le Légué fairway buoy, actual position	48°34.39'N	02°41.08'W
45-17	Le Légué approach, ½ M E of Pointe de Chatel Renault	48°32.45'N	02°42.26'W
45-18	Binic E approach, 1½ M 096°T from E b/water head	48°35.98'N	02°46.59'W
45-19	Binic entrance, ½ ca SE of E b/water head	48°36.10'N	02°48.80'W
45-20	St Quay SE approach, 2 ca S of Roselière W-card buoy	48°37.32'N	02°46.33'W
45-21	St Quay entrance, 200m 138°T of E b/water head	48°38.82'N	02°48.73'W
45-22	St Quay N approach, 6 ca 289°T from Madeux beacon tr	48°40.67'N	02°49.58'W
45-23	Grandes Moulières, 6 ca 259°T from Ile Harbour lighthouse	48°39.95'N	02°49.31'W
45-24	Rade de St Quay, 2 ca S of Les Noirs W-card buoy	48°38.95'N	02°48.38'W

COASTAL DANGERS

Refer to Admiralty charts 3674, 3672

Roches d'Erquy

An extensive area of drying and above-water rocks lies up to 2½ miles offshore to the north and north-east of Cap d'Erquy. Rohinet, 6 metres high, is the most obvious above-water rock near high water, but the reefs around Le Grand Pourier become prominent as the tide falls away.

There is a navigable channel, known as Chenal d'Erquy, between these rocks and the shore, passing south of Les Justières and Basses du Courant S-cardinal buoys. The north-west corner of Roches d'Erquy is marked by Les Landas N-cardinal buoy. The north-east corner is unmarked, except by reference to Les Justières S-cardinal buoy.

Plateau des Portes d'Erquy

This fairly compact plateau of drying and underwater rocks, not quite ¾ mile wide from west to east, lies about 1¼ miles west of Cap d'Erquy and is marked on its north-east edge by L'Evette N-cardinal beacon tower. Les Portes d'Erquy should be left clear to the north if you are coasting inshore between Erquy and Dahouet, Binic or St Quay-Portrieux.

Plateau des Jaunes

This plateau of drying and above-water rocks extends up to 1¾ miles north-west of Pointe de Pléneuf and must be rounded with care when coasting between Erquy and Dahouet. Le Petit Bignon W-cardinal beacon guards the west edge of the plateau, but the highest rock of the plateau should be skirted by a good ¾ mile as you come round.

Rohein

Towards the middle of Baie de St Brieuc, the Rohein W-cardinal tower marks the south-west corner of quite a wide but well-spaced, almost rectangular area of shoals and drying rocks. At the south-east corner are Les Comtesses reefs and at the north-west corner the long Banc des Dahouetins, parts of which have less than 1 metre depth at chart datum.

Yachts coasting between Erquy and Binic or St Quay-Portrieux would normally pass south of these dangers, leaving Rohein tower a mile or so to the north. Yachts making for Dahouet from Paimpol or Ile de Bréhat would come in through the wide gap between Rohein and the Roches de St Quay, leaving Rohein tower about 1 mile to the east.

Petit Léjon

This small outlying reef, which dries 3.1 metres, lies a couple of miles north of the Rohein plateau and is marked on its west side by Petit Léjon W-cardinal buoy. Yachts on passage between Cap Fréhel and Paimpol would normally

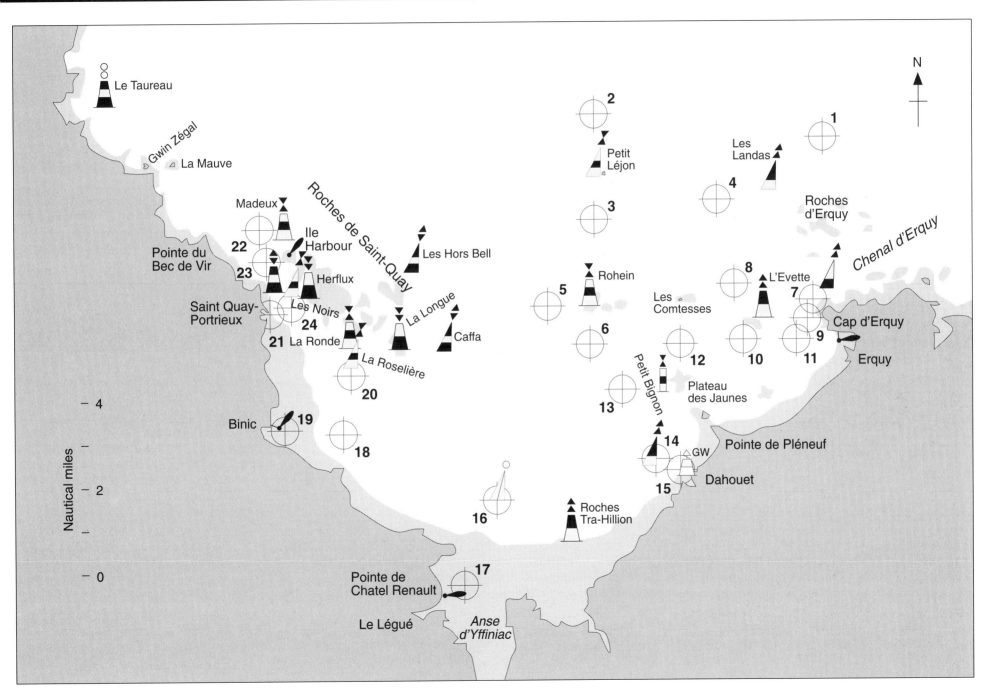

Le Taureau

Gwin Zégal

La Mauve

Madeux

Ile Harbour

Roches de Saint-Quay

Pointe du Bec de Vir

Herflux

Saint Quay-Portrieux

Les Noirs

La Ronde

La Roselière

Binic

Les Hors Bell

La Longue

Caffa

22

23

24

21

20

19

18

2

Petit Léjon

3

4

5

Rohein

6

1

Les Landas

Roches d'Erquy

Chenal d'Erquy

8

L'Evette

Les Comtesses

7

Cap d'Erquy

9

11

10

Erquy

12

13

Petit Bignon

Plateau des Jaunes

14

GW

Pointe de Pléneuf

15

Dahouet

Roches Tra-Hillion

16

Pointe de Chatel Renault

17

Le Légué

Anse d'Yffiniac

N

Nautical miles

— 4

— 2

— 0

WP No	Waypoint name and position	Latitude	Longitude
45-1	Roches d'Erquy N clearing, 4 M N of Cap d'Erquy N tip	48°42.80'N	02°29.18'W
45-2	Petit Léjon N, 1.4 M N of W-card buoy	48°43.27'N	02°37.48'W
45-3	Petit Léjon S, 1 M S of W-card buoy	48°40.87'N	02°37.48'W
45-4	Roches d'Erquy W clearing, 1¼ M 260°T from Landas buoy	48°41.31'N	02°33.09'W
45-5	Rohein W clearing, 1 M W of Rohein W-card tower	48°38.88'N	02°39.19'W
45-6	Rohein S clearing, 9 ca S of Rohein W-card tower	48°37.98'N	02°37.68'W
45-7	Chenal d'Erquy SW, 3 ca NW of Cap d'Erquy N tip	48°39.01'N	02°29.50'W
45-8	Erquy NW approach outer, 1 M 317°T from L'Evette beacon	48°39.30'N	02°32.40'W
45-9	Erquy NW approach inner, 9 ca 295°T of outer mole head	48°38.50'N	02°29.82'W
45-10	Erquy W approach outer, 7 ca 219°T from L'Evette beacon	48°38.03'N	02°32.06'W
45-11	Erquy W approach inner 1 M 268°T from outer mole head	48°38.09'N	02°30.10'W
45-12	Les Jaunes north, 1 M S of Les Comtesses main rock	48°37.98'N	02°34.37'W
45-13	Petit Bignon west, 1 M W of W-card beacon	48°36.92'N	02°36.45'W
45-14	Dahouet approach, 1 ca NE of Dahouet N-card buoy	48°35.35'N	02°35.18'W
45-15	Dahouet entrance, 200 m NW of La Petite Muette tower	48°34.99'N	02°34.32'W
45-16	Le Légué fairway buoy, actual position	48°34.39'N	02°41.08'W
45-17	Le Légué approach, ½ M E of Pointe de Chatel Renault	48°32.45'N	02°42.26'W
45-18	Binic E approach, 1½ M 096°T from E b/water head	48°35.98'N	02°46.59'W
45-19	Binic entrance, ½ ca SE of E b/water head	48°36.10'N	02°48.80'W
45-20	St Quay SE approach, 2 ca S of Roselière W-card buoy	48°37.32'N	02°46.33'W
45-21	St Quay entrance, 200m 138°T of E b/water head	48°38.82'N	02°48.73'W
45-22	St Quay N approach, 6 ca 289°T from Madeux beacon tr	48°40.67'N	02°49.58'W
45-23	Grandes Moulières, 6 ca 259°T from Ile Harbour lighthouse	48°39.95'N	02°49.31'W
45-24	Rade de St Quay, 2 ca S of Les Noirs W-card buoy	48°38.95'N	02°48.38'W

Roches de St Quay

To the north of Binic, an extensive area of drying reefs and islets fringes the coast opposite St Quay-Portrieux. The eastern edge of these dangers, some 4 miles offshore, is marked by the Caffa and Les Hors E-cardinal buoys. At the north-west corner are Madeux W-cardinal tower and the distinctive lighthouse on Ile Harbour. The southern extremity of the plateau is marked by La Roselière W-cardinal buoy and La Longue S-cardinal beacon tower.

Boats approaching St Quay from the south or south-east would normally make for La Roselière buoy before heading north-west towards St Quay harbour entrance, leaving an E-cardinal wreck buoy fairly close to port. Yachts arriving from the north, perhaps from Paimpol, Bréhat or direct from the Channel Islands, would make for a position clear to the north-west of Madeux beacon tower before continuing SSE into the Rade de St Quay-Portrieux.

pass between Petit Léjon and Le Grand Léjon lighthouse, but the Petit Léjon buoy, being a *W-cardinal*, should be left well clear to the south in this case.

Approaches to Le Légué and St Brieuc

The head of Baie de St Brieuc is shoal and should only be approached towards high water and in quiet conditions. Le Légué, in any case, is not the most attractive of harbours, although the locked basin is snug once you are safely inside. It may appeal to those with a taste for off-beat ports of call.

Approaches to Binic

The approaches to Binic dry out for about ¾ mile from the outer pierheads. This corner of the Baie de St Brieuc is well sheltered from between north-west through west to south, but is rather exposed to easterlies and north-easterlies. Boats should approach Binic about two hours before high water. The lock gate into the wet basin is open from about an hour before high water to high water at springs or so long as the height of tide reaches 9.5 metres, but the gate may not open at all at neaps.

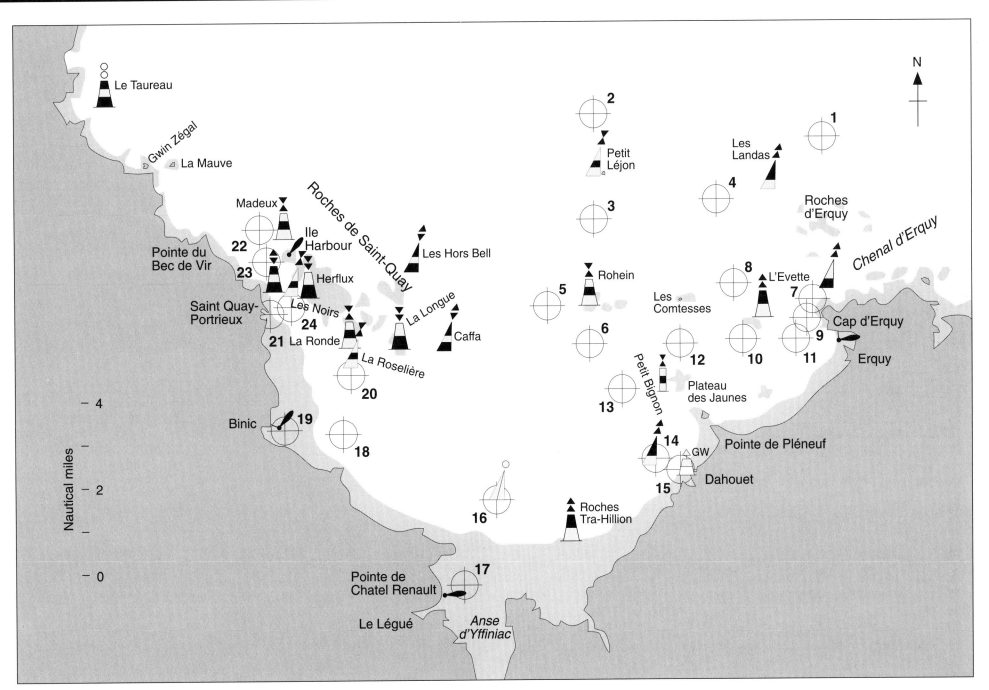

Le Taureau

Gwin Zégal

La Mauve

Madeux

Roches de Saint-Quay

Ile Harbour

Pointe du Bec de Vir

Les Hors Bell

Herflux

Saint Quay-Portrieux

Les Noirs

La Longue

La Ronde

Caffa

La Roselière

Binic

2

Petit Léjon

1

Les Landas

Roches d'Erquy

4

3

Chenal d'Erquy

Rohein

L'Evette

5

Les Comtesses

8

7

Cap d'Erquy

9

Erquy

6

12

10

11

Petit Bignon

13

Plateau des Jaunes

22

23

24

21

20

19

18

14

GW

Pointe de Pléneuf

15

Dahouet

16

Roches Tra-Hillion

17

Pointe de Chatel Renault

Le Légué

Anse d'Yffiniac

N

Nautical miles

— 4

— 2

— 0

109

Cap Fréhel to Ile de Bréhat

WP No	Waypoint name and position	Latitude	Longitude
46-1	Cap Fréhel N clearing, ¾ M N of Cap Fréhel lighthouse	48°41.86'N	02°19.04'W
46-2	Cap Fréhel W, 1 M W of Cap Fréhel N tip	48°41.36'N	02°20.57'W
46-3	Roches d'Erquy N clearing, 4 M N of Cap d'Erquy N tip	48°42.80'N	02°29.18'W
46-4	Grand Léjon S, 1½ M 170°T from Grand Léjon lighthouse	48°43.49'N	02°39.39'W
46-5	Grand Léjon N, 2 M N of Grand Léjon lighthouse	48°46.98'N	02°39.78'W
46-6	Roches d'Erquy W clearing, 1¼ M 260°T from Landas buoy	48°41.31'N	02°33.09'W
46-7	Petit Léjon N, 1.4 M N of W-card buoy	48°43.27'N	02°37.48'W
46-8	Petit Léjon S, 1 M S of W-card buoy	48°40.87'N	02°37.48'W
46-9	Rohein W clearing, 1 M W of Rohein W-card tower	48°38.88'N	02°39.19'W
46-10	Rohein S clearing, 9 ca S of Rohein W-card tower	48°37.98'N	02°37.68'W
46-11	Binic E approach, 1½ M 096°T from E b/water head	48°35.98'N	02°46.59'W
46-12	St Quay SE approach, 2 ca S of Roselière W-card buoy	48°37.32'N	02°46.33'W
46-13	St Quay N approach, 6 ca 289°T from Madeux beacon tower	48°40.67'N	02°49.58'W
46-14	Paimpol outer approach, 6.6 M 090½°T from Porz-Don L/H	48°47.47'N	02°51.50'W
46-15	Basse St Brieuc, 2 ca 060°T from E-card buoy	48°46.43'N	02°53.33'W
46-16	Les Calemarguiers, 2 ca 060°T from E-card buoy	48°47.15'N	02°54.48'W
46-17	Ferlas SE outer, 3.9 M 100°T from Men Joliguet tower	48°49.51'N	02°54.70'W
46-18	Ferlas SE inner, ½ ca S of Lel ar Serive S-card buoy	48°49.97'N	02°58.67'W
46-19	Cain ar Monse, ¼ M 307°T from N-card buoy	48°50.36'N	02°57.03'W
46-20	Men-Marc'h E approach, 2 M 121°T from Men Marc'h buoy	48°52.20'N	02°49.23'W

COASTAL DANGERS

Refer to Admiralty charts 3673, 3674, 3670

Roches d'Erquy

An extensive area of drying and above-water rocks lies up to 2½ miles offshore to the north and north-east of Cap d'Erquy. Rohinet, 6 metres high, is the most obvious above-water rock near high water, but the reefs around Le Grand Pourier become prominent as the tide falls away.

There is a navigable channel, known as Chenal d'Erquy, between these rocks and the shore, passing south of Les Justières and Basses du Courant S-cardinal buoys. The north-west corner of Roches d'Erquy is marked by Les Landas N-cardinal buoy. The north-east corner is unmarked, except by reference to Les Justières S-cardinal buoy.

Rohein

Towards the middle of Baie de St Brieuc, the Rohein W-cardinal tower marks the south-west corner of quite a wide but well-spaced, almost rectangular area of shoals and drying rocks. At the south-east corner are Les Comtesses reefs and at the north-west corner the long Banc des Dahouetins, parts of which have less than a metre depth at chart datum.

Boats coasting between Erquy and Binic or St Quay-Portrieux would normally pass south of these dangers, leaving Rohein tower a mile or so to the north. Yachts making for Dahouet from Paimpol or Ile de Bréhat would come in through the wide gap between Rohein and the Roches de St Quay, leaving Rohein tower about a mile to the east.

Petit Léjon

This small outlying reef, which dries 3.1 metres, lies a couple of miles north of the Rohein plateau and is marked on its west side by Petit Léjon W-cardinal buoy. Boats on passage between Cap Fréhel and Paimpol would normally pass between Petit Léjon and Le Grand Léjon lighthouse, but the Petit Léjon buoy, being a *W-cardinal*, should be left well clear to the south in this case.

Grand Léjon

The Grand Léjon reef, marked by a lighthouse, lies right in the north approaches to Baie de St Brieuc, more or less on a direct line between Cap Fréhel and Paimpol. The reef is steep-to on its south side but patchy on its north side. Les Bouillons, an outlying head with 1 metre over it at chart datum, lies 3 cables north-east of the lighthouse.

Roches de St Quay

See page 108

L'Ost-Pic

The distinctive headland and lighthouse of L'Ost-Pic form the southern arm of the Anse de Paimpol. Two small rocky banks lie to the east of L'Ost-Pic, both marked by E-cardinal buoys. Les Calemarguiers banks lie between ½ and 1 mile east of L'Ost-Pic lighthouse, with depths of less than ½ metre on the inshore side and a rocky patch drying 1.8 metres further out.

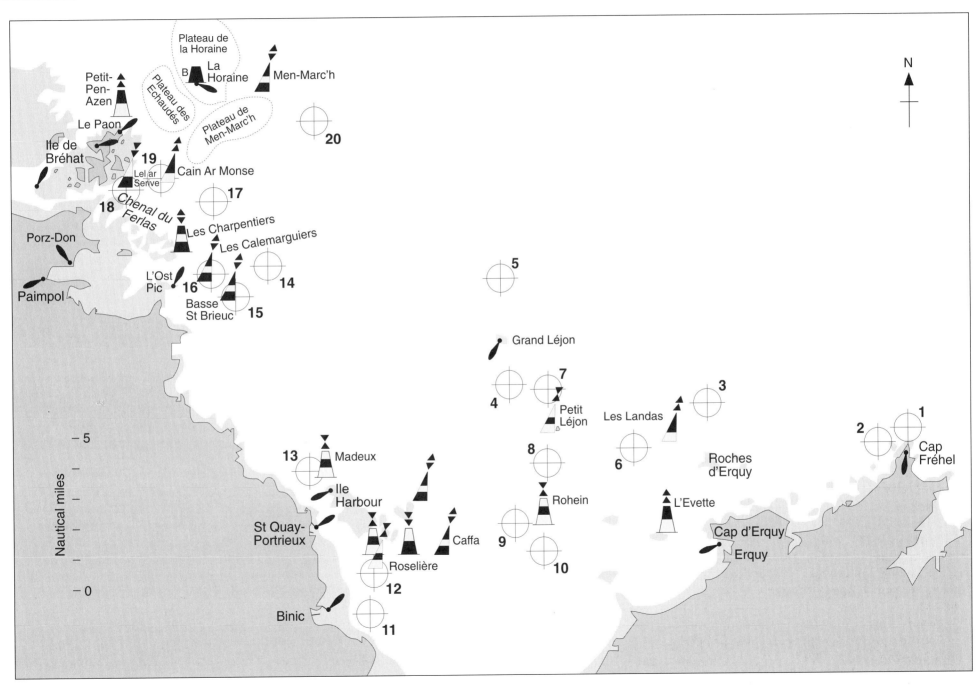

Plateau de
la Horaine

B La
Horaine

Men-Marc'h

Plateau des
Echaudés

Plateau de
Men-Marc'h

20

N

Petit-
Pen-
Azen

Le Paon

Ile de
Bréhat

19

Lel ar
Serive

Cain Ar Monse

Chenal du
Ferlas

18

17

Les Charpentiers

Porz-Don

Les Calemarguiers

L'Ost
Pic

16

14

5

Paimpol

Basse
St Brieuc

15

Grand Léjon

7

3

Les Landas

4

Petit
Léjon

Roches
d'Erquy

2

1

Cap
Fréhel

Nautical miles

— 5

13

Madeux

8

6

Ile
Harbour

Rohein

L'Evette

St Quay-
Portrieux

9

Cap d'Erquy

Caffa

Erquy

Roselière

12

10

— 0

Binic

11

WP No	Waypoint name and position	Latitude	Longitude
46-1	Cap Fréhel N clearing, ¾ M N of Cap Fréhel lighthouse	48°41.86'N	02°19.04'W
46-2	Cap Fréhel W, 1 M W of Cap Fréhel N tip	48°41.36'N	02°20.57'W
46-3	Roches d'Erquy N clearing, 4 M N of Cap d'Erquy N tip	48°42.80'N	02°29.18'W
46-4	Grand Léjon S, 1½ M 170°T from Grand Léjon lighthouse	48°43.49'N	02°39.39'W
46-5	Grand Léjon N, 2 M N of Grand Léjon lighthouse	48°46.98'N	02°39.78'W
46-6	Roches d'Erquy W clearing, 1¼ M 260°T from Landas buoy	48°41.31'N	02°33.09'W
46-7	Petit Léjon N, 1.4 M N of W-card buoy	48°43.27'N	02°37.48'W
46-8	Petit Léjon S, 1 M S of W-card buoy	48°40.87'N	02°37.48'W
46-9	Rohein W clearing, 1 M W of Rohein W-card tower	48°38.88'N	02°39.19'W
46-10	Rohein S clearing, 9 ca S of Rohein W-card tower	48°37.98'N	02°37.68'W
46-11	Binic E approach, 1½ M 096°T from E b/water head	48°35.98'N	02°46.59'W
46-12	St Quay SE approach, 2 ca S of Roselière W-card buoy	48°37.32'N	02°46.33'W
46-13	St Quay N approach, 6 ca 289°T from Madeux beacon tower	48°40.67'N	02°49.58'W
46-14	Paimpol outer approach, 6.6 M 090½°T from Porz-Don L/H	48°47.47'N	02°51.50'W
46-15	Basse St Brieuc, 2 ca 060°T from E-card buoy	48°46.43'N	02°53.33'W
46-16	Les Calemarguiers, 2 ca 060°T from E-card buoy	48°47.15'N	02°54.48'W
46-17	Ferlas SE outer, 3.9 M 100°T from Men Joliguet tower	48°49.51'N	02°54.70'W
46-18	Ferlas SE inner, ½ ca S of Lel ar Serive S-card buoy	48°49.97'N	02°58.67'W
46-19	Cain ar Monse, ¼ M 307°T from N-card buoy	48°50.36'N	02°57.03'W
46-20	Men-Marc'h E approach, 2 M 121°T from Men Marc'h buoy	48°52.20'N	02°49.23'W

Basse St Brieuc bank lies 1¾ miles ESE of L'Ost-Pic, with a depth of ½ metre over its shallowest part. Yachts can safely pass over these banks above half tide, and even near low water you can cut inside Les Calemarguiers ¼ mile off L'Ost-Pic.

Paimpol approaches

Boats making for Paimpol from St Malo would normally carry a full ebb tide westwards and thus arrive off Paimpol near low water. A rock with less than 1 metre over it at chart datum lies just over 6 cables south-east of Les Charpentiers E-cardinal beacon tower and just over 1 mile north-east of L'Ost-Pic lighthouse. This rock is in the white sector of Porz-Don light and very close

north of the direct line between waypoints 47–1 and 47–5, so yachts should take care to avoid it near low water springs.

Dangers between Paimpol and Ile de Bréhat

A broad area of islets and drying rocks extends up to 3 miles seawards to form the sheltering north arm of the Anse de Paimpol. Les Charpentiers E-cardinal beacon tower stands near the south-east edge of these dangers, but Les Barbottes Rocks, almost awash at chart datum, lie 3½ cables *east* of Les Charpentiers tower. Banc de la Cormorandière extends just over 1¼ miles north of La Cormorandière

white pyramid, its north tip with only 0.8 metres over it lying very close south of the white sector of Men Joliguet light. Yachts approaching Chenal du Ferlas from the east or south-east should make for a position near the Ferlas SE outer waypoint (No 46–17) before closing further with the shore.

East approaches to Bréhat

There are numerous wide rocky banks to the east and north-east of Ile de Bréhat. They are all well covered above half-tide, but cause uneasy turbulence and steep overfalls during the strongest hours of both the flood and ebb.

Plateau de la Horaine, with the highest area of drying rocks, lies from 3–4 miles north-east of Ile de Bréhat, guarded by La Horaine tower. Plateau des Echaudés is closer to Ile de Bréhat, its shallowest patch drying 2.6 metres. A narrow passage, Chenal de Bréhat, leads NNW–SSE between Les Echaudés and the Guarine E-cardinal buoy off the east side of Bréhat.

Plateau de Men-Marc'h is a wide shoal area south-east of La Horaine and Les Echaudés. Most of Men-Marc'h is relatively deep, with only a few patches with around ½ metre depth at chart datum; Men-Marc'h Rock itself, on the south-east edge of the plateau, drying 0.6 metres. There is a passage of deep water just to the south of Plateau de Men-Marc'h and north of Plateau du Ringue-Bras; this route leads in towards the Chenal du Ferlas from the ENE and can be a useful approach to Ile de Bréhat for boats arriving direct from Jersey, provided you allow carefully for any cross-tide.

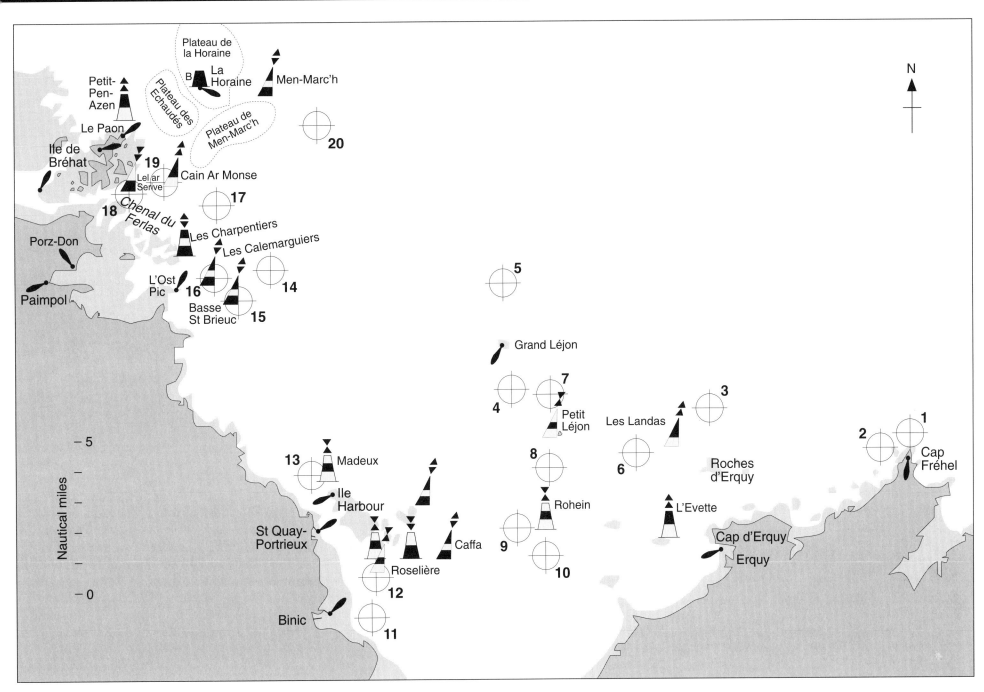

Plateau de
la Horaine

B La
Horaine
Men-Marc'h

Plateau des
Echaudés

Plateau de
Men-Marc'h

20

Petit-
Pen-
Azen

Le Paon

Ile de
Bréhat

Lel ar
Serive

Cain Ar Monse

19

18

Chenal du
Ferlas

17

Les Charpentiers

Porz-Don

Les Calemarguiers

L'Ost
Pic

16

14

Paimpol

Basse
St Brieuc

15

5

Grand Léjon

7

3

4

Petit
Léjon

Les Landas

2

1

13

Madeux

8

6

Roches
d'Erquy

Cap
Fréhel

Ile
Harbour

Rohein

L'Evette

St Quay-
Portrieux

9

Cap d'Erquy

Caffa

10

Erquy

Roselière

12

Binic

11

N

−5

Nautical miles

−0

WP No	Waypoint name and position	Latitude	Longitude
47-1	Paimpol outer approach, 6.6 M 090½°T from Porz-Don L/H	48°47.47'N	02°51.50'W
47-2	Basse St Brieuc, 2 ca 060°T from E-card buoy	48°46.43'N	02°53.33'W
47-3	Les Calemarguiers, 2 ca 060°T from E-card buoy	48°47.15'N	02°54.48'W
47-4	L'Ost Pic inner, 3½ ca due E of lighthouse	48°46.81'N	02°55.81'W
47-5	Paimpol middle approach, 800 m S of Charpentiers beacon tr	48°47.52'N	02°55.92'W
47-6	Roche Gueule, 1 ca N of red buoy on leading line	48°47.57'N	02°57.21'W
47-7	Paimpol outer anchorage, 6 ca 216°T from Dénou W pyramid	48°47.43'N	02°58.49'W
47-8	Paimpol inner approach, ½ M 034°T from Pointe Guilben sp ht	48°47.34'N	03°00.16'W
47-9	Paimpol entrance, outer pierhead light actual position	48°47.15'N	03°02.35'W
47-10	Ferlas SE outer, 3.9 M 100°T from Men Joliguet tower	48°49.51'N	02°54.70'W
47-11	Ferlas SE inner, ½ ca S of Lel ar Serive S-card buoy	48°49.97'N	02°58.67'W
47-12	Chenal de Bréhat middle, Guarine buoy, actual position	48°51.68'N	02°57.51'W
47-13	Cain ar Monse, ¼ M 307°T from N-card buoy	48°50.36'N	02°57.03'W
47-14	La Chambre, 1 ca 230°T from La Chambre S-card beacon	48°50.14'N	02°59.62'W
47-15	Rade de Bréhat, 500 m 127°T from Men Joliguet tower	48°50.01'N	02°59.79'W
47-16	Ferlas middle, 120 m S of Receveur S-card beacon	48°49.69'N	03°01.87'W
47-17	Trieux River entrance, 6½ ca E of Kermouster light	48°49.60'N	03°04.12'W
47-18	La Croix inner, 3 ca 026°T from La Croix lighthouse	48°50.56'N	03°02.98'W
47-19	La Croix outer, 9 ca 045°T from La Croix lighthouse	48°50.93'N	03°02.20'W
47-20	La Moisie inner, 3 ca 339°T from Rosédo white pyramid	48°51.83'N	03°00.84'W

COASTAL DANGERS

Refer to Admiralty charts 3670, 3673

L'Ost-Pic

The distinctive headland and lighthouse of L'Ost-Pic form the southern arm of the Anse de Paimpol. Two small rocky banks lie to the east of L'Ost-Pic, both marked by E-cardinal buoys. Les Calemarguiers banks lie between ½ mile and 1 mile east of L'Ost-Pic lighthouse, with depths of less than ½ metre on the inshore side and a rocky patch drying 1.8 metres further out.

Basse St Brieuc bank lies 1¾ miles ESE of L'Ost-Pic, with a depth of ½ metre over its shallowest part. Boats can safely pass over these banks above half tide, and even near low water you can cut inside Les Calemarguiers ¼ mile off L'Ost-Pic.

Paimpol approaches

Boats making for Paimpol from St Malo would normally carry a full ebb tide westwards and thus arrive off Paimpol near low water. A rock with less than 1 metre over it at chart datum lies just over 6 cables south-east of Les Charpentiers E-cardinal beacon tower and just over 1 mile north-east of L'Ost-Pic lighthouse. This rock is in the white sector of Porz-Don light and very close north of the direct line between waypoints 47–1 and 47–5, so boats should take care to avoid it near low water springs.

Anse de Paimpol

Most of the Anse de Paimpol dries at chart datum. Boats arriving in the bay near low water will need to anchor in one of the outer anchorages south or south-west of Ile St Rion until two hours before high water when the Paimpol lock gates open.

When arriving from seaward, most boats come north of Les Calemarguiers E-cardinal buoy to line up on a more or less westerly approach which leaves Les Charpentiers E-cardinal beacon tower about 4 cables to the north and Gouayan red beacon tower not quite ¼ mile to the south. You then pass north of Roche Gueule red buoy and La Jument red beacon tower before sounding in towards a suitable anchorage. Care must be taken to avoid the numerous patches of withies which mark the extensive oyster beds in the Anse de Paimpol.

Dangers between Paimpol and Ile de Bréhat

A broad area of islets and drying rocks extends up to 3 miles seawards to form the sheltering north arm of the Anse de Paimpol. Les Charpentiers E-cardinal beacon tower stands near the south-east edge of these dangers, but Les Barbottes Rocks, almost awash at chart datum, lie 3½ cables *east* of Les Charpentiers tower.

Banc de la Cormorandière extends just over 1¼ miles north of La Cormorandière white pyramid, its north tip with only 0.8 metres over it lying very close south of the white sector of Men Joliguet light. Boats approaching Chenal du Ferlas from the east or south-east should make for a position near the Ferlas SE outer waypoint (No 46–17) before closing further with the shore.

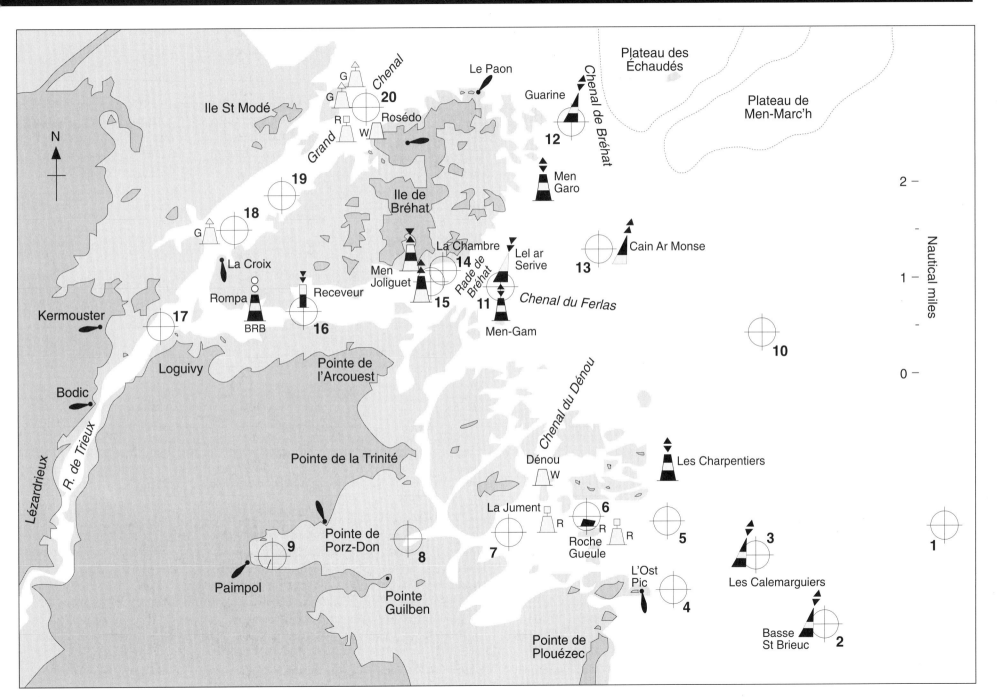

WP No	Waypoint name and position	Latitude	Longitude
47-1	Paimpol outer approach, 6.6 M 090½°T from Porz-Don L/H	48°47.47'N	02°51.50'W
47-2	Basse St Brieuc, 2 ca 060°T from E-card buoy	48°46.43'N	02°53.33'W
47-3	Les Calemarguiers, 2 ca 060°T from E-card buoy	48°47.15'N	02°54.48'W
47-4	L'Ost Pic inner, 3½ ca due E of lighthouse	48°46.81'N	02°55.81'W
47-5	Paimpol middle approach, 800 m S of Charpentiers beacon tr	48°47.52'N	02°55.92'W
47-6	Roche Gueule, 1 ca N of red buoy on leading line	48°47.57'N	02°57.21'W
47-7	Paimpol outer anchorage, 6 ca 216°T of Dénou W pyramid	48°47.43'N	02°58.49'W
47-8	Paimpol inner approach, ½ M 034°T from Pointe Guilben sp ht	48°47.34'N	03°00.16'W
47-9	Paimpol entrance, outer pierhead light actual position	48°47.15'N	03°02.35'W
47-10	Ferlas SE outer, 3.9 M 100°T from Men Joliguet tower	48°49.51'N	02°54.70'W
47-11	Ferlas SE inner, ½ ca S of Lel ar Serive S-card buoy	48°49.97'N	02°58.67'W
47-12	Chenal de Bréhat middle, Guarine buoy, actual position	48°51.68'N	02°57.51'W
47-13	Cain ar Monse, ¼ M 307°T from N-card buoy	48°50.36'N	02°57.03'W
47-14	La Chambre, 1 ca 230°T from La Chambre S-card beacon	48°50.14'N	02°59.62'W
47-15	Rade de Bréhat, 500 m 127°T from Men Joliguet tower	48°50.01'N	02°59.79'W
47-16	Ferlas middle, 120 m S of Receveur S-card beacon	48°49.69'N	03°01.87'W
47-17	Trieux River entrance, 6½ ca E of Kermouster light	48°49.60'N	03°04.12'W
47-18	La Croix inner, 3 ca 026°T from La Croix lighthouse	48°50.56'N	03°02.98'W
47-19	La Croix outer, 9 ca 045°T from La Croix lighthouse	48°50.93'N	03°02.20'W
47-20	La Moisie inner, 3 ca 339°T from Rosédo white pyramid	48°51.83'N	03°00.84'W

A narrow but well marked passage, Chenal de la Trinité, cuts inside all these dangers, providing a useful short-cut above half-tide between the Anse de Paimpol and the Chenal du Ferlas just south of Ile de Bréhat.

East approaches to Bréhat

There are numerous wide rocky banks to the east and north-east of Ile de Bréhat. They are all well covered above half-tide, but cause uneasy turbulence and steep overfalls during the strongest hours of both the flood and ebb.

Plateau des Échaudés extends between Ile de Bréhat and the drying reefs of Plateau de la Horaine. The shallowest part of Les Échaudés dries 2.6 metres. A narrow passage, Chenal de Bréhat, leads NNW–SSE between Les Échaudés and the Guarine E-cardinal buoy off the east side of Bréhat.

Plateau de Men-Marc'h is a wide shoal area south-east of La Horaine and Les Échaudés. Most of Men-Marc'h is relatively deep, with only a few patches having around ½ metre depth at chart datum; Men-Marc'h rock itself, on the south-east edge of the plateau, dries 0.6 metres. There is a passage of deep water just south of Plateau de Men-Marc'h and north of Plateau du Ringue-Bras; this route leads in towards the Chenal du Ferlas from the ENE and can be a useful approach to Ile de Bréhat for boats arriving direct from Jersey, provided you allow carefully for any cross-tide.

Chenal du Ferlas

The Ferlas channel leads between the south side of Ile de Bréhat and the Brittany mainland just east of the Trieux River. It is well marked and straightforward above half-tide, but care must be taken through parts of the channel near low water. At the east end, Cain Ar Monse Rock, almost awash at chart datum, is marked on its north side by a N-cardinal buoy, although the leading line and the white sector of Men Joliguet normally bring you in 4 cables or so south of the rock. Opposite Cain Ar Monse, on the south side of the normal leading line, the north tip of Banc de la Cormorandière has only 0.8 metres over it at chart datum.

Towards the middle of Chenal du Ferlas, between Ile de Bréhat and Rompa isolated danger beacon tower, there are various patches which are shallow near low water. The south side of the channel is shallow as you approach Roc'h Rouray and there is a patch on the north side with only 0.8 metres at chart datum, just under 1 cable *south* and a shade east of Trebeyou S-cardinal beacon tower. Rompa beacon tower has a small drying rock close off its south side.

Grand Chenal de Trieux

Once you are abreast Ile de Bréhat, the Grand Chenal de Trieux is straightforward and well marked, sheltered by land and rocks on both sides. However, until you draw south of the north tip of Bréhat, allow for a strong cross-tide across the outer Trieux estuary, especially during the middle hours of the flood.

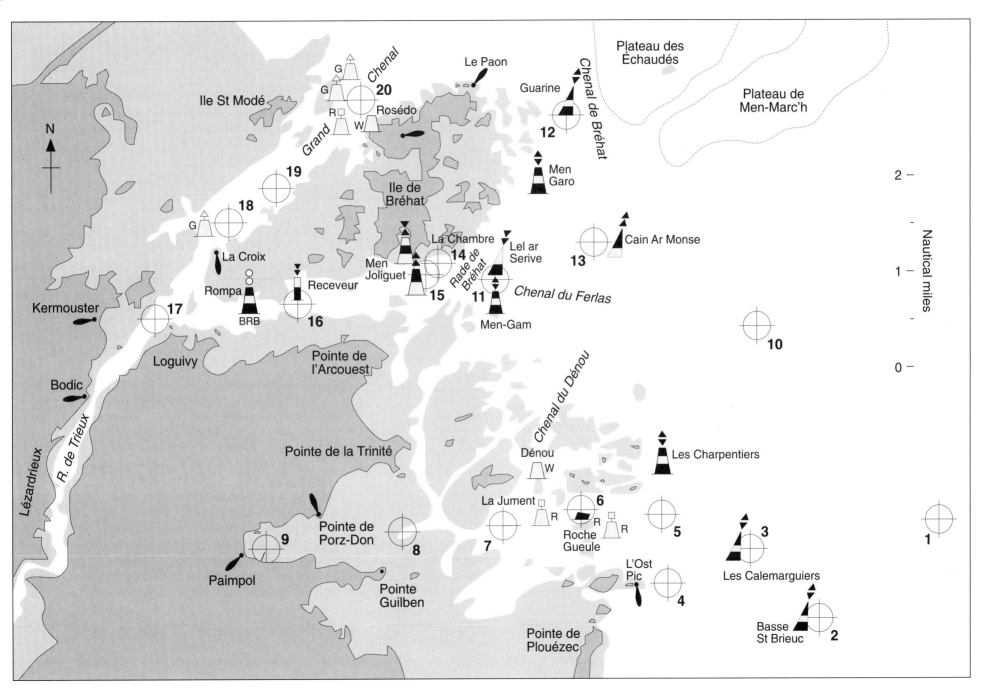

Ile St Modé

Chenal

Grand

G △
G ○
R □
W ▽

20

Rosédo

Le Paon

Plateau des
Échaudés

Guarine

Chenal de Bréhat

Plateau de
Men-Marc'h

12

N

19

Men
Garo

18

G

Ile de
Bréhat

La Croix

La Chambre

Cain Ar Monse

13

Rompa

Men
Joliguet

14

Lel ar
Serive

Receveur

Rade de Bréhat

Kermouster

BRB

15

11

Chenal du Ferlas

16

Men-Gam

17

10

Loguivy

Pointe de
l'Arcouest

Bodic

Chenal du Dénou

R. de Trieux

Pointe de la Trinité

Les Charpentiers

Dénou
W

Lézardrieux

La Jument □
R

6

9

Pointe de
Porz-Don

Roche
Gueule R
R

5

Les Calemarguiers

3

Paimpol

7

8

L'Ost
Pic

4

2

Pointe
Guilben

Basse
St Brieuc

Pointe de
Plouézec

2 —

1 —

0 —

Nautical miles

1

Approaches to the Trieux River

WP No	Waypoint name and position	Latitude	Longitude
48-1	Grand Chenal approach, 8 ca NW of Basses du Nord buoy	48°55.08'N	02°55.93'W
48-2	Chenal de Bréhat N, 1¾ M 021°T from Le Paon light	48°53.63'N	02°58.11'W
48-3	Chenal de Bréhat middle, Guarine buoy, actual position	48°51.68'N	02°57.51'W
48-4	La Moisie inner, 3 ca 339°T from Rosédo white pyramid	48°51.83'N	03°00.84'W
48-5	La Moisie outer, 8 ca 343°T from La Moisie beacon	48°54.65'N	03°02.45'W
48-6	La Gaine NE, 1 M E of Les Heaux lighthouse on leading line	48°54.57'N	03°03.59'W
48-7	Les Heaux N clearing inner, 1¼ M N of lighthouse	48°55.82'N	03°05.09'W
48-8	Les Heaux N clearing outer, 2½ M N of lighthouse	48°57.07'N	03°05.09'W
48-9	Roch ar Bel clearing, 4.3 M 067°T from Les Heaux L/H	48°56.25'N	02°59.00'W

COASTAL DANGERS

Refer to Admiralty charts 3670, 3673

Strong cross-tides

The Grand Chenal into the Trieux River is not difficult, but there are dangers several miles from the low-lying coast and you need to allow for the powerful cross-tides that sweep round this corner of Brittany between Les Heaux and La Horaine, especially during the middle hours of the flood. The cross-tide cuts off as you draw abreast the north end of Ile de Bréhat.

Plateau de la Horaine

Plateau de la Horaine, the most seaward area of shoals and rocks on the east side of the Grand Chenal, lies from 3–4 miles north-east of Ile de Bréhat. The drying dangers on the south-west side of the plateau are guarded by La Horaine tower, but the whole area around these shoals is uneasy with turbulence and overfalls as the tide rushes across it. The north tip of La Horaine is marked by the Basses du Nord N-cardinal buoy (sometimes referred to as Nord Horaine) which is the outer buoy for the Grand Chenal.

Dangers east of Bréhat

There are several other wide rocky banks south of La Horaine and to the east of Ile de Bréhat. These are mostly well covered above half-tide, but again cause uneasy turbulence and steep overfalls during the strongest hours of both the flood and ebb.

Plateau des Échaudés lies between Ile de Bréhat and La Horaine, its shallowest patch drying 2.6 metres. A narrow passage, Chenal de Bréhat, leads NNW–SSE between Les Échaudés and the Guarine E-cardinal buoy off the east side of Bréhat.

Plateau de Men-Marc'h is a wide shoal area south-east of La Horaine and Les Échaudés. Most of Men-Marc'h is relatively deep, with only a few patches having around ½ metre depth at chart datum; Men-Marc'h rock itself, on the south-east edge of the plateau, dries 0.6 metres. There is a passage of deep water just to the south of Plateau de Men-Marc'h and north of Plateau du Ringue-Bras; this route leads in towards the Chenal du Ferlas from the ENE and can be a useful approach to Ile de Bréhat for boats arriving direct from Jersey, provided you allow carefully for any cross-tide.

Outer overfalls

Not quite 3½ miles north and a shade west of the north tip of Bréhat, well to the west of the Grand Chenal approaches, two rocky shoals – Roch ar Bel and Carrec Mingui – have a safe depth over them for boats, but cause turbulent overfalls during the strongest hours of the tide. They should be avoided in fresh winds if you are arriving off the Grand Chenal from the west or leaving the Grand Chenal to round Les Heaux.

Les Sirlots and Basse Plate

Basse Plate shoals lie about 1 mile south of Roch ar Bel and Carrec Mingui on the west side of the estuary. Although well covered above half-tide, Basse Plate should be avoided on account of its overfalls and turbulent water, especially during the strongest part of the flood.

The Plateau des Sirlots lies further into the estuary, about ¾ mile south of Basse Plate, and is left clear to starboard as you come in through the Grand Chenal. Les Sirlots green whistle buoy guards the east edge of these shoals and is a strategic mark for the inner part of the estuary.

West side of Trieux estuary

The west side of the Trieux estuary is a maze of drying rocks and shoals which, providing a natural continuation of the mainland, straggles north-eastwards for a good 3 miles. The long sandspit known as Sillon de Talber forms the backbone of these dangers and their north-east edge is guarded by several beacons, of which the most seaward is La Moisie E-cardinal beacon tower.

La Moisie passage

This narrow channel leads into the Trieux estuary from the NNW, skirting the edge of the

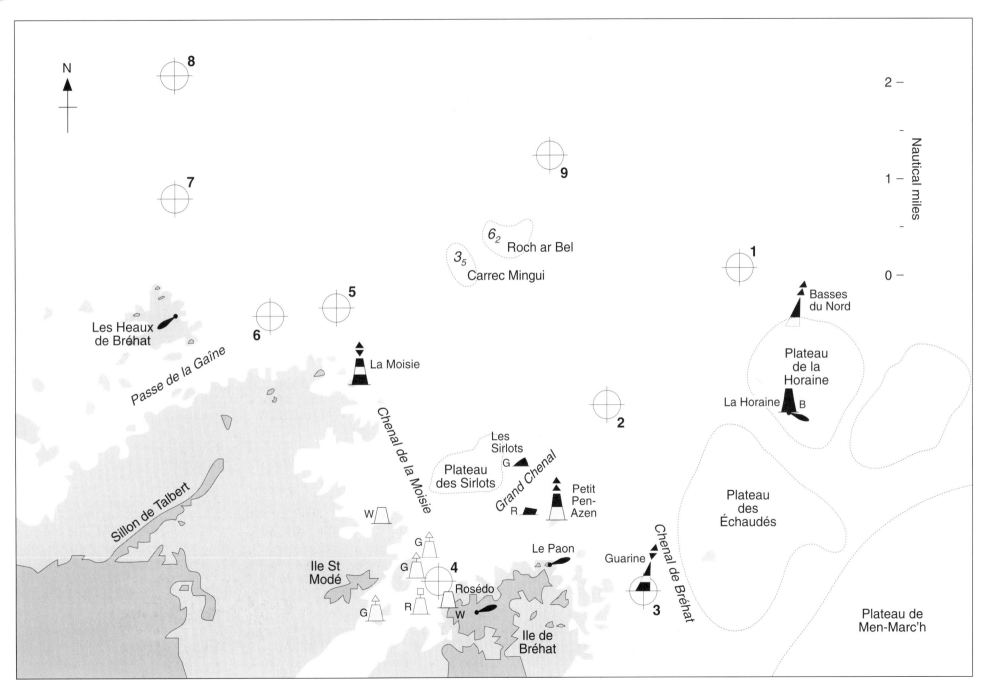

N

8

7

6

5

Les Heaux
de Bréhat

Passe de la Gaîne

La Moisie

Sillon de Talbert

Chenal de la Moisie

W

G

G

Ile St
Modé

R

G

Rosédo

W

4

Le Paon

Les
Sirlots

Plateau
des Sirlots

G

Grand Chenal

R

Petit
Pen-
Azen

Guarine

Ile de
Bréhat

3

9

6₂ Roch ar Bel

3₅

Carrec Mingui

2

1

Basses
du Nord

Plateau
de la
Horaine

La Horaine B

Chenal de Bréhat

Plateau
des
Échaudés

Plateau de
Men-Marc'h

2 –

Nautical miles

1 –

0 –

WP No	Waypoint name and position	Latitude	Longitude
48-1	Grand Chenal approach, 8 ca NW of Basses du Nord buoy	48°55.08'N	02°55.93'W
48-2	Chenal de Bréhat N, 1¾ M 021°T from Le Paon light	48°53.63'N	02°58.11'W
48-3	Chenal de Bréhat middle, Guarine buoy, actual position	48°51.68'N	02°57.51'W
48-4	La Moisie inner, 3 ca 339°T from Rosédo white pyramid	48°51.83'N	03°00.84'W
48-5	La Moisie outer, 8 ca 343°T from La Moisie beacon	48°54.65'N	03°02.45'W
48-6	La Gaine NE, 1 M E of Les Heaux lighthouse on leading line	48°54.57'N	03°03.59'W
48-7	Les Heaux N clearing inner, 1¼ M N of lighthouse	48°55.82'N	03°05.09'W
48-8	Les Heaux N clearing outer, 2½ M N of lighthouse	48°57.07'N	03°05.09'W
48-9	Roch ar Bel clearing, 4.3 M 067°T from Les Heaux L/H	48°56.25'N	02°59.00'W

reefs that extend north-east from Sillon de Talber and keeping west of Basse Plate, Plateau des Sirlots and several smaller drying rocks – Ar Mesclek, Pierre Rouge, La Traverse and Roc ar Gazec. The Moisie passage needs reasonable visibility and is best taken above half-tide.

Les Heaux

The cluster of above-water and drying rocks known as Les Heaux de Bréhat are almost the most northerly rocks on the west side of the Trieux estuary. Les Heaux lighthouse is nearly 50 metres high and provides an unmistakable landfall mark as you approach the Trieux from seaward. When rounding Les Heaux, perhaps bound between Lézardrieux and Tréguier, you must be sure of clearing the various drying dangers which extend WNW of the lighthouse for almost 2 miles. La Jument N-cardinal buoy is the corner mark for these dangers.

Passe de la Gaîne

This narrow, rather delicate passage leads inside Les Heaux lighthouse towards the Tréguier estuary. In good visibility though, and above half-tide, Pass de la Gaîne presents no great difficulty for those familiar with the rocks and strong tides along this coast.

Boats entering Passe de la Gaîne at the east end have usually just left the Trieux estuary via Chenal de la Moisie. As you emerge seawards, once Moisie E-cardinal beacon tower is half a mile astern and before Les Heaux lighthouse bears due west true, come to port to make good due west true and so bring the lighthouse fine on the starboard bow.

About a quarter of a mile south-east of Les Heaux lighthouse is a 2 metre above-water rock, Roc'h ar Hanap. You enter Passe de la Gaîne by steering to make good 241°T and leaving Roc'h ar Harap 1½–2 cables to starboard.

Thereafter, leave the first green beacon a cable to starboard and steer to leave the second green beacon only 150 metres to starboard. The leading marks for Passe de la Gaîne will be 4–6 miles distant in the Tréguier estuary, a little to the right of Plougrescant church spire. These marks are often hidden in haze until you get much closer, so it's best to steer by the beacons until the transit comes into view.

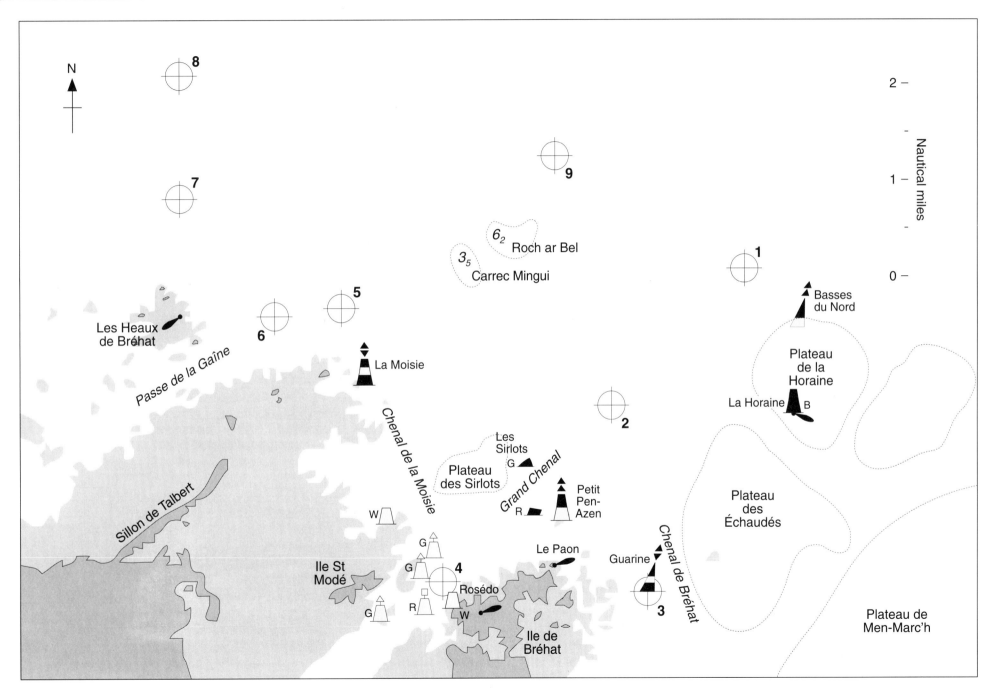

N

2 —

Nautical miles

1 —

0 —

8

7

9

6₂ Roch ar Bel

3₅ Carrec Mingui

1

Basses
du Nord

Plateau
de la
Horaine

La Horaine B

5

Les Heaux
de Bréhat

6

Passe de la Gaîne

La Moisie

Chenal de la Moisie

2

Les
Sirlots

Plateau
des Sirlots

Grand Chenal

G

R

Petit
Pen-
Azen

Plateau
des
Échaudés

Sillon de Talbert

W

G

G

4

G

Le Paon

Rosédo

R

W

Guarine

Chenal de Bréhat

3

Ile St
Modé

G

Ile de
Bréhat

Plateau de
Men-Marc'h

WP No	Waypoint name and position	Latitude	Longitude
49-1	Roches Douvres West, 3 M WNW of lighthouse	49°07.80'N	02°52.79'W
49-2	Roches Douvres East, 3½ M due E of lighthouse	49°06.48'N	02°43.34'W
49-3	Barnouic SW, 1.1 M W of Roche Gautier W-card buoy	49°00.49'N	02°54.59'W
49-4	Barnouic SE inner, 1½ M SE of Barnouic E-card tower	49°00.65'N	02°46.71'W
49-5	Barnouic SE outer, 3.6 M SE of Barnouic E-card tower	48°59.09'N	02°44.50'W
49-6	Grand Chenal approach, 8 ca NW of Basses du Nord buoy	48°55.08'N	02°55.93'W
49-7	Chenal de Bréhat N, 1¾ M 021°T from Le Paon light	48°53.63'N	02°58.11'W
49-8	Chenal de Bréhat middle, Guarine buoy, actual position	48°51.68'N	02°57.51'W
49-9	Men-Marc'h E approach, 2 M 121°T from Men Marc'h buoy	48°52.20'N	02°49.23'W
49-10	Grand Léjon NW, 6 M NW of Grand Léjon lighthouse	48°49.19'N	02°46.20'W
49-11	Ferlas SE outer, 3.9 M 100°T from Men Joliguet tower	48°49.51'N	02°54.70'W
49-12	Ferlas SE inner, ½ ca S of Lel ar Serive S-card buoy	48°49.97'N	02°58.67'W
49-13	Cain ar Monse, ¼ M 307°T from N-card buoy	48°50.36'N	02°57.03'W
49-14	Roch ar Bel clearing, 4.3 M 067°T from Les Heaux lighthouse	48°56.25'N	02°59.00'W
49-15	La Moisie outer, 8 ca 343°T from La Moisie beacon	48°54.65'N	03°02.45'W
49-16	La Gaine NE, 1 M E of Les Heaux lighthouse on leading line	48°54.57'N	03°03.59'W
49-17	Les Heaux N clearing inner, 1¼ M N of lighthouse	48°55.82'N	03°05.09'W
49-18	Les Heaux N clearing outer, 2½ M N of lighthouse	48°57.07'N	03°05.09'W

COASTAL DANGERS

Refer to Admiralty charts 2668, 3670

Roches Douvres

The Roches Douvres plateau is about 2 miles from west to east and 1½ miles from north to south. The tides set strongly in this area, especially between Roches Douvres and Plateau de Barnouic. It's important to pass a safe distance off, preferably keeping 'down-tide' of the dangers ie passing west-about when the tide is west-going and east-about when the tide is east-going. Note that local magnetic anomalies can be experienced to the east and south-east of Roches Douvres, which may affect an autopilot as well as a steering compass.

Plateau de Barnouic

This patchy area of rocky shoals about 3 miles south of Roches Douvres is more spread out than the latter and only has one reef, Roche Gautier, that dries. In some ways, however, its relative invisibility makes Barnouic potentially more sinister than Roches Douvres in this area of powerful tides. Barnouic E-cardinal beacon tower guards the east edge of the main shoals and the Roche Gautier W-cardinal buoy lies to the south-west of the plateau. The north-west shoals of the plateau have only a metre over them at datum and produce nasty overfalls during the strongest part of the tide.

Trieux approaches – strong cross-tides

The approach to the Trieux estuary is not difficult, but there are dangers several miles from the low-lying coast and you need to allow for the powerful cross-tides that sweep round this corner of Brittany between Les Heaux and La Horaine, especially during the middle hours of the flood. Entering the Grand Chenal de Trieux, the cross-tide cuts off as you draw abreast of the north end of Ile de Bréhat.

Outer overfalls

Basse Maurice, a deepish rocky shoal with 13 metres over it, lies 3 miles south-west of the Barnouic Roche Gautier W-cardinal buoy; more or less on the line most yachts take if bound from St Peter Port to Lézardrieux westabout Roches Douvres. There are often overfalls over Basse Maurice, especially with wind over tide, and it's a patch worth avoiding in boisterous weather. In calm conditions, you often see turbulent 'slicks' of oily smooth water near Basse Maurice, caused by the strong tidal stream surging over the shoal.

Not quite 3½ miles north and a shade west of the north tip of Bréhat, well to the west of the Grand Chenal approaches, are two rocky shoals: Roch ar Bel and Carrec Mingui. These have a safe depth over them for yachts, but cause turbulent overfalls during the strongest hours of the tide. They should be avoided in fresh winds if you are arriving off the Grand Chenal from the west or leaving the Grand Chenal to round Les Heaux.

Plateau de la Horaine

Plateau de la Horaine, the most seaward area of shoals and rocks on the east side of the Trieux estuary, lies from 3–4 miles north-east of Ile de Bréhat. The drying dangers on the south-west side of the plateau are guarded by La Horaine tower, but the whole area around these shoals is uneasy with turbulence and overfalls as the tide

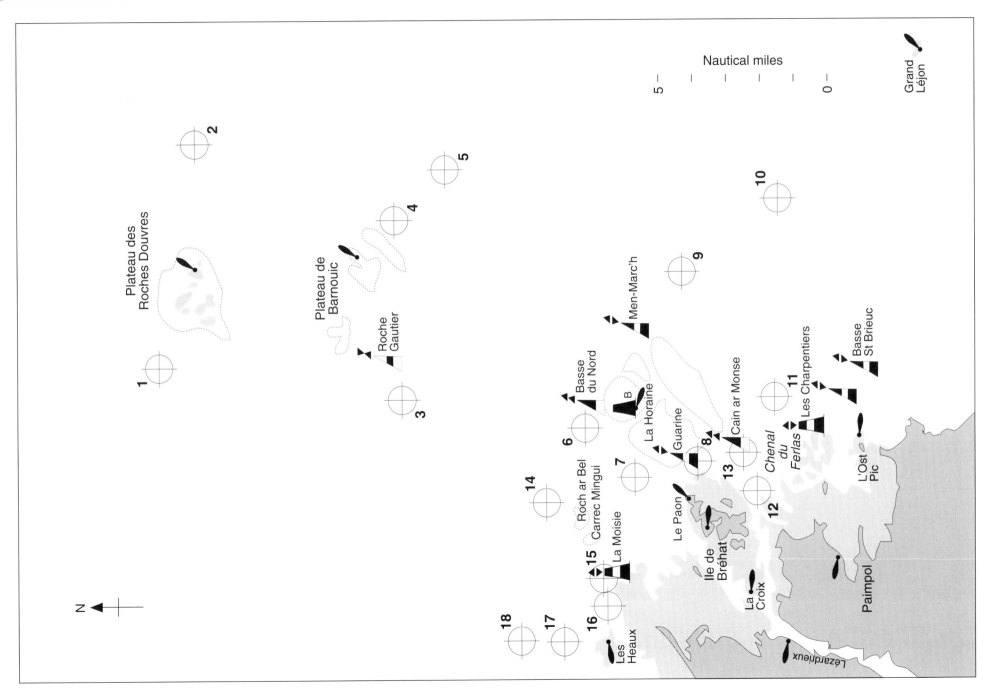

Nautical miles

5

0

Grand Léjon

Plateau des Roches Douvres

2

5

4

Plateau de Barnouic

Roche Gautier

3

1

Men-Marc'h

Basse du Nord

B

La Horaine

Guarine

Cain ar Monse

9

10

Basse St Brieuc

Les Charpentiers

11

Chenal du Ferlas

L'Ost Pic

6

7

8

13

12

Roch ar Bel

Carrec Mingui

14

La Moisie

15

Le Paon

Ile de Bréhat

La Croix

Paimpol

Les Heaux

16

17

18

N

Lézardrieux

123

WP No	Waypoint name and position	Latitude	Longitude
49-1	Roches Douvres West, 3 M WNW of lighthouse	49°07.80'N	02°52.79'W
49-2	Roches Douvres East, 3½ M due E of lighthouse	49°06.48'N	02°43.34'W
49-3	Barnouic SW, 1.1 M W of Roche Gautier W-card buoy	49°00.49'N	02°54.59'W
49-4	Barnouic SE inner, 1½ M SE of Barnouic E-card tower	49°00.65'N	02°46.71'W
49-5	Barnouic SE outer, 3.6 M SE of Barnouic E-card tower	48°59.09'N	02°44.50'W
49-6	Grand Chenal approach, 8 ca NW of Basses du Nord buoy	48°55.08'N	02°55.93'W
49-7	Chenal de Bréhat N, 1¾ M 021°T from Le Paon light	48°53.63'N	02°58.11'W
49-8	Chenal de Bréhat middle, Guarine buoy, actual position	48°51.68'N	02°57.51'W
49-9	Men-Marc'h E approach, 2 M 121°T from Men-Marc'h buoy	48°52.20'N	02°49.23'W
49-10	Grand Léjon NW, 6 M NW of Grand Léjon lighthouse	48°49.19'N	02°46.20'W
49-11	Ferlas SE outer, 3.9 M 100°T from Men Joliguet tower	48°49.51'N	02°54.70'W
49-12	Ferlas SE inner, ½ ca S of Lel ar Serive S-card buoy	48°49.97'N	02°58.67'W
49-13	Cain ar Monse, ¼ M 307°T from N-card buoy	48°50.36'N	02°57.03'W
49-14	Roch ar Bel clearing, 4.3 M 067°T from Les Heaux lighthouse	48°56.25'N	02°59.00'W
49-15	La Moisie outer, 8 ca 343°T from La Moisie beacon	48°54.65'N	03°02.45'W
49-16	La Gaine NE, 1 M E of Les Heaux lighthouse on leading line	48°54.57'N	03°03.59'W
49-17	Les Heaux N clearing inner, 1¼ M N of lighthouse	48°55.82'N	03°05.09'W
49-18	Les Heaux N clearing outer, 2½ M N of lighthouse	48°57.07'N	03°05.09'W

rushes across it. The north tip of La Horaine is marked by the Basses du Nord N-cardinal buoy (sometimes referred to as Nord Horaine) which is the outer buoy for the Grand Chenal de Trieux.

Dangers east of Bréhat
There are several other wide rocky banks south of La Horaine and to the east of Ile de Bréhat. These are mostly well covered above half-tide, but again cause uneasy turbulence and steep overfalls during the strongest hours of both the flood and ebb. Plateau des Échaudés lies between Ile de Bréhat and La Horaine, its shallowest patch drying 2.6 metres. A narrow passage, Chenal de Bréhat, leads NNW–SSE between Les Échaudés and the Guarine E-cardinal buoy off the east side of Bréhat.

Plateau de Men-Marc'h is a wide shoal area south-east of La Horaine and Les Échaudés. Most of Men-Marc'h is relatively deep, with only a few patches having around ½ metre depth at datum; Men-Marc'h rock itself, on the south-east edge of the plateau, dries 0.6 metres. There is a passage of deep water just to the south of Plateau de Men-Marc'h and north of Plateau du Ringue-Bras; this route leads in towards the Chenal du Ferlas from the ENE and can be a useful approach to Ile de Bréhat for yachts arriving direct from Jersey, provided you make careful allowance for any cross-tide.

Les Heaux
The cluster of above-water and drying rocks known as Les Heaux de Bréhat are almost the most northerly rocks on the west side of the Trieux estuary. Les Heaux lighthouse is nearly 50 metres high and provides an unmistakable landfall mark as you approach the Trieux from seaward. When rounding Les Heaux, perhaps bound between Lézardrieux and Tréguier, you must be sure of clearing the various drying dangers which extend WNW of the lighthouse for almost 2 miles. La Jument N-cardinal buoy is the corner mark for these dangers.

Magnetic anomalies
You can experience local magnetic interference in the sea area immediately south-east of Roches Douvres, an eerie sensation for any navigator. This effect is said to be due to the high ferrous content of the Roches Douvres granite, although I have found that you have to be reasonably close to the plateau before noticing anything odd. These anomalies will affect electronic compasses and autopilot fluxgates as well as ordinary steering and hand-bearing compasses.

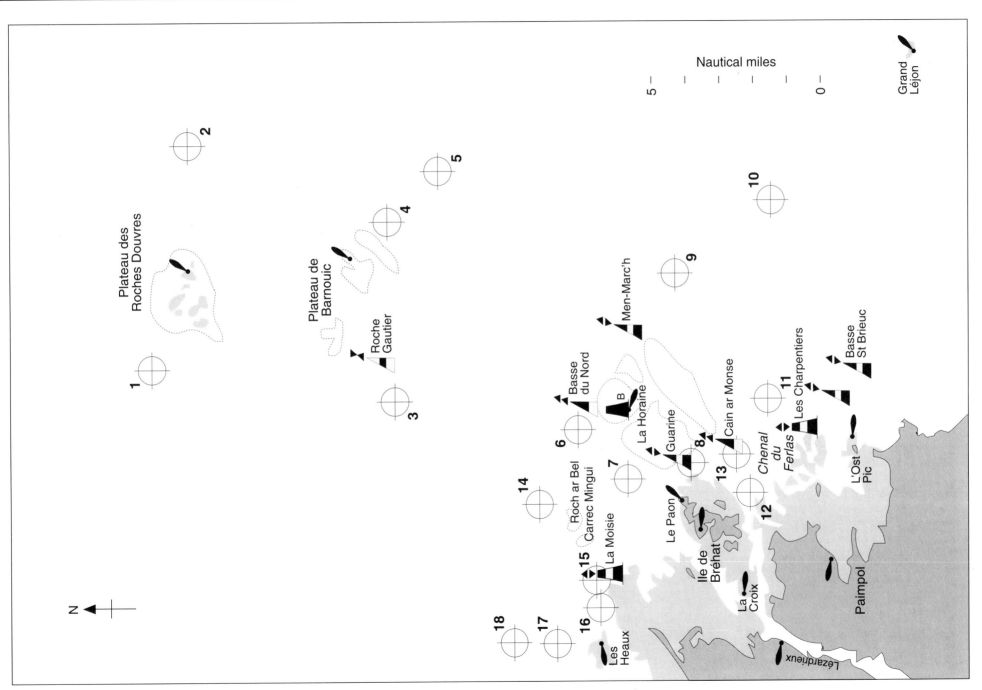

Nautical miles

Plateau des
Roches Douvres

1

2

Plateau de
Barnouic

3

Roche
Gautier

4

5

Men-Marc'h

Basse
du Nord

6

7

B

La Horaine

Guarine

8

9

Cain ar Monse

13

Chenal
du
Ferlas

12

11

Les Charpentiers

Basse
St Brieuc

10

L'Ost
Pic

Paimpol

Le Paon

Île de
Bréhat

La
Croix

Lézardrieux

La Moisie

Carrec Mingui

Roch ar Bel

15

16

17

18

14

Les
Heaux

N

Grand
Léjon

WP No	Waypoint name and position	Latitude	Longitude
50-1	Les Heaux N clearing inner, 1¼ M N of lighthouse	48°55.82'N	03°05.09'W
50-2	Les Heaux N clearing outer, 2½ M N of lighthouse	48°57.07'N	03°05.09'W
50-3	La Jument clearing, ¼ M N of N-card buoy	48°55.66'N	03°07.94'W
50-4	Tréguier outer, 3 ca 287°T of Basse Crublent red buoy	48°54.44'N	03°11.51'W
50-5	Tréguier inner, 1 ca E of Petit Pen ar Guézec green buoy	48°52.58'N	03°09.17'W
50-6	La Corne, 1 ca due N of La Corne lighthouse	48°51.50'N	03°10.53'W
50-7	Perros E outer, ¾ M 038°T of Basse Guazer buoy on leading line	48°52.23'N	03°20.16'W
50-8	Port Blanc inner, 6 ca E of Le Four rock on leading line	48°51.13'N	03°19.20'W
50-9	Perros inner, ¼ M 207°T of Pierre du Chenal beacon tower	48°49.14'N	03°24.76'W
50-10	Perros W outer, ¾ M W of Les Couillons de Tomé buoy	48°50.92'N	03°26.73'W
50-11	Sept Iles E, 2.9 M E of Ile Rouzic E tip in Port Blanc W sector	48°53.98'N	03°21.61'W
50-12	Sept Iles SE, midway between Dervinis and Couillons buoys	48°51.68'N	03°26.45'W
50-13	Sept Iles S, 1.2 M S of Ile aux Moines lighthouse	48°51.59'N	03°29.34'W
50-14	Sept Iles W, 2¼ M W of Ile aux Moines lighthouse	48°52.79'N	03°32.77'W
50-15	Sept Iles N clearing, 4¼ M due N of Ile aux Moines L/H	48°57.04'N	03°29.34'W
50-16	Ploumanac'h entrance, 2 ca NW of Pointe de Mean Ruz L/H	48°50.44'N	03°29.16'W

COASTAL DANGERS

Refer to Admiralty charts 2668, 3670, 3672, 3669

Les Heaux

The cluster of above-water and drying rocks known as Les Heaux de Bréhat are almost the most northerly dangers on the west side of the Trieux estuary. Les Heaux lighthouse is nearly 50 metres high and provides an unmistakable landfall mark as you approach the Trieux from seaward. When rounding Les Heaux, perhaps bound between Lézardrieux and Tréguier, you must be sure of clearing the various drying dangers which extend WNW of the lighthouse for almost 2 miles. La Jument N-cardinal buoy is the corner mark for these dangers.

Approaches to the Tréguier River

There are numerous drying and above-water rocks between Les Heaux and the entrance to Tréguier. One normally gives a wide berth to these when passing outside Les Heaux, round La Jument N-cardinal buoy and then in through the Grande Passe via Basse Crublent red buoy. An inner channel, Passe de la Gaine, leads inside Les Heaux providing a useful short cut between the Lézardrieux and Tréguier estuaries in suitable conditions. Passe de la Gaine should only be taken above half-tide and in reasonable visibility.

There is an intermediate channel into the Tréguier estuary, known as Passe du Nord-Est, leading from La Jument N-cardinal buoy inside Le Corbeau rock and Basses du Corbeau. The marks for this entrance are not always easy to make out and, for the minimal distance saved, most boats will find it best to use the Grande Passe when approaching Tréguier outside Les Heaux.

Dangers between Tréguier and Perros

Between Basse Crublent red buoy and Basse Guazer red buoy in the outer north-east approaches to Perros-Guirec, there are various rocky dangers up to 1¾ miles offshore. A direct line between Basse Crublent and Basse Guazer buoys leads just outside these dangers, clearing Basse Laéres (dries 0.6 metres) by barely a cable. Yachts must be careful to stay safely outside this direct line, especially with onshore winds and when the tide is east-going, when the set tends to be inshore.

Approaches to Perros-Guirec

The north-east approach to Perros-Guirec leads inshore from Basse Guazer red buoy inside Ile Tomé, converging slowly with the Brittany coast. The Basse Guazer shoal lies 1½ miles offshore, but between Guazer red buoy and the red beacon towers in the Anse de Perros, you pass a wide area of reefs on the port hand that extends well over a mile offshore between Port Blanc and Kerjean. Yachts approaching Perros by this Passe de l'Est should keep well off these dangers and follow the leading line carefully, making good a more or less direct line between Basse Guazer buoy and the green conical buoy off the south tip of Ile Tomé.

The north-west approach to the Anse de Perros is less encumbered than the north-east but better marked and generally more straightforward. Various drying reefs extend westward for up to ¾ mile from the west side of Ile Tomé, marked at the extremity by Bilzic red beacon tower. Les Couillons de Tomé reef, ½ mile off the north-west tip of Ile Tomé, is guarded by Les Couillons de Tomé W-cardinal buoy.

On the south side of the Passe de l'Ouest, there are several drying reefs well out in the

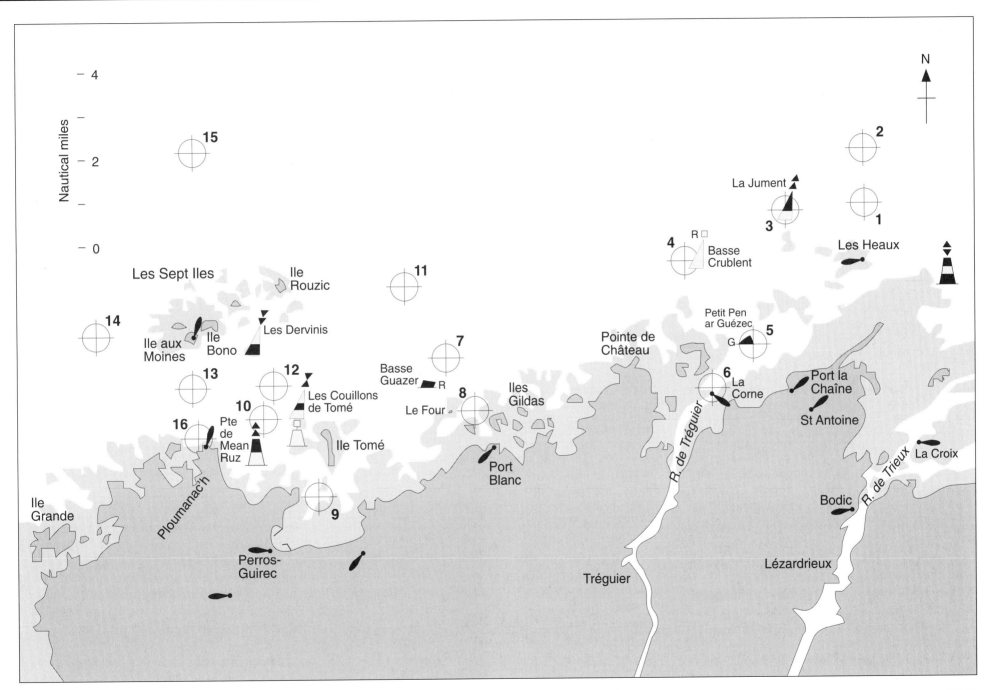

N

Nautical miles

— 4

— 2

— 0

15

2

La Jument

3

1

4 R Basse Crublent

Les Heaux

Les Sept Iles

Ile Rouzic

11

14

Les Dervinis

Petit Pen ar Guézec

Pointe de Château

5 G

Ile aux Moines

Ile Bono

7

Basse Guazer R

6 La Corne

Port la Chaîne

13

12

Les Couillons de Tomé

8

Le Four

Iles Gildas

St Antoine

10

16

Pte de Mean Ruz

Ile Tomé

Port Blanc

R. de Tréguier

R. de Trieux

La Croix

Ile Grande

Ploumanac'h

9

Bodic

Perros-Guirec

Lézardrieux

Tréguier

WP No	Waypoint name and position	Latitude	Longitude
50-1	Les Heaux N clearing inner, 1¼ M N of lighthouse	48°55.82'N	03°05.09'W
50-2	Les Heaux N clearing outer, 2½ M N of lighthouse	48°57.07'N	03°05.09'W
50-3	La Jument clearing, ¼ M N of N-card buoy	48°55.66'N	03°07.94'W
50-4	Tréguier outer, 3 ca 287°T of Basse Crublent red buoy	48°54.44'N	03°11.51'W
50-5	Tréguier inner, 1 ca E of Petit Pen ar Guézec green buoy	48°52.58'N	03°09.17'W
50-6	La Corne, 1 ca due N of La Corne lighthouse	48°51.50'N	03°10.53'W
50-7	Perros E outer, ¾ M 038°T of Basse Guazer buoy on leading line	48°52.23'N	03°20.16'W
50-8	Port Blanc inner, 6 ca E of Le Four rock on leading line	48°51.13'N	03°19.20'W
50-9	Perros inner, ¼ M 207°T of Pierre du Chenal beacon tower	48°49.14'N	03°24.76'W
50-10	Perros W outer, ¾ M W of Les Couillons de Tomé buoy	48°50.92'N	03°26.73'W
50-11	Sept Iles E, 2.9 M E of Ile Rouzic E tip in Port Blanc W sector	48°53.98'N	03°21.61'W
50-12	Sept Iles SE, midway between Dervinis and Couillons buoys	48°51.68'N	03°26.45'W
50-13	Sept Iles S, 1.2 M S of Ile aux Moines lighthouse	48°51.59'N	03°29.34'W
50-14	Sept Iles W, 2¼ M W of Ile aux Moines lighthouse	48°52.79'N	03°32.77'W
50-15	Sept Iles N clearing, 4¼ M due N of Ile aux Moines L/H	48°57.04'N	03°29.34'W
50-16	Ploumanac'h entrance, 2 ca NW of Pointe de Mean Ruz L/H	48°50.44'N	03°29.16'W

bay between Pointe du Château and Pointe de Mean Ruz, but they are well guarded on their north edge by Bernard green beacon tower, La Fronde green buoy and La Horaine north-cardinal beacon tower.

The Anse de Perros itself is shallow, most of it drying at chart datum. Depending on the tides, you can anchor or use the waiting buoys between Pointe du Château and Roc'h Hu de Perros red beacon tower. At neaps you can edge further into the bay under Pointe du Château for greater shelter.

Les Sept Iles

This string of small islands and reefs lies just offshore a few miles north of Ploumanac'h and Ile Tomé. The two largest islands, Ile aux Moines and Ile Bono, are close together on the south-west edge of the plateau. Being fairly clean on their south sides, they form a natural anchorage which is open to the south and east but reasonably sheltered in moderate winds from between north and west.

The powerful lighthouse on Ile aux Moines is a key mark if you are approaching this stretch of coast at night anywhere between Lézardrieux and Roscoff. Unlit dangers extend 1¾ miles north, nearly 3½ miles ENE and just over a mile west of the lighthouse. Les Dervinis, an isolated rock drying 3.2 metres not quite a mile south-east of Ile Bono, is marked on its south side by an unlit south-cardinal buoy.

The tides are very strong locally between Les Sept Iles and the mainland, especially in the narrows between Ile aux Moines and Pointe de Mean Ruz. The bottom is uneven and relatively shallow in several patches through this strait, and this can cause steep overfalls locally, especially near springs with wind-over-tide.

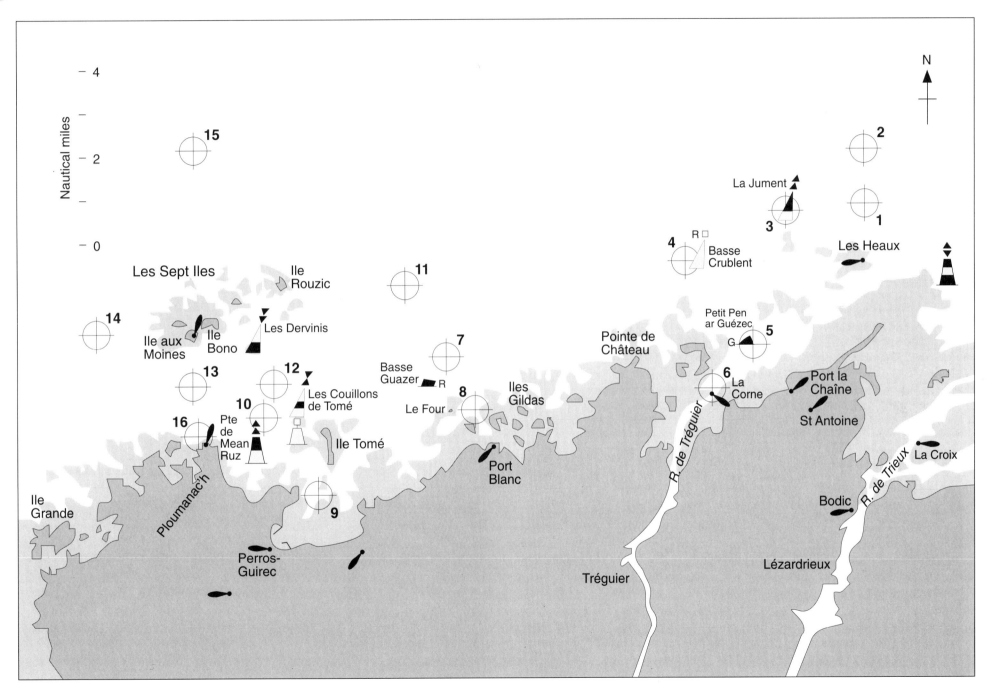

N

Nautical miles

— 4

— 2

— 0

15

2

La Jument

3

1

Les Heaux

4 R □

Basse
Crublent

Les Sept Iles

Ile
Rouzic

11

Pointe de
Château

Petit Pen
ar Guézec

G **5**

14

Ile aux
Moines

Ile
Bono

Les Dervinis

7

6 La Corne

Port la
Chaîne

13

12

Les Couillons
de Tomé

Basse
Guazer R

8

Le Four

Iles
Gildas

St Antoine

10

Ile Tomé

La Croix

16

Pte
de
Mean
Ruz

Port
Blanc

Bodic

Ile
Grande

Ploumanac'h

9

Perros-
Guirec

R. de Tréguier

R. de Trieux

Tréguier

Lézardrieux

WP No	Waypoint name and position	Latitude	Longitude
51-1	Les Sept Iles S, 1.2 M S of Ile aux Moines lighthouse	48°51.59'N	03°29.34'W
51-2	Les Sept Iles W, 2¼ M W of Ile aux Moines lighthouse	48°52.79'N	03°32.77'W
51-3	Ploumanac'h entrance, 2 ca NW of Pointe de Mean Ruz L/H	48°50.44'N	03°29.16'W
51-4	Trégastel entrance, 1½ ca NW of Ile Dhu red beacon	48°50.53'N	03°31.30'W
51-5	Les Sept Iles SW, 3½ M 250°T from Ile aux Moines L/H	48°51.61'N	03°34.36'W
51-6	Bar all Gall, ¼ M NW of Bar all Gall W-card buoy	48°49.99'N	03°36.23'W
51-7	Triagoz South, 1¾ M due S of Les Triagoz lighthouse	48°50.60'N	03°38.71'W
51-8	Méloine NE, 2½ M 019°T of La Méloine Grande Roche	48°48.93'N	03°45.77'W
51-9	Trébeurden NW outer, 1.3 M 247°T from Bar all Gall buoy	48°49.29'N	03°37.80'W
51-10	Trébeurden W inner, 6 ca 236°T from Ar Veskleg rock	48°46.21'N	03°37.57'W
51-11	Trébeurden approach, 150 m S of Ar Gourédec S-card buoy	48°46.40'N	03°36.40'W
51-12	Le Crapaud W, ¼ M W of Le Crapaud W-card buoy	48°46.64'N	03°40.75'W
51-13	Le Crapaud SW, ½ M SW of Le Crapaud W-card buoy	48°46.30'N	03°40.92'W
51-14	Le Crapaud S, 1.3 M S of Le Crapaud W-card buoy	48°45.34'N	03°40.39'W
51-15	Lannion outer, 4 M 270°T of Beg Léguer lighthouse	48°44.40'N	03°39.87'W
51-16	Lannion inner, 1 M 270°T of Beg Léguer lighthouse	48°44.40'N	03°34.31'W
51-17	Lannion entrance, 100 m N of inner green beacon tower	48°43.89'N	03°33.16'W
51-18	Roc'h Parou clearing, ½ M W of Roc'h Parou	48°42.97'N	03°37.87'W
51-19	Locquirec approach. ½ M E of Le Château rock E edge	48°42.04'N	03°37.67'W
51-20	Méloine South, 1.6 M S of La Méloine Grande Roche	48°44.98'N	03°47.04'W
51-21	Primel approach, on leading line 8 ca from pierhead	48°43.56'N	03°49.93'W
51-22	Méloine West, 3 ca W of Méloine W-card buoy	48°45.63'N	03°51.00'W

COASTAL DANGERS

Refer to Admiralty charts 2745, 3669

Les Sept Iles

This string of small islands and reefs lies just offshore a few miles north of Ploumanac'h and Ile Tomé. The two largest islands, Ile aux Moines and Ile Bono, are close together on the SW edge of the plateau. They form a natural anchorage which is open to the south and east but reasonably sheltered in moderate winds from between north and west.

The powerful lighthouse on Ile aux Moines is a key mark if you are approaching this stretch of coast at night anywhere between Lézardrieux and Roscoff. Unlit dangers extend 1¾ miles north, nearly 3½ miles ENE and just over a mile west of the lighthouse. Les Dervinis, an isolated rock drying 3.2 metres not quite a mile south-east of Ile Bono, is marked on its south side by an unlit S-cardinal buoy.

The tides are very strong locally between Les Sept Iles and the mainland, especially in the narrows between Ile aux Moines and Pointe de Mean Ruz. The bottom is uneven and relatively shallow in several patches through this strait, and this can cause steep overfalls locally, especially near springs with wind-over-tide.

Dangers between Ploumanac'h and Trébeurden

The rather austere corner of North Brittany mainland between Ploumanac'h and Trébeurden is well littered with off-lying rocks, which need to be given a wide berth as you come round the coast inside Les Sept Iles and Plateau des Triagoz.

This can be a tricky corner for gauging safe distances off, partly because there is no prominent landmark on the mainland, partly because of the strong tidal streams whose direction can vary depending on your distance offshore, and also because the only buoy off this section of coast, the Bar all Gall W-cardinal, is not moored right on the corner of the off-lying dangers but well round to the south of some of them.

Plateau des Triagoz

This low group of drying and above-water rocks lies 4 miles west of Les Sept Iles, marked on its south side by a lighthouse. Triagoz lighthouse is useful for gauging your position as you come round the rocky corner of mainland between Ploumanac'h and Trébeurden. Cruising west with the west-going tide, be careful not to be set too close to Triagoz as you hold offshore to avoid the coastal dangers. You would normally need to be turning south of west just as the Bar all Gall W-cardinal buoy bears south.

Dangers west of Ile Grande and Trébeurden

There are numerous small islands and rocks to the west of Ile Grande and Trébeurden, but the islands make it easier to assess your position on this side of the corner than on the north side between Ploumanac'h and the Bar all Gall buoy. Rather more tricky is the wide plateau of shoals

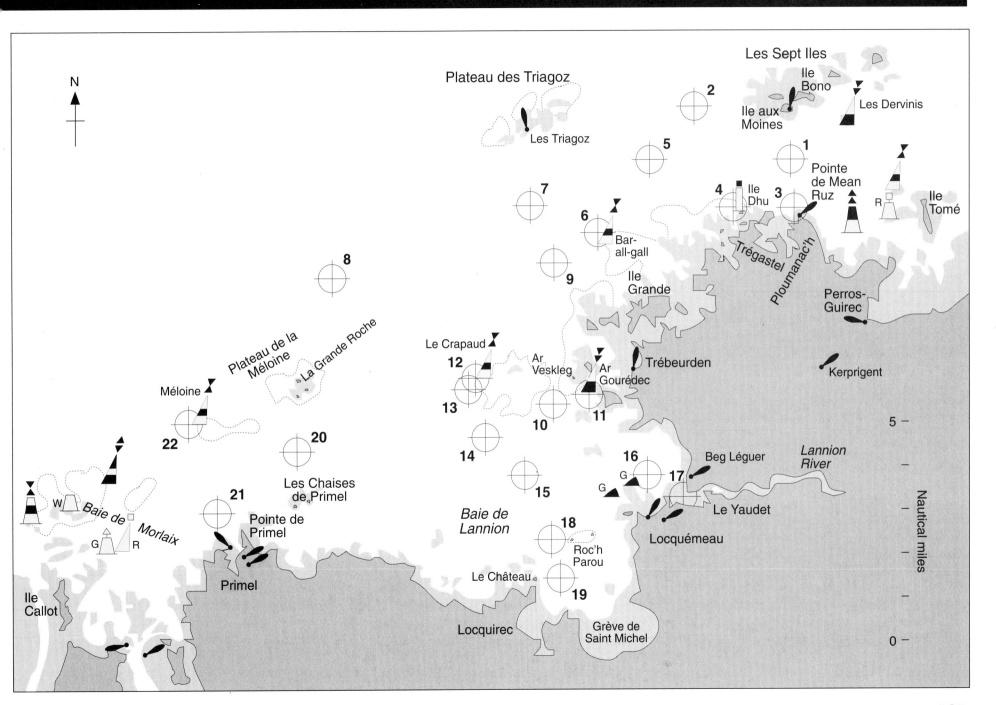

Les Sept Iles

Plateau des Triagoz

2

Ile Bono

Les Dervinis

Ile aux Moines

Les Triagoz

5

1

Pointe de Mean Ruz

7

4 Ile Dhu **3**

Ile Tomé

R

6 Bar-all-gall

Trégastel

Ploumanac'h

Perros-Guirec

N

8

9 Ile Grande

Plateau de la Méloine

La Grande Roche

Le Crapaud

12

Ar Veskleg

Ar Gourédec

Trébeurden

Kerprigent

Méloine

13

22

11

10

5 —

20

14

15

16

Beg Léguer

Lannion River

G **17**

G

Le Yaudet

Nautical miles

Les Chaises de Primel

21

Baie de Lannion

18

Locquémeau

W Baie de Morlaix

Pointe de Primel

Roc'h Parou

G R

Le Château

19

Primel

Ile Callot

Locquirec

Grève de Saint Michel

0 —

WP No	Waypoint name and position	Latitude	Longitude
51-1	Les Sept Iles S, 1.2 M S of Ile aux Moines lighthouse	48°51.59'N	03°29.34'W
51-2	Les Sept Iles W, 2¼ M W of Ile aux Moines lighthouse	48°52.79'N	03°32.77'W
51-3	Ploumanac'h entrance, 2 ca NW of Pointe de Mean Ruz L/H	48°50.44'N	03°29.16'W
51-4	Trégastel entrance, 1½ ca NW of Ile Dhu red beacon	48°50.53'N	03°31.30'W
51-5	Les Sept Iles SW, 3½ M 250°T from Ile aux Moines L/H	48°51.61'N	03°34.36'W
51-6	Bar all Gall, ¼ M NW of Bar all Gall W-card buoy	48°49.99'N	03°36.23'W
51-7	Triagoz South, 1¾ M due S of Les Triagoz lighthouse	48°50.60'N	03°38.71'W
51-8	Méloine NE, 2½ M 019°T of La Méloine Grande Roche	48°48.93'N	03°45.77'W
51-9	Trébeurden NW outer, 1.3 M 247°T from Bar all Gall buoy	48°49.29'N	03°37.80'W
51-10	Trébeurden W inner, 6 ca 236°T from Ar Veskleg rock	48°46.21'N	03°37.57'W
51-11	Trébeurden approach, 150 m S of Ar Gourédec S-card buoy	48°46.40'N	03°36.40'W
51-12	Le Crapaud W, ¼ M W of Le Crapaud W-card buoy	48°46.64'N	03°40.75'W
51-13	Le Crapaud SW, ½ M SW of Le Crapaud W-card buoy	48°46.30'N	03°40.92'W
51-14	Le Crapaud S, 1.3 M S of Le Crapaud W-card buoy	48°45.34'N	03°40.39'W
51-15	Lannion outer, 4 M 270°T of Beg Léguer lighthouse	48°44.40'N	03°39.87'W
51-16	Lannion inner, 1 M 270°T of Beg Léguer lighthouse	48°44.40'N	03°34.31'W
51-17	Lannion entrance, 100 m N of inner green beacon tower	48°43.89'N	03°33.16'W
51-18	Roc'h Parou clearing, ½ M W of Roc'h Parou	48°42.97'N	03°37.87'W
51-19	Locquirec approach. ½ M E of Le Château rock E edge	48°42.04'N	03°37.67'W
51-20	Méloine South, 1.6 M S of La Méloine Grande Roche	48°44.98'N	03°47.04'W
51-21	Primel approach, on leading line 8 ca from pierhead	48°43.56'N	03°49.93'W
51-22	Méloine West, 3 ca W of Méloine W-card buoy	48°45.63'N	03°51.00'W

a mile or so west of the islands, which has Le Crapaud rock (dries 3.9 metres) on the north.

Boats coming round from the east towards Trébeurden can cut between Le Crapaud shoals and Ile Molène with care, using waypoints 51–9 and 51–10 and making good due south between them to keep ½ mile west of Ar Veskleg rock. If in doubt though, take the outside passage west of Le Crapaud, dropping safely south of the shoal area before heading ENE towards the north-west tip of Ile Milliau and the entrance to Trébeurden.

Approaches to the Lannion River

There are various off-lying rocks in the approaches to the Lannion River, especially if you come round from Trébeurden. Les Roches lie almost a mile south-west of Ile Milliau, with the isolated heads of Le Four (drying 1 metre and 3.5 metres) another 6 cables or so further south-west. Bonnieg (dries 4.9 metres) and Le Taureau are about a mile seaward of Pointe de Bihit, but the south tip of Le Taureau, which is almost 2 metres above water, is the southernmost danger on the port hand as you approach the Lannion estuary from the west. On the south side of the Lannion approaches, the drying reefs north of Pointe de Séhar are guarded by Locquémeau and Kinierbel green buoys.

Plateau de la Méloine

This long tail of rocks and rocky shoals runs NE-SW a few miles offshore in the east approaches to the Bay of Morlaix. The northeast out-lier is Pongaro Rock, just awash at datum, which lurks about 1¼ miles north-east of the main cluster of above-water rocks. The south-western dangers are Les Trépieds, a couple of miles WSW of the main rocks, guarded on their west side by Méloine W-cardinal buoy.

Les Chaises de Primel

This distinctive line of rocks extends north-east from Pointe de Primel for a couple of miles. The most prominent of the outer rocks, Le Pigeonnier, is 10 metres high, but drying dangers extend for ½ mile beyond Le Pigeonnier and must be given a wide berth if you are approaching the Bay of Morlaix from the east inside Plateau de la Méloine, especially if coming across from Trébeurden or Lannion.

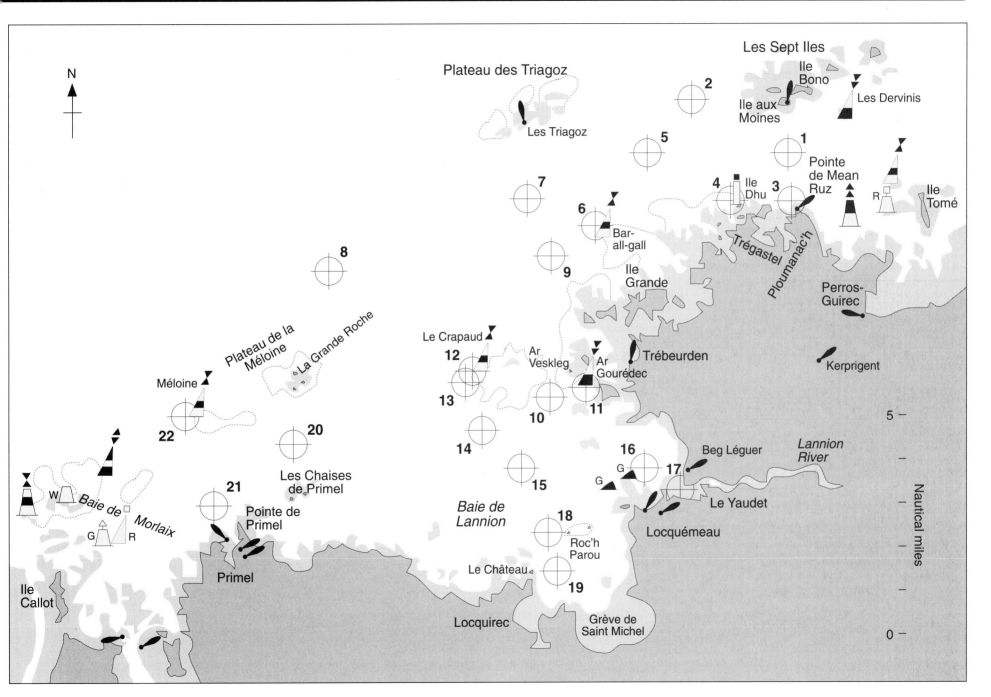

N

Les Sept Iles

Plateau des Triagoz

Ile Bono

2

Ile aux Moines

Les Dervinis

Les Triagoz

5

1

Ile Tomé

7

4 Ile Dhu 3

Pointe de Mean Ruz

R

6

Bar-all-gall

Trégastel

Ploumanac'h

9

Ile Grande

Perros-Guirec

8

Plateau de la Méloine

La Grande Roche

Le Crapaud

Trébeurden

Kerprigent

Méloine

12

Ar Veskleg

Ar Gourédec

13

11

10

22

5 —

20

14

16

Beg Léguer

Lannion River

Les Chaises de Primel

15

G

17

21

Pointe de Primel

Baie de Lannion

G

Le Yaudet

W

Baie de Morlaix

18

Roc'h Parou

Locquémeau

Nautical miles

Primel

G R

Le Château

Ile Callot

19

Locquirec

Grève de Saint Michel

0 —

133

Approaches to Morlaix River

WP No	Waypoint name and position	Latitude	Longitude
52-1	Primel approach, on leading line 8 ca from pierhead	48°43.56'N	03°49.93'W
52-2	Méloine West, 3 ca W of Méloine W-card buoy	48°45.63'N	03°51.00'W
52-3	Chenal de Tréguier outer, 2 ca ENE of La Pierre Noire beacon	48°42.70'N	03°51.80'W
52-4	Chenal de Tréguier inner, 3½ ca 010°T from Ile Noire lighthouse	48°40.76'N	03°52.35'W
52-5	Grand Chenal outer, 2 ca NE of Pot de Fer E-card buoy	48°44.43'N	03°53.71'W
52-6	Stolvezen, 2 ca NW of Stolvezen red buoy	48°42.83'N	03°53.44'W
52-7	Grand Chenal inner, ½ M 356°T from Ile Louet lighthouse	48°40.98'N	03°53.29'W
52-8	Les Duons south, ½ M S of Les Duons white pyramid	48°43.20'N	03°55.28'W
52-9	Bloscon inner approach, 5½ ca 030°T from Bloscon pierhead	48°43.75'N	03°57.20'W
52-10	Bloscon outer approach, 1.1 M E of Astan E-card buoy	48°44.96'N	03°55.87'W
52-11	Batz inner north clearing, 2½ M N of Ile de Batz L/H	48°47.28'N	04°01.52'W
52-12	Chenal de Batz west inner, 130 m N of Basse Plate beacon tr	48°44.39'N	04°02.44'W

COASTAL DANGERS

Refer to Admiralty charts 2745, 3669

General

The Bay of Morlaix, some 3 miles wide between Primel and the Plateau des Duons, is littered with rocks and islets but well marked with buoys and beacon towers. The two main entrance channels, the Grand Chenal and Chenal de Tréguier, lead south through the cordon of dangers into the sheltered but mostly shallow lower reaches of the Morlaix River. In reasonable visibility, you can enter the estuary by the Grand Chenal at any state of tide, by day or night, to anchor or pick up a mooring close east of Pen Lann point.

Plateau des Duons

This outer group of rocks lies about 1½ miles east of the east end of the Chenal de Batz and effectively separates the approaches to the Morlaix estuary and the approaches to Roscoff and the Penzé River. The north-east corner of Plateau des Duons is guarded by Pot de Fer E-cardinal buoy, while the main body of reefs is surmounted by a white pyramid. It is easy enough to cut south of Les Duons when passing between, say, the anchorage at Bloscon and the Grand Chenal de Morlaix.

Chenal de Tréguier

This eastern-most channel into the Morlaix estuary is relatively shallow and should only be taken above half-flood, but provides the shortest way in if you are coming round from Primel, or if you are approaching Morlaix from the east inside Plateau de la Méloine. The Chenal de Tréguier can be taken at night with care, using the leading lights on Ile Noire and up on La Lande.

Grand Chenal de Morlaix

The Grand Chenal, although rather narrow between Ile Ricard and the extensive reefs around Ile aux Dames, is deep for most of its length and can be taken by most boats at any state of tide, by day or night. In poor visibility, however, the Chenal de Tréguier is usually a safer bet, especially if you arrive from the east.

Chenal Ouest de Ricard

This western-most channel into the Morlaix estuary, just west of the Grand Chenal, carries the deepest water of all three entrance channels but is only feasible in daylight.

Approaches to the Penzé River

The various rocky shoals at the entrance to the Penzé River form a kind of outer bar. It is best for strangers to treat these as drying at least a metre. The best time to approach Penzé is about half-flood, when it is straightforward to come in between Guerhéon green and Le Cordonnier red beacon towers and follow the marked channel south into the river.

Ile de Batz

The north-facing coast near Roscoff and the Ile de Batz just opposite are well littered with rocky dangers. The Chenal de Batz between Roscoff and the island is shallow at its east end, but is well marked and straightforward enough with at least a couple of hours' rise of tide. Seaward of Ile de Batz, the dangers extend up to a mile offshore.

Most boats on passage between Morlaix and L'Abervrac'h will find the Chenal de Batz easier and quicker than keeping outside Ile de Batz, especially as one will be leaving Morlaix, perforce, near high water. Similarly, yachts carrying a fair stream eastwards from L'Abervrac'h will normally find themselves arriving off Batz with plenty of depth in the Chenal de Batz.

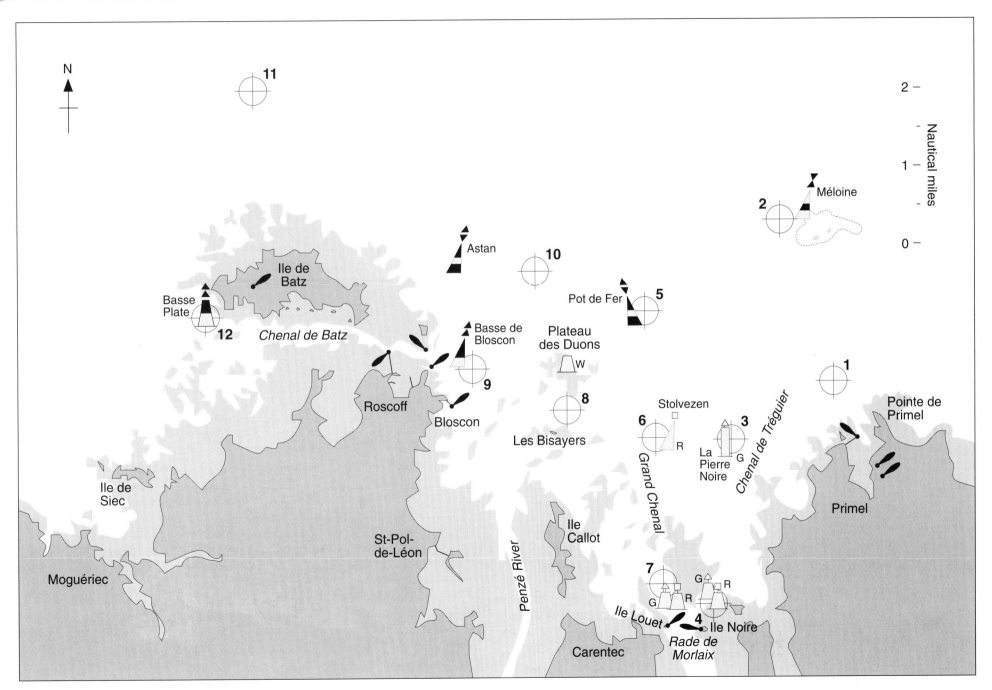

N

11

2 —

Nautical miles

1 —

0 —

▼▼ Méloine

2 Pot de Fer

Astan

10

Basse
Plate

12 *Chenal de Batz*

Ile de
Batz

Basse de
Bloscon

9

Plateau
des Duons

W

5

Pot de Fer

Roscoff

Bloscon

8

Les Bisayers

Stolvezen

6 R

La
Pierre
Noire

△ **3**

G

Chenal de Tréguier

1

Pointe de
Primel

Ile de
Siec

Grand Chenal

Primel

St-Pol-
de-Léon

Ile
Callot

Moguériec

Penzé River

7

G   R

G   R

Ile Louet   **4** Ile Noire

Carentec

*Rade de
Morlaix*

WP No	Waypoint name and position	Latitude	Longitude
53-1	Batz inner north clearing, 2½ M N of Ile de Batz lighthouse	48°47.28'N	04°01.52'W
53-2	Batz outer north clearing, 4 M N of Ile de Batz lighthouse	48°48.78'N	04°01.52'W
53-3	Chenal de Batz west inner, 130 m N of Basse Plate Bn Tr	48°44.39'N	04°02.44'W
53-4	Chenal de Batz west outer, 3 M W of Ile de Batz lighthouse	48°44.78'N	04°06.10'W
53-5	Anse de Kernic offing, 4 M N of Benven rock	48°44.10'N	04°13.77'W
53-6	Pontusval outer, 1.7 M N of Pontusval E-card buoy	48°43.21'N	04°19.13'W
53-7	Pontusval E-card buoy, actual position	48°41.51'N	04°19.13'W
53-8	Pontusval entrance, 50 m W of An Neudenn beacon tower	48°40.72'N	04°19.04'W
53-9	Aman ar Ross N-card buoy, actual position	48°41.95'N	04°26.96'W
53-10	Lizen Ven Ouest W-card buoy, actual position	48°40.58'N	04°33.60'W

COASTAL DANGERS

Refer to Admiralty charts 3668, 3669

Ile de Batz

The north-facing coast near Roscoff and the Ile de Batz just opposite are well littered with rocky dangers. The Chenal de Batz between Roscoff and the island is shallow at its east end, but is well marked and straightforward enough with at least a couple of hours' rise of tide. Seaward of Ile de Batz, the dangers extend up to a mile offshore.

Most boats on passage between the Morlaix estuary and L'Abervrac'h will find the Chenal de Batz easier and quicker than keeping outside Ile de Batz, especially as one will be leaving Morlaix, perforce, near high water. Similarly, yachts carrying a fair stream eastwards from L'Abervrac'h will normally arrive off Batz with plenty of depth in the Chenal de Batz.

Dangers between Ile de Batz and Ile Vierge

The North Brittany coast between Roscoff and Ile Vierge is rather featureless and austere, with off-lying dangers extending over 2 miles offshore in parts, particularly down towards Ile Vierge. It is prudent to stay on or outside a direct line between Ile de Batz lighthouse and Aman ar Ross N-cardinal buoy, or say between waypoints 53–4 and 53–9 in the table above.

Shallow draught boats venturing into Pontusval should make for waypoint 53–6 before turning inshore for waypoint 53–7, which is the Pontusval E-cardinal buoy.

Poor visibility

Poor visibility is not uncommon towards the west end of this stretch of coast. Boats on passage between Ile de Batz and L'Abervrac'h can sometimes find conditions much hazier off Ile Vierge than they were further east. However, it is not difficult to pick your way between Aman ar Ross and Lizen Ven Ouest buoys, and then make for waypoint 54–3 before turning south for 54–4 and Le Libenter W-cardinal buoy at the entrance to L'Abervrac'h.

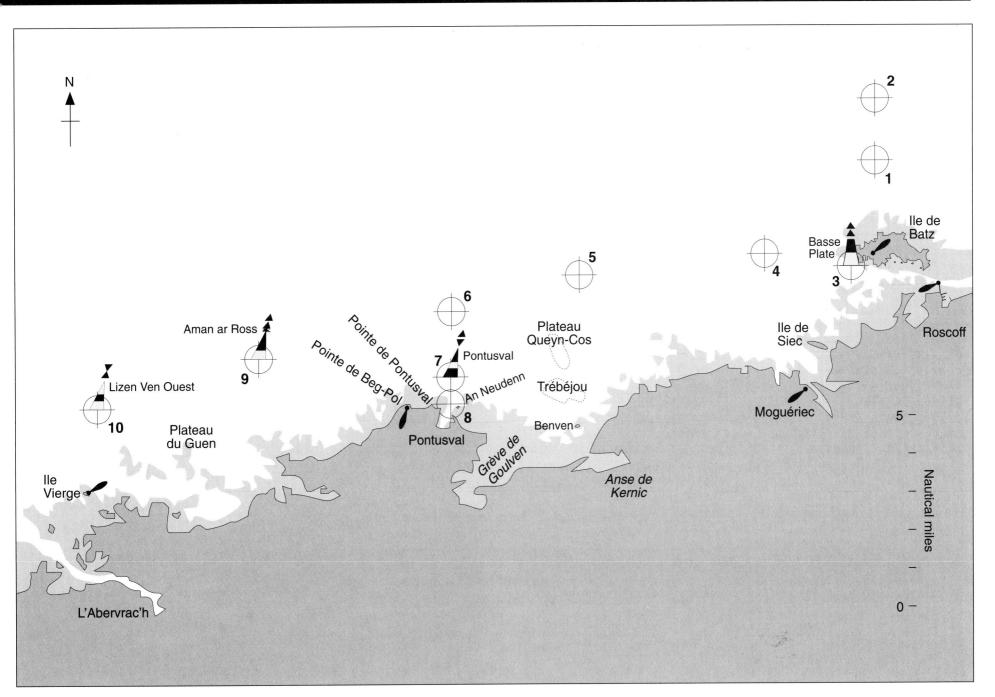

N

2

1

Ile de Batz

Basse Plate

5

4

3

6

Aman ar Ross

Pointe de Pontusval

Plateau Queyn-Cos

Ile de Siec

Roscoff

Pointe de Beg-Pol

7 Pontusval

9

An Neudenn

Trébéjou

Lizen Ven Ouest

8

Benven

Moguériec

10

Plateau du Guen

Pontusval

Grève de Goulven

Anse de Kernic

Ile Vierge

Nautical miles

5 —

—

—

—

—

0 —

L'Abervrac'h

WP No	Waypoint name and position	Latitude	Longitude
54-1	Aman ar Ross N-card buoy, actual position	48°41.95'N	04°26.96'W
54-2	Lizen Ven Ouest W-card buoy, actual position	48°40.58'N	04°33.60'W
54-3	L'Abervrac'h north approach, 1.2 M N of Le Libenter buoy	48°38.77'N	04°38.31'W
54-4	L'Abervrac'h entrance, 2 ca SW of Le Libenter buoy	48°37.43'N	04°38.53'W
54-5	L'Abervrac'h middle, 1 M 280°T from Ile Vrac'h lighthouse	48°37.12'N	04°35.96'W
54-6	L'Abervrac'h inner, ¼ M 308°T from La Palue directional light	48°36.12'N	04°34.03'W
54-7	Corn Carhai clearing, 1¼ M 340°T from Corn Carhai lighthouse	48°36.44'N	04°44.48'W
54-8	Grande Basse de Portsall W-card buoy, actual position	48°36.77'N	04°46.04'W
54-9	Brividic W-card buoy, actual position	48°35.38'N	04°46.16'W

COASTAL DANGERS

Refer to Admiralty charts 1432, 3668, 3669

Poor visibility

Poor visibility is not uncommon towards the west end of this stretch of coast. Boats on passage between Ile de Batz and L'Abervrac'h can sometimes find conditions much hazier off Ile Vierge than they were further east. However, it is not difficult to pick your way between Aman ar Ross and Lizen Ven Ouest buoys, and then make for waypoint 54–3 before turning south for 54–4 and Le Libenter W-cardinal buoy at the entrance to L'Abervrac'h.

Le Libenter

Yachts arriving off L'Abervrac'h from the east must make the final approach to Le Libenter W-cardinal buoy from due north or just west of north i.e. making for waypoint 54–3 before turning south for 54–4. This is to stay well clear of Le Libenter reef, a dangerous plateau over which the sea breaks heavily at the least provocation.

Approaches to L'Aberbenoit

L'Aberbenoit is easy enough to enter in moderate weather with sufficient rise of tide, but should be avoided in a heavy north-westerly swell, when the relatively small buoys and beacons of the approach channel will be difficult to identify in good time. The outer mark for L'Aberbenoit is La Petite Fourche W-cardinal buoy, which lies about 6 cables SSW of Le Libenter buoy.

Roches de Portsall

This dangerous area of rocks, right on the north-west corner of Brittany, is where the tanker Amoco Cadiz came to grief notoriously in the late 1970s. These reefs are marked by Corn Carhai lighthouse, but drying rocks extend not quite ½ mile north of the lighthouse.

Yachts and motorboats rounding this corner will normally pass a good mile north of Corn Carhai, making towards the Grande Basse de Portsall W-cardinal buoy although not necessarily keeping outside it. Waypoints 54–7 and 54–9 make useful turning points for this corner, although the Grande Basse de Portsall buoy is a useful landfall mark if you are arriving off the north end of the Chenal du Four direct from across the Channel.

Swell

This far north-west corner of Brittany is often subject to a heavy swell from between west and north-west, even in quite moderate winds. This can make the area feel more menacing than it really is, and the deep troughs of the swell can sometimes make it difficult to pick out landmarks from some distance offshore.

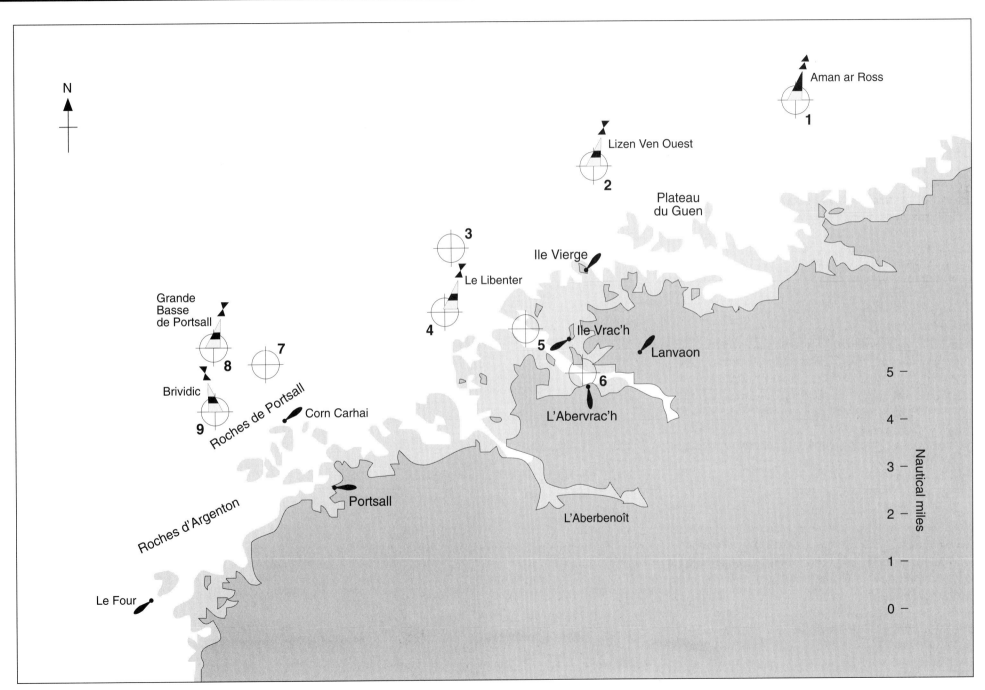

N

Aman ar Ross
1

Lizen Ven Ouest
2

Plateau
du Guen

3

Ile Vierge

Le Libenter

4

Ile Vrac'h

Grande
Basse
de Portsall

5
Lanvaon

8

7

6

Brividic

L'Abervrac'h

9

Roches de Portsall

Corn Carhai

Portsall

L'Aberbenoît

Roches d'Argenton

Le Four

Nautical miles

5 –

4 –

3 –

2 –

1 –

0 –

Approaches to Chenal du Four

WP No	Waypoint name and position	Latitude	Longitude
55-1	Corn Carhai clearing, 1¼ M 340°T from Corn Carhai L/H	48°36.44'N	04°44.48'W
55-2	Grande Basse de Portsall W-card buoy, actual position	48°36.77'N	04°46.04'W
55-3	Brividic W-card buoy, actual position	48°35.38'N	04°46.16'W
55-4	Portsall outer, 3¼ M 266°T from Portsall directional lighthouse	48°33.68'N	04°47.06'W
55-5	Portsall inner, ½ M 266°T from Portsall directional lighthouse	48°33.86'N	04°42.93'W
55-6	Le Four inner, ½ M W of Le Four lighthouse	48°31.45'N	04°48.97'W
55-7	Le Four outer, 1½ M W of Le Four lighthouse	48°31.45'N	04°50.47'W
55-8	L' Aberildut outer, 2½ M 263°T from L' Aberildut directional light	48°28.01'N	04°49.20'W
55-9	L' Aberildut inner, 130 m S of Le Lieu red beacon tower	48°28.24'N	04°46.55'W
55-10	La Valbelle, 200 m W of La Valbelle buoy on leading line	48°26.49'N	04°50.10'W

COASTAL DANGERS

Refer to Admiralty charts 1432, 3345

General

The Chenal du Four is a well-marked passage between the far north-west corner of Brittany and the off-lying islands of Ushant, Molène, Quémènes and Béniguet. It provides the most common route for yachts cruising between the English Channel and the Bay of Biscay. The Chenal du Four is wider than it appears from a small-scale chart and is quite straightforward in reasonable visibility, by day or night, so long as you carry the tide in your favour.

You often meet a somewhat forbidding Atlantic swell in the north approaches between L'Abervrac'h and Le Four lighthouse, especially off the Roches de Portsall, but further south the islands provide some shelter and the swell usually dies away.

Roches de Portsall

This dangerous area of rocks, right on the north-west corner of Brittany, is where the tanker Amoco Cadiz came to grief notoriously in the late 1970s. These reefs are marked by Corn Carhai lighthouse, but drying rocks extend not quite ½ mile north of the lighthouse.

Yachts rounding this corner will normally pass a good mile north of Corn Carhai, making towards the Grande Basse de Portsall W-cardinal buoy although not necessarily keeping outside it. Waypoints 54–7 and 54–9 make useful turning points for this corner, although the Grande Basse de Portsall buoy is a good landfall mark if you are arriving off the north end of the Chenal du Four direct from across the Channel.

Roches d'Argenton

This long tail of drying and above-water rocks lies up to a mile offshore and stretches north-east from Le Four lighthouse for more than 2 miles. Yachts coming down from Brividic W-cardinal buoy should not make for Le Four lighthouse directly but for a clearing position safely off to the west, in order to be sure of keeping well off Roches d'Argenton.

Les Liniou

This distinctive group of mainly above-water rocks are the next features you see as you draw south of Le Four lighthouse. In moderate weather Les Liniou provide useful steering marks because it is safe to pass ½ mile west of the outer above-water rocks. From here you can make good just west of south towards La Valbelle red buoy, which marks the entrance to the southern, usually more sheltered part of the Chenal du Four.

Plateau des Fourches

This rather nasty plateau of reefs lies about a mile south of the normal leading line approach to L'Aberildut. You need to take particular care to clear Plateau des Fourches if cutting close inshore to cheat the tide in the Chenal du Four; perhaps while northbound towards L'Aberildut when the stream in the Four is already running south. With any swell in the offing, the sea breaks heavily over Plateau des Fourches below about half-tide.

Poor visibility

It is not uncommon to meet poor visibility in the Chenal du Four, particularly towards the north end even having passed Le Conquet in quite sunny conditions. With GPS, this is not such a trial as it once was, so long as you keep your head and work systematically from waypoint to waypoint.

Having come up through the Chenal du Four in murky visibility, it is not usually difficult to find Le Libenter buoy with GPS and thus to enter L'Abervrac'h safely. However, when approaching L'Abervrac'h entrance from the west in mist or fog, it is vital to find Le Libenter buoy before proceeding any further east. The buoy's mournful whistle can be a surprising help in the final approach.

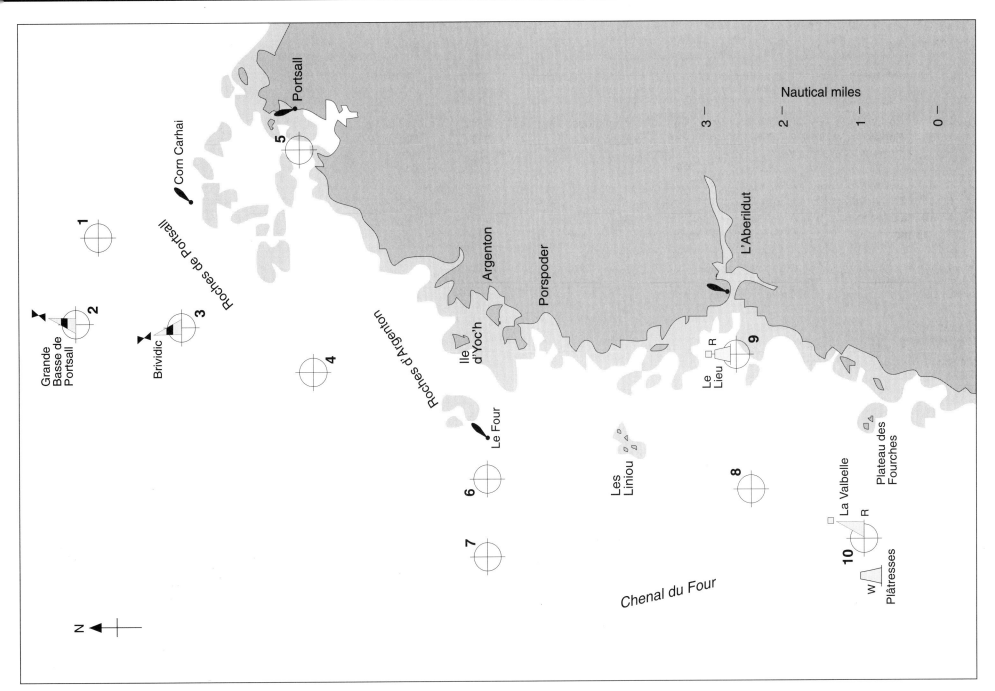

Nautical miles

3 —

2 —

1 —

0 —

Portsall

Corn Carhai

1

Grande
Basse de
Portsall

2

Brividic

3

Roches de Portsall

5

4

Roches d'Argenton

Argenton

Porspoder

Ile
d'Yoc'h

L'Aberildut

Le
Lieu

R

9

Le Four

Les
Liniou

6

7

8

La Valbelle

R

10

W

Plâtresses

Plateau des
Fourches

Chenal du Four

N